HOW TO PROBATE AND SETTLE AN ESTATE IN FLORIDA

Fourth Edition

Gudrun Maria Nickel
Attorney at Law

SPHINX® PUBLISHING
AN IMPRINT OF SOURCEBOOKS, INC.®
NAPERVILLE, ILLINOIS

D1159425

Fourth Edition, 2001

Published by: **Sphinx® Publishing, An Imprint of Sourcebooks, Inc.®**

Naperville Office
P.O. Box 4410
Naperville, Illinois 60567-4410
630-961-3900
Fax: 630-961-2168
http://www.sourcebooks.com

This publication is designed to provide accurate and authoritative information in regard to the subject matter covered. It is sold with the understanding that the publisher is not engaged in rendering legal, accounting, or other professional service. If legal advice or other expert assistance is required, the services of a competent professional person should be sought.

From a Declaration of Principles Jointly Adopted by a Committee of the
American Bar Association and a Committee of Publishers and Associations

This product is not a substitute for legal advice.

Disclaimer required by Texas statutes.

Library of Congress Cataloging-in-Publication Data
Nickel, Gudrun M.
      How to probate and settle an estate in Florida /Gudrun Maria Nickel-- 4th ed.
         p. cm. -- (Legal survival guides)
      Rev. ed. of: How to probate an estate in Florida. 3rd ed. 1998.
      Includes index.
      ISBN 1-57248-144-7
      1. Probate law and practice--Florida--Popular works. 2. Probate law and
practice--Florida--Forms. I. Nickel, Gudrun M. How to probate an estate in Florida. II.
Title. III. Series.

   KFF144.Z9N53   2001
   346.7305'2'0269--dc21   2001020722

Printed and bound in the United States of America.

VHG Paperback — 10 9 8 7 6 5 4 3 2 1

CONTENTS

Using Self-Help Law Books

Before using a self-help law book, you should realize the advantages and disadvantages of doing your own legal work and understand the challenges and diligence that this requires.

THE GROWING TREND

Rest assured that you won't be the first or only person handling your own legal matter. For example, in some states, more than seventy-five percent of divorces and other cases have at least one party representing him or herself. Because of the high cost of legal services, this is a major trend and many courts are struggling to make it easier for people to represent themselves. However, some courts are not happy with people who do not use attorneys and refuse to help them in any way. For some, the attitude is, "Go to the law library and figure it out for yourself."

We at Sphinx write and publish self-help law books to give people an alternative to the often complicated and confusing legal books found in most law libraries. We have made the explanations of the law as simple and easy to understand as possible. Of course, unlike an attorney advising an individual client, we cannot cover every conceivable possibility.

COST/VALUE ANALYSIS

Whenever you shop for a product or service, you are faced with various levels of quality and price. In deciding what product or service to buy, you make a cost/value analysis on the basis of your willingness to pay and the quality you desire.

When buying a car, you decide whether you want transportation, comfort, status, or sex appeal. Accordingly, you decide among such choices as a Neon, a Lincoln, a Rolls Royce, or a Porsche. Before making a decision, you usually weigh the merits of each option against the cost.

When you get a headache, you can take a pain reliever (such as aspirin) or visit a medical specialist for a neurological examination. Given this choice, most people, of course, take a pain reliever, since it costs only pennies; whereas a medical examination costs hundreds of dollars and takes a lot of time. This is usually a logical choice because it is rare to need anything more than a pain reliever for a headache. But in some cases, a headache may indicate a brain tumor and failing to see a specialist right away can result in complications. Should everyone with a headache go to a specialist? Of course not, but people treating their own illnesses must realize that they are betting on the basis of their cost/value analysis of the situation. They are taking the most logical option.

The same cost/value analysis must be made when deciding to do one's own legal work. Many legal situations are very straight forward, requiring a simple form and no complicated analysis. Anyone with a little intelligence and a book of instructions can handle the matter without outside help.

But there is always the chance that complications are involved that only an attorney would notice. To simplify the law into a book like this, several legal cases often must be condensed into a single sentence or paragraph. Otherwise, the book would be several hundred pages long and too complicated for most people. However, this simplification necessarily leaves out many details and nuances that would apply to special or unusual situations. Also, there are many ways to interpret most legal questions. Your case may come before a judge who disagrees with the analysis of our authors.

Therefore, in deciding to use a self-help law book and to do your own legal work, you must realize that you are making a cost/value analysis. You have decided that the money you will save in doing it yourself outweighs the chance that your case will not turn out to your satisfaction. Most people handling their own simple legal matters never have a problem, but occasionally people find that it ended up costing them more to have an attorney straighten out the situation than it would have if they had hired an attorney in the beginning. Keep this in mind if you decide to handle your own case, and be sure to consult an attorney if you feel you might need further guidance.

LOCAL RULES   The next thing to remember is that a book which covers the law for the entire nation, or even for an entire state, cannot possibly include every procedural difference of every county court. Whenever possible, we provide the exact form needed; however, in some areas, each county, or even each judge, may require unique forms and procedures. In our *state* books, our forms usually cover the majority of counties in the state, or provide examples of the type of form that will be required. In our *national* books, our forms are sometimes even more general in nature but are designed to give a good idea of the type of form that will be needed in most locations. Nonetheless, keep in mind that your *state*, county, or judge may have a requirement, or use a form, that is not included in this book.

You should not necessarily expect to be able to get all of the information and resources you need solely from within the pages of this book. This book will serve as your guide, giving you specific information whenever possible and helping you to find out what else you will need to know. This is just like if you decided to build your own backyard deck. You might purchase a book on how to build decks. However, such a book would not include the building codes and permit requirements of every city, town, county, and township in the nation; nor would it include the lumber, nails, saws, hammers, and other materials and tools you would need to actually build the deck. You would use the book as your guide, and then do some work and research involving such matters as whether you need a permit of some kind, what type and grade of wood are available in your area, whether to use hand tools or power tools, and how to use those tools.

Before using the forms in a book like this, you should check with your court clerk to see if there are any local rules of which you should be aware, or local forms you will need to use. Often, such forms will require the same information as the forms in the book but are merely laid out differently, use slightly different language, or use different color paper so the clerks can easily find them. They will sometimes require additional information.

CHANGES IN
THE LAW

Besides being subject to local rules and practices, the law is subject to change at any time. The courts and the legislatures of all fifty states are constantly revising the laws. It is possible that while you are reading this book, some aspect of the law is being changed.

In most cases, the change will be of minimal significance. A form will be redesigned, additional information will be required, or a waiting period will be extended. As a result, you might need to revise a form, file an extra form, or wait out a longer time period; these types of changes will not usually affect the outcome of your case. On the other hand, sometimes a major part of the law is changed, the entire law in a particular area is rewritten, or a case that was the basis of a central legal point is overruled. In such instances, your entire ability to pursue your case may be impaired.

Again, you should weigh the value of your case against the cost of an attorney and make a decision as to what you believe is in your best interest.

INTRODUCTION

Joint ownership of property, trusts, and other forms of estate planning may often eliminate the need for the probate procedure. However, even with careful and proper planning it may be necessary to proceed through the courts to finally distribute property to a deceased person's heirs.

Although many simple legal matters in Florida may be handled without lawyers, the Florida Probate Rule 5.030 states that every guardian or personal representative, unless the personal representative is also an attorney, must be represented by an attorney. The Florida law seeks to protect all of the heirs and creditors of an estate.

While the employment of an attorney to bring the probate proceeding through the court may be required by Florida law, there is a great deal of information available about the process to the heirs and beneficiaries. This information can help the reader and can be a guide in assisting an attorney. Resources, referenced in the text, are available on the Internet. Using this book as a guide will provide a better understanding of the procedures, forms, and time frames. This will help the reader understand how probate in Florida works, how to get an estate closed, and how to get the property distributed as expeditiously as possible.

Chapter 1 will untangle the mystery of probate and help the reader get started. The probate procedure can be complicated and lengthy. Chapter 2 describes the steps that the reader or an attorney will take through formal probate. Chapter 3 and 4 give alternative administration avenues, and Chapter 5 has a few details on property that does not require probate at all.

For convenience, there is a glossary, selected statutes, checklists, and blank forms to further assist in the probate process. The Florida Bar Association also provides information about the probate process via the Internet at:

http://www.flabar.org/newflabar/consumerservices

NOTE: *At the time of this publication, all statutes and forms are current. However, as of January 1, 2002, many statutes and some forms relating to probate are expected to change. The new laws will affect the way in which wills are signed and notarized, the manner in which creditors are notified about estate openings, and the amount of cash exempt as a family allowance. As always, check with the court clerk and a law library to ensure you are using the most current information.*

AN OVERVIEW OF PROBATE

1

WHAT IS PROBATE?

Probate is simply the legal process by which property in an estate is transferred to the heirs or beneficiaries of the deceased person (the *decedent*). The difference between heirs and beneficiaries is that *heirs* are persons who are entitled to property if the decedent died without a will, and the *beneficiaries* are persons who are given property in a will.

The process begins by presenting to a judge a petition listing the property of the decedent and the people to whom it is proposed the property be given. If the petition is proper, all necessary people have been notified, and taxes and debts have been paid, then the judge will sign an order distributing the property.

In large estates particularly, there are often conflicting interests among family members or heirs, and the probate process can become emotional and sometimes bitter. An estate may consist of a large amount of property and potential conflicting claims. If there are conflicting claims, it is most likely that an heir with a conflicting interest will hire an attorney to represent his or her claim. You will be best served by a knowledgeable probate attorney properly prepared to handle your interest in the estate.

When Is Probate Necessary?

Contrary to a popular misconception, probate may be necessary whether or not the decedent had a will. A *will* does not eliminate the requirement for probate; rather, it is the main instrument used in the probate process. If the decedent owned property in his or her individual name alone at the time of his or her death, probate is required.

If the decedent died without having signed a will, he died *intestate*. If he died leaving a properly signed will, he died *testate*. If the decedent died intestate, then his property will pass to his *heirs at law*. These are the heirs listed in the Florida Statutes (Fla. Stat.) in the order in which they will inherit. If the decedent died testate, his property will be distributed to those individuals he named in his will. (If someone contests the validity of the will, the court may get involved in determining whether those persons named in the decedent's will are actually entitled to receive the property.)

Different Probate Procedures

Florida has four different probate procedures depending upon the size and nature of the estate. If the estate is over $60,000, *formal probate* is used and the procedures are generally the same regardless of how large the estate is. However, Florida has several streamlined procedures if the estate is under $60,000 without real estate (see Chapter 3), or under $25,000 if provision is made to pay any claims against the estate (see Chapter 4). If there is only a small amount of personal property or an income tax refund of under $500, this property can be distributed without administration (see Chapter 5).

The process need not be complicated, provided all the necessary forms are completed for the court, all required persons are notified, and the proper procedures are followed. In most cases, if there are no objections to the probate proceeding and no conflicting claims, there will be no need for a court hearing—the entire procedure can be handled by mail or in person with the clerk of the probate court. Unless there is a delay in selling some of the assets, the probate process can often be completed shortly after the ninety-day period for claims expires.

TYPES OF OWNERSHIP OF PROPERTY

There are three common types of ownership for property other than sole ownership: *tenancy by the entireties*, *joint tenancy*, and *tenancy in common*.

Only husband and wife can own property as *tenants by entireties*. If real property is owned by two persons as "husband and wife," it is assumed that title is held as tenants by the entireties. This means that husband and wife own the property as one entity—if one spouse dies, the other gets the entire property. It does not have to go through probate.

If two or more unmarried persons own property as *joint tenants with rights of survivorship*, the surviving persons will own all of the property upon the death of the decedent, and it also does not have to go through probate.

If title to the property does not specifically state "joint tenants with rights of survivorship," it will be assumed that the parties own the property as *tenants in common*. Each tenant in common leaves his share of the property to his heirs or beneficiaries, either by will or by law. In a probate proceeding, a court may decide who the heirs or beneficiaries are. These persons then become the tenants in common with the surviving tenants, or owners.

WHAT PROPERTY IS SUBJECT TO PROBATE?

Not all property owned by a person at death has to go through the probate process. In some situations, such as where a husband and wife owned all property jointly (as tenants by the entireties, as explained above and in later paragraphs) or where property was owned by two persons as joint tenants with right of survivorship, it will only be necessary to file a certified copy of the death certificate with the clerk of the circuit court to show the entire property interest is now held by the survivor.

For example, if a husband and wife owned a home as tenants by the entireties, had a car titled in both names, and had a joint bank account, probate would be unnecessary when one spouse dies. A certified copy of the deceased spouse's death certificate should be:

- filed in the court records;

- sent to the state Department of Motor Vehicles to remove the deceased spouse's name from the car title; and

- shown to the bank to remove the deceased spouse's name from the account.

In addition, in order to clear a title to real estate held as husband and wife, the survivor should record an AFFIDAVIT OF CONTINUOUS MARRIAGE in the county records to confirm the marriage was continuous until the date of death. (see form 40, p.176.) (An intervening divorce would result in property ownership as tenants in common, regardless of a remarriage.) Contrary to popular belief, there is no need for a new deed after the death of one owner. The original deed and a death certificate is all the survivor needs to prove ownership.

Certified copies of the death certificate can be obtained from the funeral home. Before deciding what type of probate, if any, is necessary you must gather the records of all property owned by the decedent and determine whether each item must be probated or if it passed automatically at death.

NOTE: *A release from federal and state tax liability (or evidence of payment) may also be necessary. Requirements vary depending upon whether Florida was the primary or secondary resident of the decedent.*

WHO IS ENTITLED TO REPRESENT THE ESTATE?

The person responsible for the probate of an estate is the *personal representative*. (In other states he or she may be referred to as *executor*, *executrix, administrator,* or *administratrix.*) You also need to be aware of the following terms. Someone who is entitled to the decedent's property, either through the probate laws or through a will is commonly referred to as an *heir.* Traditionally, the term *heir* only referred to a person inheriting either real estate or personal property through the probate laws when there was no will. A *devisee* is a person who inherits real estate through a will. A *legatee* is someone who inherits personal property through a will.

If there is a will, it will usually name a person to be the personal representative. If the person named in the will as personal representative is not able to serve and an alternate is not named in the will (or the named alternate is also unable to serve), then the following persons, in order of preference, are considered for appointment as personal representative: (1) the person selected by a majority of the persons entitled to the estate, (2) a devisee or legatee under the will.

If the decedent died without a will, then the following persons, in order of preference, are considered for the appointment: 1) the surviving spouse, 2) the person selected by a majority of the heirs, 3) the heir closest in family relationship. If more than one heir applies, the court may exercise its discretion in selecting the one best qualified.

If the decedent had been declared incapacitated at the time of death, then the guardian of the decedent's property may be entitled to serve as personal representative. Similarly, if a person who would otherwise be entitled to appointment or to participate in selecting the personal representative is incompetent, his or her guardian may act in his or her place.

If no one applies to be a personal representative, the court shall appoint a capable person. Persons who work for or hold public office under the court, and persons who are employed by or hold office under any judge exercising jurisdiction, may not be appointed. (Fla. Stat., Sec. 733.301.)

Often someone making a will wants to name as personal representative an individual who is not a Florida resident. Florida law only allows certain nonresidents to act as personal representative, namely:

- a legally adopted child or adoptive parent of the individual;

- a *lineal* (direct) *descendant* (child or grandchild) who is related by blood (*lineal consanguinity*)

- a lineal *ascendant* (parent, grandparent) who is related by blood;

- a spouse, brother, sister, uncle, aunt, nephew, or niece of the decedent, or someone related by blood to such person; or

- the spouse of a person otherwise qualified under this section.

If no one qualifies, then a state resident as described in the previous paragraph may be appointed. The court may also appoint a *curator* to protect estate assets until a personal representative is appointed (Fla. Stat., Sec. 733.501.)

Specifically not qualified are individuals who have been convicted of a felony, those who due to sickness, intemperance, or lack of understanding are not competent to carry out the duties and responsibilities of a personal representative, or individuals under eighteen.

ESTATE AND INHERITANCE TAXES

The state of Florida does not levy either estate or inheritance taxes except on large estates, which can deduct the amount from their federal tax bill.

The federal government levies a tax only on estates $675,000 or greater. This amount will increase to $1,000,000 over the next five years.

NOTE: *The new tax bill to be signed by the president will increase the exclusion to $1,000,000 as of January 1, 2002; full repeal is scheduled by 2010.*

The manner in which the estate taxes are apportioned is beyond the scope of this book, but is detailed in Florida Statute, Section 733.817. The state of Florida receives a portion of any estate tax due the federal government. In determining if the estate is over this limit, you must include both property in probate and any other property that passed at death, such as joint property, trust interests, and life insurance benefits.

If there is any question of whether an estate is subject to tax, you should check with an accountant or probate attorney.

If there will be $600 or more in income received by the estate before December 31, the personal representative will have to file with the Internal Revenue Service (IRS) an income tax return for the estate (IRS Form 1041). The personal representative will also file a NOTICE CONCERNING FIDUCIARY RELATIONSHIP (IRS FORM 56) to state to the IRS that he is serving as the representative of an estate. (see form 17, p.135.) Income to the estate does not include money received from the sales of property, but includes only such items as interest, rents, royalties, and dividends. Be sure to check with an accountant if you have any questions about this.

If the income received by the decedent (if under sixty-five and single) between last December 31st and the date of death was over $6800 then a final income tax return must be filed for this period (IRS Form 1040). (This amount increases if the decedent was married, and/or over age sixty-five.)

NONRESIDENT DECEDENT

If the decedent was not a resident of the state of Florida, but left Florida property, the property must be probated through a process called *ancillary administration*. Such a situation is beyond the scope of this book, but the forms are very similar to those in this book. Usually, just a few words are changed. For more guidance, see Florida Statutes, Chapter 734, in Appendix A of this book.

In this situation, the primary probate proceeding will be handled in the state of the decedent's residency; a secondary proceeding must be handled in the Florida county in which the property is located in order to clear title for the heirs and any subsequent buyer. Ancillary summary administration is the ancillary probate of estates with a value of less than $25,000.

FILING FEES

A fee must be paid when a probate estate is opened. The fee will vary depending upon the value of the estate assets and may also vary somewhat from county to county. Although fees are stated in this text, it is important to check with your local probate court clerk to verify the amount. If the correct sum is not paid, the estate file will not be opened. If there is no cash available in the estate to pay the fee, the personal representative can pay it and be reimbursed later.

EXECUTION OF DOCUMENTS

Most probate documents are signed by the petitioner (usually the personal representative) and the petitioner's attorney if he has one. Most of the documents do not have to be notarized, but on those that must be notarized, the date of expiration of the notary's commission as well as the commission number, if any, must be included.

HOW LONG DOES PROBATE TAKE?

If there are only a few small assets that must be probated and there are no claims by creditors, a small family or summary estate could be settled in a few weeks. If a formal probate must be conducted, it could be completed in as quickly as four months or as long as several years, depending upon how long it takes to gather all the assets and distribute them to the proper parties.

WHAT TYPE OF PROBATE IS SIMPLE?

This book does not cover every conceivable situation that may arise in a probate proceeding. However, the basic steps for the different forms of proceedings are set forth in each chapter as simply and concisely as possible.

You should consult with an attorney who has experience in probate law if the estate you are in charge of:

- is subject to federal taxation;

- includes partnership interests or complicated royalties;

- has an ambiguous will;

- is difficult to determine the beneficiaries of;

- has claims against it that are questionable; or

- has anyone contesting the will.

DO YOU NEED AN ATTORNEY?

Since there is no personal representative in family administration (Chapter 3), summary administration (Chapter 4), or disposition of personal property without administration (Chapter 5), no attorney should be necessary for these actions. Florida guarantees the right of every person to represent him or herself in court. (Fla. Stat., Sec. 454.18.)

Florida Probate Rule 5.030 requires that a personal representative be represented by an attorney unless he is the sole interested party. A good argument can be made that if two or three heirs ask to be appointed co-personal representatives, they will not need an attorney if there are no other interested parties. If all bills of the estate have been paid, the heirs should be the sole interested parties. But one Florida court has ruled that until three years after death, there might be other interested parties and therefore an attorney is required. Other Florida courts or the Florida Supreme Court might rule differently. (The Florida Supreme Court has said that people should have access to the courts without the need for lawyers.)

How to Find an Attorney

The most common, and perhaps best, way to find a lawyer is to ask friends and acquaintances for referrals. Once you have several names, contact those offices and ask the cost of an initial consultation. If those lawyers you have been referred to are not able to handle your probate matter, perhaps they can refer you to other attorneys. In most counties there are local bar associations that should be able to refer you to several lawyers who do probate work. The phone number should be listed in your local telephone directory. If not, call your county court clerk's office. Finally, you may have a group legal plan through your employer or prepaid legal service available (several credit card companies now offer prepaid legal services). Some plans provide for a limited amount of legal work for the cost of membership, or at a reduced fee.

No matter how you find an attorney, be sure to have an understanding of the fee before the work begins. For many years, attorneys regularly charged a percentage of the estate, typically three to five percent, as the fee. The Florida Supreme Court recently ruled that this was not acceptable and that the fee should be based upon the number of hours of work performed by the attorney. However, the law now allows a base charge plus a percentage of the total estate. The calculation of fees is detailed in the Florida Statutes, Section 733.6171. Also, the statute allows for further compensation for extraordinary services. (Fla. Stat., Sec. 733.6171(4)(a).) Different arrangements for compensation may be made if all parties involved in the proceedings agree.

Also, be sure you have a clear understanding of the differences between the fees and the *costs*, as costs can add considerably to the total charges. For example, the filing fee, charges for mailing, and cost of publication can exceed $200.

Other Things to Do

In addition to filing the proper papers with the probate court, other matters must also be taken care of when handling an estate. For example:

1. The decedent's safe deposit box, if one exists, should be opened immediately. In many cases, the original will has been placed in the decedent's safe deposit box. The initial opening of the safe deposit box must be in the presence of an employee of the institution where the box is located and the personal representative. The contents of the box must also be inventoried in the presence of the employee and the personal representative, and both must verify the contents by signing an inventory. The personal representative is required to file the inventory of the contents within ten days after the box is opened. Only the following documents must be delivered, upon request, by the lessor, typically a bank:

    - The will of the decedent must be delivered to the court having probate jurisdiction where the bank is located.

    - A life insurance policy on the life of the decedent must be delivered to the beneficiary of the policy.

    - Any written instructions regarding burial, or a deed to a burial plot, must be delivered to the person requesting the information.

    The PETITION TO OPEN SAFE DEPOSIT BOX is in Appendix C. (see form 1, p.117.) Before opening, an ORDER TO OPEN SAFE DEPOSIT BOX must be issued. (see form 2, p.118.) After the LETTERS OF ADMINISTRATION are issued and presented, the lessor of the safe deposit box must deliver all contents to the personal representative. (see form 9, p.127.)

2. The Social Security office should be notified of the decedent's death. A Social Security check received after the month in which the death occurred must be returned. The estate will be required to reimburse the government for any checks received in the month of and after the decedent's death. (Any Social Security checks should be kept separate from the estate assets and returned to the government, along with a letter explaining they are being returned because the payee is deceased.)

3. All mail addressed to the decedent should be collected and sorted carefully to obtain additional information about any debts and assets the decedent may have had. A change of address form can be obtained and filed at the local post office, so that the mail will be forwarded directly to the personal representative.

4. All of the decedent's credit cards should be cancelled (some companies may cancel small, outstanding balances if notified). The credit card companies should be sent a letter of cancellation, giving the date of death. Other creditors and vendors should be notified as well, including any newspaper and magazine subscriptions.

5. Social Security benefits should be claimed through the decedent's local Social Security office. In addition to a death benefit to help cover funeral expenses, Social Security may provide survivors' benefits to the spouse and minor children.

6. The decedent's employer should be contacted about any death benefits through the employer's insurance. There may also be additional company benefits, such as a company profit-sharing plan or pension plan, or railroad retirement benefits (contact the nearest Railroad Retirement Board). The decedent's family or beneficiaries may be entitled to benefits if he was a federal employee. Check with Medicare also.

7. Information on veteran's benefits which may be available to dependents of deceased veterans is provided by the nearest Veterans Administration Office.

8. Determine whether there are any benefits available through worker's compensation for employment-related deaths. There may be other organizations or companies that owe benefits to the decedent and/or survivors. For example, some credit card companies and travel clubs (such as AAA) offer accidental death benefits to their card-holders. Check with all of them.

FORMAL ADMINISTRATION 2

The *formal administration* procedure is used if the estate does not qualify for either family or summary administration. (Fla. Stat., Chapter (Ch.) 733.) Generally, the estate must meet the following three criteria:

1.   The value of the estate must be greater than $25,000 if it includes real estate (otherwise summary administration may be allowed);

2.   The value must be greater than $60,000 with no real estate (otherwise family administration may be allowed); *and*

3.   The death occurred within the two years prior to filing for probate (otherwise summary administration may be allowed).

THE PROBATE PROCESS

The probate procedure is a step by step process, most with specific time limitations. To begin formal administration, a petition must be filed with the court, along with a certified copy of the death certificate of the decedent, and the original will. If the original will cannot be located, you should see an attorney. If the decedent did not have a will, then the certified copy of the death certificate may be attached to the petition alone.

In the next sections there are lists of the steps in a formal administration with and without a will. Following this is an explanation of each of the steps. (There are FORMAL ADMINISTRATION CHECKLISTS for your convenience in Appendix B.)

PETITION FOR ADMINISTRATION

WITH A WILL   If there is a will, fill out the PETITION FOR ADMINISTRATION WITH WILL (PETITION). (see form 3, p.119.)

☞ Write the county name at the top right, and leave the "file no." line blank (the court clerk will fill that in).

☞ Write the name of the person who has died in the space above the word "Deceased."

☞ The interest the *petitioner* (the one who is signing the petition) has in the decedent's estate (such as "heir and daughter" or "personal representative named in will," etc.) goes on the first blank.

☞ Write the petitioner's name and address, and the name and office address of the petitioner's attorney on the next two blanks.

☞ Write the name, last address (including county), date of death, and place of death of the decedent in Item 2.

☞ In Item 3 write the names and addresses of all heirs and beneficiaries and the ages of any who are under age eighteen. Also, write their relationship to the decedent.

☞ Explain at Item 4 why the proceeding is being filed in the particular county.

☞ Write the petitioner's name at Item 5 and then briefly explain the legal and other qualifications of the individual asking to be appointed personal representative.

☞ At Item 6 write an approximate list of the assets of the estate and their respective values. (You may need extra space, so write "see attachment" and then write this information on a separate piece of paper.) Check off whether estate taxes will be required.

☞ Write the date of the will at Item 7. If there are any *codicils*, or revisions to the will, write that date as well.

☞ Sign and date the form.

The petition must also state that the petitioner is not aware of any other wills or codicils, and that the original is either (a) accompanying the petition, or (b) in the possession of the court.

WITHOUT A WILL

If there is no will, file a PETITION FOR ADMINISTRATION WITHOUT WILL. (see form 4, p.121.) Follow the instructions for form 3.

NOTE: *Probate for residents' estates should be filed with the probate division of the clerk of the circuit court in the county in which the decedent was domiciled (had his or her primary residence).*

NOTICE OF PETITION FOR ADMINISTRATION

A NOTICE OF PETITION FOR ADMINISTRATION WITH WILL (NOTICE) must be filed by the petitioner. (see form 14, p.132.) (If there is no will, see form 13, p.131.) File this form in either of the following situations: First, if an heir or beneficiary under a will other than the will being offered for probate files a caveat with the court. (A *caveat* is a paper claiming an interest in the estate or in some way challenging the will. If a caveat is filed, it is time to see an attorney.) Second, a NOTICE must be served on all persons who are known to be qualified to act as personal representative and who are entitled to *preference*. This must be done before LETTERS OF ADMINISTRATION are granted to anyone not entitled to preference (see the section on "Who Is Entitled to Represent the Estate," p.5 for information about preferences).

If either of the above situations applies, a copy of the PETITION, signed by the personal representative, should be sent to all persons who may have an interest in the estate. If the decedent died *testate* (with a properly signed will), it should be sent to all persons named in the will, the decedent's spouse, and any other persons who are known to be named in a prior will. If the decedent died *intestate* (with no will), the PETITION should be sent to all legal heirs and those persons who may have an interest in the estate. A NOTICE OF PETITION FOR ADMINISTRATION should be included with the PETITION, giving the recipient twenty days from receipt in which to respond or object. Once the PETITION is filed and the time for response to the NOTICE OF PETITION FOR ADMINISTRATION has expired, the court can admit the will to probate (or open the estate if there is no will).

SERVICE   The petitioner may *serve* (deliver) the NOTICE OF PETITION FOR ADMINISTRATION on interested persons. The NOTICE must have a copy of the will attached. No one who is served with formal NOTICE before the LETTERS OF ADMINISTRATION are signed by the court, or who has in writing waived receipt of the formal NOTICE, may then challenge the validity of the will and other related issues *except* in court proceedings before the LETTERS OF ADMINISTRATION are signed. (see form 9, p.127.)

OATH OF PERSONAL REPRESENTATIVE

Before LETTERS OF ADMINISTRATION will be signed by the court, an OATH OF PERSONAL REPRESENTATIVE must be signed by the personal representative. (see form 5, p.123.) It must state that he or she has been appointed personal representative and that he or she will "faithfully administer the decedent's estate in accordance with the law of the state of Florida." Although a separate form for the OATH OF PERSONAL REPRESENTATIVE has been included in this text, the oath may be included in the DESIGNATION OF RESIDENT AGENT AND ACCEPTANCE. (see form 6, p.124.) It may also be included in the PETITION FOR ADMINISTRATION.

DESIGNATION OF RESIDENT AGENT

The personal representative must then appoint another person to be a *resident agent* for the purpose of accepting any notice or service of summons in the county where the estate is to be probated. (see form 6, p.124.) Often an attorney will act as the resident agent; however, any adult residing in the county may act as resident agent. The resident agent must also sign to accept the appointment.

OATH OF WITNESS

Self-proved wills (signed as required under Florida law) may be admitted to probate without any additional documentation. *Self-proved* means that the witnesses took an oath at the time the will was signed, the oath is included in the last will and testament, and the decedent's signature was notarized by a qualified notary public. There is an OATH OF WITNESS TO WILL in this book. (see form 10, p.128.)

If the will was not self-proved, then the will may be admitted to probate only after the attesting witnesses provide an oath before a circuit judge, clerk, or court-appointed commissioner. This means that you must contact one of the witnesses and ask that they appear at the courthouse to sign the oath.

If the witness cannot appear at the courthouse without great hardship then the court will appoint a *commissioner* to take the oath of the witness. (See "Commission" in the next section.)

If there is no competent witness available, the will may be admitted upon the oath of the personal representative or any other interested person before a circuit judge, clerk or court-appointed commissioner, stating that he/she believes the will to be the true last will and testament of the decedent.

Wills signed outside of the state of Florida are accepted immediately in Florida if they are self-proved. That is, they must be executed with two witnesses and a notary public who notarizes the signatures of the testator/testatrix and the witnesses. If the will was not self-proved, a commissioner may be appointed as explained below.

COMMISSION

If the will is not self-proved and the witness is unable to appear before the circuit court judge or clerk, the court may appoint a commissioner to take the oath of any person who witnessed the signing of the will. A commissioner is usually a notary public.

The procedure is to first locate a witness to the will and ask who the nearest notary is. Then prepare a PETITION FOR APPOINTMENT OF COMMISSIONER. (see form 11, p.129.) Also, prepare a COMMISSION and file both with the court clerk. (see form 12, p.130.) After the judge signs the COMMISSION it is sent to the notary who executes it along with the witness and mails it back to the court.

If the court determines that a witness cannot be found, has become incompetent since the will was signed, or the witness' testimony cannot be obtained within a reasonable time period, the court may admit the will to probate. The personal representative or any other person with no interest in the estate under the will must sign an oath stating that he or she believes the will to be the true last will of the decedent.

If the will was prepared outside of Florida, the witnesses were probably employees of the law office that prepared the will. In such a case, call that out-of-state law office, explain the situation, and ask for the name of a notary in the law office. Then have that notary appointed as commissioner.

LOST OR MISPLACED WILL

If the original will has been lost or misplaced, the PETITION FOR ADMINISTRATION of the will must include a copy of the will or its substance, and the testimony of the witnesses must be reduced to writing and filed. This information will be used as evidence in any contest of the will if the witness has died or moved from the state. The lost or destroyed will shall not be admitted to probate unless formal notice has been given to all those who would have been entitled to property of the decedent if there was no will. (Fla. Stat., Sec. 733.207.)

DEATH CERTIFICATE

A certified copy of the decedent's death certificate should be filed with the court within three months of the date the NOTICE OF ADMINISTRATION is first published. (see form 15, p.133.) (Usually this is filed with the PETITION FOR ADMINISTRATION.) Certified copies of the death certificate can be obtained from the funeral home.

FILING FEES

Special charges for handling the probate estate may vary from county to county. For example the basic filing fee for formal administration in Collier County, which must be paid at the time the PETITION FOR ADMINISTRATION is filed, is currently $103.50, in Palm Beach County the filing fee is over $200. This amount should be paid from the probate estate. Be sure to check with the court clerk before filing.

BOND

Even if a bond is waived in the will, the court may require one. A *bond* is a guaranty by a bonding or insurance company that the personal representative will properly perform the required duties and not misuse the funds of the estate. By calling the clerk of the probate division of your court, you may be able to find out what amount of bond will be required for your estate or whether it will be waived. A BOND OF PERSONAL REPRESENTATIVE form is included in this book. (see form 39, p.175.)

Insurance companies issue bonds for a fee, or a cash bond can be posted with the clerk. If the will waived the bond requirement, this should be stated in the PETITION FOR ADMINISTRATION, as well as in the ORDER ADMITTING WILL TO PROBATE AND APPOINTING PERSONAL REPRESENTATIVE. (see form 7, p.125.)

ORDER ADMITTING WILL TO PROBATE AND APPOINTING PERSONAL REPRESENTATIVE

After the above steps have been successfully completed, the judge will sign an ORDER ADMITTING WILL TO PROBATE AND APPOINTING PERSONAL REPRESENTATIVE. (see form 7, p.125.) If there is no will, an ORDER APPOINTING PERSONAL REPRESENTATIVE will be issued. (see form 8, p.126.) One of these forms must be prepared and submitted to the court for the judge's signature.

LETTERS OF ADMINISTRATION

Once the above process is completed, the court will sign the LETTERS OF ADMINISTRATION to the personal representative, giving the power and authority to act on behalf of the estate. (see form 9, p.127.) (In testate estates, the courts give preference as personal representative to the person, or his or her successor, named in the will or pursuant to a power granted in the will. After the court has signed the LETTERS OF ADMINISTRATION in either a testate or intestate estate, and another person who was entitled to act as personal representative did not waive his or her preference or didn't receive formal notice, then the LETTERS OF ADMINISTRATION can be revoked by the court and new ones issued.)

A bond or *surety* from the personal representative will also be required, unless waived by the will. The cost of the bond may be included in the administration expenses. Several certified copies of the LETTERS OF ADMINISTRATION should be kept by the personal representative, as they will be required in dealing with the decedent's property. In some counties in Florida the court will prepare the LETTERS OF ADMINISTRATION, but in most counties the personal representative must submit the form to the court. It may be less expensive to request several certified copies of the LETTERS OF ADMINISTRATION when they are signed. Check with the clerk.

Except as provided for in the will or by court order, the powers of the personal representative are as follows:

- retain estate assets until distribution to beneficiaries or heirs;

- convey or lease real property;

- receive assets from fiduciaries or other sources;

- deposit or invest liquid assets;

- acquire or dispose of an asset, including real property;

- make repairs or alterations on buildings;

- enter into leases of property that extend beyond the period of administration;

- enter into mineral leases;

- abandon property of no value;

- vote stock or securities of the estate;

- pay calls or assessments against the securities of the estate;

- hold property in the name of a nominee;

- insure the assets of the estate, and himself or herself, against liability;

- borrow money, with or without security, to be paid from estate assets (other than real property);

- extend, renew, or modify an obligation due the estate;

- pay taxes, assessments, and other expenses incident to the administration of the estate;

- exercise stock subscriptions;

- allocate items of income or expense;

- employ persons including attorneys;

- prosecute or defend claims for or against the estate;

- sell, mortgage, or lease personal property;

- continue any business of the decedent;

- provide for exoneration from personal liability;

- satisfy and settle claims and distribute the assets of the estate;

- enter into agreements concerning federal estate taxes;

- make partial distributions to beneficiaries of any part of the estate that are not required to satisfy costs of administration; and

- execute all instruments (sign documents or papers) necessary in the exercise of the personal representative's powers.

"The personal representative is required to use the same standard of care required of trustees, must settle and distribute the estate as expeditiously and efficiently as possible in accordance with the terms of the will." (Florida Statute 733.602)

The personal representative also has specific powers under Florida law to deal with estate property contaminated with hazardous or toxic substances, including ordering property inspections and tests, taking actions necessary to prevent or remedy a violation of environmental law, and charging costs of testing, clean-up, or related expenses to the estate. The personal representative specifically has no personal liability to any beneficiary or other party as a result of a decrease in the affected estate's assets.

A successor personal representative will have the same powers as the original personal representative to complete the administration of the estate.

If the personal representative is specifically denied any of the above powers, then the court must first authorize the exercise of such a power. For example, if the will does not grant the personal representative the right to sell the decedent's real estate, the personal representative must first obtain authorization from the court to sell.

A personal representative may also be removed and the LETTERS OF ADMINISTRATION revoked in certain instances, including failure to comply with a court order, failure to account for the sale of property or to produce and exhibit the estate assets when required, failure to give security when required, insolvency of a corporate personal representative, conviction of a felony, and change to a residence outside of Florida if not otherwise qualified.

NOTICE OF ADMINISTRATION AND STATEMENT REGARDING CREDITORS

After the court signs the LETTERS OF ADMINISTRATION, a NOTICE OF ADMINISTRATION must be sent to the newspaper that publishes legal notices in your area, where it must be published once a week for two consecutive weeks. (see form 15, p.133.) In some counties the NOTICE OF ADMINISTRATION is arranged for by the court, but in most, the personal representative places the ad. It should be placed in a paper that regularly runs legal notices, but it need not be in the most expensive paper. Often you can find a small paper that has much better rates than the large dailies. Just be sure to ask if the paper is legally authorized for legal notices. The primary purpose of the NOTICE OF ADMINISTRATION is to notify any creditors of the estate, who will then have three months from the date of the first publication to file their form called a *statement of claim*. A copy of the NOTICE OF ADMINISTRATION must also be sent to all known creditors, who then have thirty days after the date they received notice in which to file their claims.

Effective January 1, 1993, the personal representative must file a STATEMENT REGARDING CREDITORS confirming that a diligent search has been made for creditors of the decedent. (see form 41, p.177.)

Once a statement of claim is filed by the creditor, the clerk of the court then sends a copy to the personal representative. If the personal representative or an interested person objects to the claim (does not believe the claim is valid or that it should be paid), then an objection to the claim must be filed with the court. The objection must be filed either within four months after the date the NOTICE OF ADMINISTRATION is first published, or thirty days after the claim is filed, whichever date is later. Within ten days after filing the objection, it must be sent by registered or certified mail, return receipt requested, to the person who filed the claim. After the receipts have come back, they should be stapled to a sheet of paper with the name of the court, case name, and case number at the top and filed with the court. You should keep a photocopy of these for your file.

If the person filing the claim disagrees with the objection, he or she has thirty days after receipt of the objection to file an independent lawsuit to allow the court to determine the validity of the claim.

If the NOTICE OF ADMINISTRATION was not sent to the spouse of the decedent, those beneficiaries named in the will, and those known to have been named in a previous will, then it must also be sent at this time. Those persons to whom this NOTICE OF ADMINISTRATION is sent also have three months from the date it is first published to question (a) whether the will is valid; (b) whether the personal representative is qualified to act; (c) the location (*venue*) where the probate proceeding has been filed; and (d) whether the court has *jurisdiction* over the proceeding.

After the NOTICE OF ADMINISTRATION has been published, the newspaper should send the personal representative a copy of it as published, along with an *affidavit* giving the dates of publication. This affidavit, a RECEIPT FOR NOTICE BY MAIL, must then be filed with the court. (see form 16, p.134.)

WHEN DEBTS EXCEED ASSETS

The personal representative must pay the expenses of administration and obligations in a specific order. The expenses and obligations are divided into classes. (Fla. Stat., Sec. 733.707.)

After paying any preceding class, if the estate does not have sufficient assets to pay all of the next class, the creditors of that class will be paid *pro rata* (a percentage) according to the respective claims. If the assets are not sufficient to pay the first class, the creditors in the first class will be paid pro rata according to their respective claims as well.

Administering the Estate

Once the LETTERS OF ADMINISTRATION have been issued, you can begin administering the estate. This means you must gather all of the assets of the estate and pay any legitimate claims against the estate.

One of the first things you will need to do is to open a checking account in the name of the estate with yourself as the personal representative (example: "Jane Jones as Personal Representative of the Estate of Howard Smith"). To do this you will need a tax identification number as explained in the next section.

One of the duties of the personal representative is to convert the assets of the estate into cash so that it may be divided among the heirs or beneficiaries. If heirs or beneficiaries of the estate wish to receive certain items in the estate, such as personal items or real estate or stocks and bonds, these items can be distributed to them at the value as of the date of death.

Some of the things you may have to do in administering the estate are close out bank accounts, sell or dispose of clothes and furniture, and sell stocks and bonds.

A personal representative must promptly carry out the duties of settlement and distribution of the estate without court order unless a court order is required.

IRS FORM SS-4

In the event a fiduciary tax return is required (explanation below) or to open a bank account, the estate will need a federal employer identification number (FEIN). The federal APPLICATION FOR EMPLOYER IDENTIFICATION NUMBER (IRS FORM SS-4) must be completed and sent by the personal representative to the Internal Revenue Service (IRS) in Atlanta, Georgia. (see form 18, p.137.) A federal identification number for the estate will be assigned and the personal representative will be notified by mail within approximately three to four weeks.

The personal representative may also be able to obtain a number by telephone, by calling (770) 455-2360. However, the form should first be completed, because the IRS officer asks how the questions are completed on the IRS FORM SS-4. After the number is assigned, the form must nevertheless be mailed in or faxed to 678-530-6156, along with the assigned FEIN number written on the upper right-hand corner.

INVENTORY

Within sixty days after the court signs the LETTERS OF ADMINISTRATION, the personal representative must prepare and file with the court an INVENTORY of the property of the decedent. (see form 20, p.143.) It must include a reasonably detailed list with an estimated fair market value for each item, and it must be served on the surviving spouse of the decedent, any heirs if the decedent died intestate, the beneficiaries under the will if he or she died testate, any interested persons who may have requested a copy (through the court), and the Florida Department of Revenue. The Florida Department of Revenue's address is:

> Florida Department of Revenue
> Compliance Support
> 5050 W. Tahnessee St.
> Bldg. K
> Tallahassee, FL 32399-0100

The Inventory should be amended or supplemented if the personal representative later learns of any changes. Appraisers may be employed without court order.

The decedent's safe deposit box may initially be opened only in the presence of an employee of the institution where the box is located and the personal representative. An INVENTORY of the contents must also be made in the presence of an employee and the personal representative, each of whom is required to verify the contents by signing a copy of the INVENTORY. The INVENTORY must be filed with the court within ten days after the box is opened.

INVENTORY AND EXEMPT PROPERTY

In preparing the INVENTORY, the personal representative must note any property that is *exempt* from the estate (property that is not included in the estate to be distributed to the heirs or beneficiaries, and that is not subject to any creditors' claims, except those creditors who have a security interest in the property). Property that is exempt from the probate proceeding and that should be immediately transferred to the surviving spouse (or minor children jointly if there is no surviving spouse) is as follows:

- household furniture, furnishings and appliances in the decedent's home up to $10,000 in value, as well as any automobiles held in the decedent's name for personal use;

- unless otherwise dealt with in the will, personal property of the decedent up to a total of $1000 in value; and

- Florida prepaid college program contracts and Florida college savings.

If the decedent left a will, the exempt property is over and above any share passing to the spouse or minor children under the will, unless the will provides otherwise.

A PETITION TO DETERMINE EXEMPT PROPERTY should be filed by those persons claiming the property. (see form 37, p.172.) An ORDER DETERMINING EXEMPT PROPERTY is then issued. (see form 38, p.174.)

In addition, if the decedent died leaving a spouse and lineal heirs (children, grandchildren), ascendants (parents, grandparents), or descendants, who were supported by the decedent, these persons are entitled to a $6000 allowance for their support during the administration of the estate. A petition for a family allowance is filed either after all persons have been served or have filed waivers.

HOMESTEAD

Florida's *homestead* laws create unique problems with respect to probate. There is much confusion among Florida lawyers and judges about the law when homestead property is involved. This section will give a very general explanation. Keep in mind that this can become very complicated in some circumstances.

The Florida Constitution, Article X, specifically protects the home that was owned by the decedent, if the decedent has a spouse and/or minor children. To qualify as homestead, all of the following requirements must be met at the time of the decedent's death:

- it was owned by the decedent,

- the decedent was a Florida resident,

- the property was the residence of the decedent or his or her family, and

- the property meets the size limitation specified in the Florida Constitution.

The size limitation is a maximum $^1/_2$ acre within a town or city, or 160 acres outside of the town or city limits (this is determined as of the date the property became the owner's homestead, not as of the date of death). The owner's creditors may not force the sale of such homestead property to satisfy debts owed by the owner.

Upon the owner's death, two questions arise:

1. Who gets the property?

2. What happens to the exemption from claims of creditors?

The answer to the first question depends on who survives the decedent. If the decedent leaves a spouse, but no minor children, the spouse gets the property (regardless of what the decedent's will says). If the decedent leaves a spouse and a minor child, the spouse gets a life estate in the property with the property going to the minor child upon the spouse's death (regardless of what the will says). If the decedent leaves a spouse and any *lineal* descendants (i.e., adult children, grandchildren, great grandchildren, etc.), the spouse gets a life estate in the property with the property going to the lineal descendants upon the spouse's death (regardless of what the will says, except that the will may give the property exclusively to the spouse). If the decedent leaves no spouse, but does leave lineal descendants, at least one of whom is a minor, the property goes to the lineal descendants (regardless of what the will says). Finally, if the decedent does not leave a spouse nor any minor lineal descendant, the property goes to the adult lineal descendants (except that the decedent if free to leave the property to anyone in his or her will). Therefore, if the decedent is survived by a spouse or a minor lineal descendant, the decedent is not free to give the property to just anyone in a will. (See Fla. Stat., Sec., 733.607.)

Whether the exemption from creditors of the decedent continues after death depends upon who gets the property. In general, if the property goes to the spouse or an heir at law (i.e., a person who would be an heir if there was no will), it is still exempt from the decedent's creditors.

To clarify the status of homestead property, and to have the transfer of title officially recognized, it is necessary to file a PETITION TO DETERMINE HOMESTEAD REAL PROPERTY. (see form 42, p.178.) You will also need to prepare an ORDER DETERMINING HOMESTEAD REAL PROPERTY for the judge to sign. (see form 43, p.180.) In some counties, the judge may also require an affidavit or some other document, to verify the claim that the property was the decedent's homestead. The court will let you know if any additional papers are required.

If the decedent and surviving spouse owned the property as tenants by entirety, it is not considered homestead property, but passes to the survivor by filing a death certificate and AFFIDAVIT OF CONTINUOUS MARRIAGE. (see form 40, p.176.)

The legal issues surrounding homestead property can become complicated, especially when it comes time to obtain title insurance when the property is sold. It is therefore important to identify homestead property, and obtain a signed ORDER DETERMINING HOMESTEAD REAL PROPERTY from the judge officially declaring the property to be homestead and identifying the new owners. (see form 43, p.180.) If you have any questions concerning homestead property, you should contact an attorney.

NOTE: *If the estate would qualify for the summary administration procedure (see Chapter 4) without the homestead property, you can still use the summary procedure because the homestead property is not part of the probate estate.*

SPOUSE'S SHARE

IF DECEDENT LEFT A WILL

Under Florida law, the surviving spouse of a person who dies a resident of Florida has the right to elect to take thirty percent of the fair market value of all of the estate assets at the time of the decedent's death, regardless of the provisions in the decedent's will. The election must be filed with the court within the earlier of six months of the date of the first publication of notice of administration, or two years after the date of the decedent's death. Any estate tax consequences for filing this election should be carefully considered.

The elective share is in addition to homestead, exempt property, and other allowances. The valuation of property used to satisfy the spouse's elective share is detailed in the Florida Statutes, Chapter 732, Part II.

IF DECEDENT DIES WITHOUT A WILL

If the decedent died without a will and left no lineal descendants (children, grandchildren, great grandchildren), the surviving spouse is entitled to the entire estate. If there are lineal descendants of the decedent and the surviving spouse, then the spouse is entitled to the first $20,000 of the estate, plus one-half of the balance of the estate. The remainder of the estate is distributed among the remaining heirs. If the decedent died leaving lineal descendants who are not also the lineal descendants of the surviving spouse (children from a previous marriage), then the surviving spouse is entitled to one-half of the estate, with the remainder going to the other heirs.

PRELIMINARY NOTICE AND REPORT

Effective January 1, 2000, for decedents dying after January 1, 2000, estates are no longer required to file a PRELIMINARY NOTICE AND REPORT (DR-301). If Florida estate tax is not due, and no IRS Form 706 is required, the personal representative should file the AFFIDAVIT OF NO FLORIDA ESTATE TAX DUE (DR-312), with the clerk of the Circuit Court in the county or counties in which the decedent owned property. (see form 19, p.141.). For decedents dying before January 1, 2000, the PRELIMINARY NOTICE AND REPORT (DR-301) form must still be filed with the Florida Department of Revenue. (see form 45, p.182.)

ADVERSARY PROCEEDINGS

If any beneficiary, personal representative, or other interested person questions who is entitled to receive all or part of the estate, a petition should be filed with the court, with notice to all interested persons (beneficiaries, heirs, and others who may have an interest in the outcome). This petition is then handled like any other civil litigation, with the individual claiming an interest in the estate then being named as the *plaintiff*, and the personal representative (in his or her capacity as personal representative) as the *defendant*. Anyone considering this type of action should seek the assistance of a competent attorney.

ORDER OF PAYMENT

The personal representative must pay (out of the estate) the expenses of the probate administration and the other obligations of the estate in the following order of priority:

1. costs, expenses of administration, and payment for the services of the personal representative and his or her attorney. The amount is governed by statute. (Fla. Stat., Secs. 733.617 and 733.6171.);

2. reasonable funeral, interment, and grave marker expenses up to $6000;

3. debts and taxes that are required under federal law;

4. reasonable hospital and medical expenses incurred by the decedent during the last sixty days before death, including any compensation paid to attendants;

5. any family allowance;

6. arrearage from court ordered child support;

7. debts acquired by the estate after the decedent's death through the continuation of the decedent's business. However, these debts are paid only to the extent of the assets of the business; and

8. all other claims against the estate, and any excess over the reasonable amounts allowed under 2 and 4 above.

If there is not sufficient money left in the estate after a certain priority of debts are paid, then the creditors in the next priority will be paid a pro rata share according to the amount of their respective claims.

The assets of a trust may also be used to pay the expenses of administration if the assets of the estate are not sufficient. Although trusts are beyond the scope of this book, reference is found in Appendix A. (Fla. Stat., Sec. 733.707.)

A compromise may be reached on any claim after the date for filing objections to the claim has expired. The court may authorize the compromise for the *best interests* of the beneficiaries. Any unpaid or unresolved claims expire upon the one-year anniversary date the claim was filed. If a claim is not filed within two years of the decedent's death, regardless of whether LETTERS OF ADMINISTRATION have been issued, neither the personal representative nor the beneficiaries can be held liable for the claim.

The laws regarding filing claims do not affect a creditor's security interest in the decedent's property, including a mortgage, or a lien held by one in possession of the decedent's personal property.

UNCLAIMED PROPERTY

If a personal representative is unable to distribute property because the heir or lawful owner cannot be found, the court must order the personal representative to sell the property and deposit the proceeds with the court clerk. The clerk will then post a notice, depending upon the amount involved (on the courthouse door if less than $500, once a month for two months in the local newspaper if more than $500). If no one has claimed the money after six months from the date the notice was first posted or from the date of first publication, then the money is paid to the state treasurer, less any fees lawfully charged by the clerk.

FINAL ACCOUNTING AND PETITION FOR DISCHARGE

At least ninety days after the NOTICE OF ADMINISTRATION was published and within twelve months after the date the court issues the LETTERS OF

ADMINISTRATION, a FINAL ACCOUNTING (form 22) and a PETITION FOR DISCHARGE (form 23) must be filed for estates that are not required to file a federal estate tax return. If a federal estate tax return must be filed, the FINAL ACCOUNTING and PETITION FOR DISCHARGE must be filed within 12 months of the date the tax return is due. Notice of the FINAL ACCOUNTING and PETITION FOR DISCHARGE must be sent to all interested persons unless a WAIVER OF ACCOUNTING AND OF SERVICE OF PETITION FOR DISCHARGE, RECEIPT OF BENEFICIARY AND CONSENT TO DISCHARGE (WAIVER, RECEIPT, AND CONSENT) has been filed. (see form 21, p.145.) It allows the beneficiaries to a) waive the filing of a final accounting; b) waive the service of a petition for discharge; c) waive all notices; and d) consent to an order discharging the personal representative from his or her duties without notice or hearing.

The FINAL ACCOUNTING must contain certain information. (see form 22, p.146.) Fill it in as follows:

- ☞ Write in the name of the deceased, the file number and division at the top.

- ☞ Write the word "Final" in the space under the name of Deceased where requested.

- ☞ Make a full accounting of all receipts and disbursements by the estate, either from last annual accounting or since estate was opened under "Summary."

- ☞ Make sure a statement that all claims and debts of the estate have been either paid, settled, or otherwise disposed of and all tax returns filed and taxes and expenses of administration paid is written (form 22 has this language at the bottom of page 1 of the form).

- ☞ Include the proposed plan of distribution (how the property of the estate is to be distributed) on the lines indicating such information.

- ☞ Put the name of the estate in the first blank on page 2 of the form.

☞ Put the dates of the final accounting ("from____ through ____").

☞ Put the name and address of the personal representative or attorney next to indicate a fully administered estate.

NOTE: *There are schedules to fill out to make a complete detailed accounting. Only the totals go on the first page of form 22.*

The PETITION FOR DISCHARGE must contain similar information. (see form 23, p.152.)

☞ Write the county and file number at the top right.

☞ Put the name of the deceased in the space above the word "Deceased," and in the blank at Item 1.

☞ At Item 4, write what amount is paid to the personal representative, attorney, etc. as listed there.

☞ At Item 5, write the same amounts in each subsection as contained in the FINAL ACCOUNTING.

☞ At Item 8, list all persons who you serve with the FINAL ACCOUNTING and this petition.

☞ Sign and date the form.

If there is an objection to the FINAL ACCOUNTING and PETITION FOR DISCHARGE, the court must determine the plan of distribution. However, if notice has been given and no objections are filed within thirty days from the date of notice, the personal representative may distribute the estate as set forth in the PETITION FOR DISCHARGE. (If waivers were filed by the beneficiaries, the thirty-day waiting period does not apply.)

RECEIPT OF BENEFICIARIES

After the personal representative has distributed the assets according to the plan in the PETITION FOR DISCHARGE, the beneficiaries should file a WAIVER, RECEIPT, AND CONSENT with the court. (see form 21, p.145.)

If the beneficiary is a trustee or guardian, a receipt must be filed with the court before an ORDER OF DISCHARGE will be granted. (see form 24, p.154.) For example, the decedent may have set up a trust for a grandchild, providing that the assets be held in the trust until the grandchild is eighteen years of age. The trustee of that trust, having received the assets for the benefit of the child, must file a receipt with the court.

If a minor child is to receive a bequest from an estate, the parents must be appointed legal guardians of the child in order to receive the funds. They are then required to provide the court a periodic accounting of the location and disposition of the funds.

ORDER OF DISCHARGE

The judge will sign the ORDER OF DISCHARGE after a report of distribution and the WAIVER, RECEIPT, AND CONSENT (form 21) have been filed by the personal representative. The ORDER OF DISCHARGE should include release of the bond required by the court, if any. At that time the probate proceeding will be completed. (see form 24, p.154.)

TAX RETURNS

FEDERAL TAX IDENTIFICATION NUMBER

The personal representative is responsible for filing all tax returns that are required on behalf of the probate estate. These may include:

- ☛ decedent's last federal income tax return;

- ☛ annual federal income tax returns for the estate;

- ☛ federal gift tax return for the decedent;

- ☛ Florida intangible personal property tax return; or

- ☛ federal estate tax return.

Failure to file may subject the personal representative to penalties.

IRS FORM 1040	If the decedent was unmarried, under age sixty-five, and had more than $7,200 income in the year of his death, a final federal income tax form (IRS Form 1040) will have to be filed on behalf of the decedent and signed by the personal representative as "Jo Smith, Personal Representative of the Estate of Mae Brown." The name of the decedent should read "Mae Brown, Deceased 11-11-91." The word "deceased" should also be written across the top of the form. IRS Form 1310 should be filed with the return if a refund is being claimed, and the return is being filed by someone other than the surviving spouse or personal representative. Otherwise a copy of the court certificate appointing the personal representative should be attached to the IRS 1040 return.

If the decedent has a surviving spouse, and the final return is a joint return, the decedent's representative and the surviving spouse must sign.

A copy of the current IRS publication explaining this subject can be obtained from the IRS, either through your local IRS office or by calling 800-829-3676.

IRS FORM 1041	Income on the assets of the decedent is also taxable and must be shown on IRS Form 1041, a *fiduciary income tax return*. This form is typically used in formal administration, which may take more than six or nine months, and requires the personal representative to report income before the assets are actually distributed. Capital gains may have to be reported on this return if any assets are sold before probate is completed. Form 1041 should be obtained from the IRS if it is needed by calling 800-829-3676, or on the Web at:

http://www.irs.gov/forms_pubs/form.html

IRS FORM 706	The federal estate tax return must be filed within nine months from the date of death of a U.S. citizen or resident whose gross estate exceeds $675,000. Congress recently provided gradual increases in this amount—in 2002, it will increase from $675,000 to $700,000, in 2004 to $850,000, in 2005 to $950,000, and in 2006 to $1,000,000.

NOTE: *As of this printing, the president will be signing a new tax law that would increase the exemption to $1,000,000 as of January 2002, and may eliminate the estate tax by 2010.*

A tax return must be filed, even if no tax is due. Unless an extension has been granted, any tax due must be paid when the return is filed.

The manner in which the estate taxes are apportioned is beyond the scope of this book, but is detailed in the statutes (Fla. Stat., Sec. 733.817.)

FLORIDA ESTATE TAX LIEN WAIVER

In order to expedite the sale of estate property before payment of all taxes, the APPLICATION FOR WAIVER AND RELEASE OF FLORIDA ESTATE TAX LIEN (DR-308) should be filed with the Florida Department of Revenue. This form is used to request a waiver and release of the tax lien detailed in the Florida Statutes. (see form 46, p.184.)

FLORIDA ESTATE TAX

The Florida portion of the Estate Tax must be paid to the Florida Department of Revenue. The amount due is the credit shown on the IRS Form 706, less any estate taxes properly paid to other states. A check for the Florida estate tax and a copy of the IRS Form 706 (along with a copy of estate tax returns for other states and evidence of payment) must be sent to Florida.

Florida is also entitled to a credit if a non-resident owned any property in the state. The formula may be obtained from the Florida Department of Revenue:

http://www.state.fl.us/dor/taxes/how_estate.html

OTHER TAX RETURNS

There may be other tax returns due, such as partnership returns, corporate returns, sales tax returns, etc. It is important to determine what type of business, if any, the decedent was engaged in. It may also be best to let the accountant previously handling the decedent's returns complete these as well.

FAMILY ADMINISTRATION 3

Family administration is a type of simplified probate proceeding available if the *gross* value of the estate as of the date of death, for federal estate tax purposes, is less than $60,000. (Fla. Stat., Sec. 735.101.)

The estate must consist solely of personal property; *or*, if real property is involved, formal administration (see Chapter 2) must be at a point when the time for claims of creditors has lapsed and any outstanding claims have been properly handled. Because there is no personal representative, the court should not require that the heirs or beneficiaries hire an attorney to handle the paperwork. (Florida Probate Rule 5.030; Fla. Stat., Sec. 454.18.) (To help you stay organized, there is a FAMILY ADMINISTRATION CHECKLIST in Appendix B.)

LAST WILL AND TESTAMENT OR HEIRS

If the decedent left no will, then to qualify for family administration the heirs at law can only be any of the following:

- a surviving spouse,

- lineal ascendants (parents, grandparents), or

- lineal descendants (children, grandchildren).

If the decedent left a will, the beneficiaries under the will must have the following relationship to the decedent: surviving spouse, lineal descendants, or lineal ascendants. A bequest to any other person must only be a small part of the estate. In order to qualify for family administration, the will must not direct probate under Florida Statutes, Chapter 733.

THE PETITION

The requirements for a PETITION FOR FAMILY ADMINISTRATION are explained in Florida Statutes, Section 735.103 and Florida Probate Rule 5.520. (form 25—WITH WILL, and form 27—WITHOUT WILL.) It must show that the estate is entitled to family administration under Florida law. It is filed by the petitioners, which should include the surviving spouse and all the beneficiaries. If any beneficiary is a minor (under age eighteen), or mentally incapacitated, the petitioner for that individual may be his or her legal guardian, or if none, then by the natural guardian. The surviving spouse and all beneficiaries must sign the PETITION FOR FAMILY ADMINISTRATION. (The filing fee for the PETITION FOR FAMILY ADMINISTRATION may vary from county to county. You should check with your local court clerk.)

The petition should include a complete list of all assets of the gross estate and the estimated value of each asset. Those estate assets that are to be probated should be listed separately from those that are not to be probated.

The forms included in this book cover a simple estate in which either there are no debts of the estate or the debts are *barred* (for example, because no claims have been filed). If there are debts that must be paid, the easiest way to handle them is for the beneficiaries to pay them before filing the petition. Otherwise, the petition must state that provisions for payment of the debts has been made. The PETITION FOR FAMILY ADMINISTRATION should include the following information (whether with a will or without):

- the name of each creditor;

- the nature of the debt;

- the amount of the debt and whether the amount is estimated or exact; and

- when the debt is due.

If provision for payment of the debt has been made other than in the proposed order of distribution, the following information must be shown:

- the name of the person who will pay the debt;

- the creditor's written consent for substitution or assumption of the debt by another person;

- the amount to be paid if the debt has been compromised; and

- if the debt is to be paid in other than one lump sum or as directed by court order, the time and method of payment.

If the debts of the estate are not paid at the time of filing the PETITION FOR FAMILY ADMINISTRATION, you should retype the form in this book to include this information in place of paragraph 12 in form 25 or in place of paragraph 8 in form 27.

Finally, the PETITION FOR FAMILY ADMINISTRATION should include a schedule of how the assets will be distributed. If the decedent left a valid last will and testament, it should be filed with the petition.

NOTE: *A petitioner who is not a resident of Florida must meet the same requirements as a petitioner who is a resident.*

NOTE: *No formal notice is required, as all beneficiaries have signed the* PETITION FOR FAMILY ADMINISTRATION.

OATH OF WITNESS

Self-proved wills (signed as required under Florida law) may be admitted to probate without any additional documentation. *Self-proved* means that the witnesses took an oath at the time the will was signed, the statement is included in the last will and testament, and the decedent's signature was notarized by a qualified notary public.

If the will was not self-proved, it may be admitted to probate only after the attesting witnesses provide an oath before a circuit judge, clerk, or court-appointed commissioner. This means that you must contact one of the witnesses and ask that they appear at the courthouse to sign the OATH OF WITNESS TO WILL. (see form 10, p.128.)

If the witness cannot appear at the courthouse without great hardship then the court will appoint a *commissioner* to take the oath of the witness. See "Commission" in the next section.

If there is no competent witness available, the will may be admitted upon the oath of the personal representative or any other interested person before a circuit judge, clerk, or court-appointed commissioner, stating that he believes the will to be the true last will and testament of the decedent.

COMMISSION

If the will is not self-proved and the witness is unable to appear before the circuit court judge or clerk, the court may appoint a commissioner to take the oath of any person who signed as a witness to the execution of the will. A commissioner is usually a notary public.

The procedure is to first locate a witness to the will and ask who the nearest notary is. Then prepare a PETITION FOR APPOINTMENT OF COMMISSIONER. (see form 11, p.129.) Also prepare a COMMISSION, naming that notary, and file them with the court clerk. (see form 12, p.130.) After the judge signs the commission it is sent to the notary who executes it along with the witness and mails it back to the court.

If the will was prepared outside of Florida, the witnesses were probably employees of the law office that prepared the will. In such a case, call that out-of-state law office, explain the situation, and ask for the name of a notary in the law office. Then have that notary appointed as the commissioner.

NONRESIDENT DECEDENT

If the decedent was not a resident of Florida, and died leaving property in Florida, the Florida estate must qualify for family administration. This means that the total value of the Florida estate, for federal estate tax purposes, is less than $60,000, and must consist either solely of personal property or, if real property, then formal administration must be at a point where the time for filing claims by creditors has lapsed and any claims have been properly handled.

If probate proceedings were held out of state and an ORDER OF DISCHARGE was entered, the will may be admitted in Florida if it was properly executed in that state. (see form 24, p154.)

OPPOSITION TO FAMILY ADMINISTRATION

If a beneficiary is opposed to family administration, yet will receive his or her share of the estate, the other heirs will nevertheless be permitted to distribute the estate in accordance with the ORDER OF FAMILY ADMINISTRATION (ORDER). (form 26 or 28.) However, the court may hold a formal hearing, after giving notice of the objection to all beneficiaries.

Anyone who was lawfully entitled to share in the estate but who was not included in the order of distribution may enforce his or her rights against those who obtained the order.

DEBTS OF THE ESTATE

For a period of two years after the death of the decedent, the petitioners will be personally responsible for any valid debt owed by the estate, but only to the extent of the value of the portion of the estate received by each petitioner or beneficiary. The court may require proof of payment of a funeral or other bill.

TAX RELEASES

Effective January 1, 2000, for decedents dying after January 1, 2000, estates are no longer required to file a PRELIMINARY NOTICE AND REPORT (DR-301). If Florida estate tax is not due, and no IRS Form 706 is required, the personal representative should file the form AFFIDAVIT OF

NO FLORIDA ESTATE TAX DUE (DR-312). The **DR-312** form must be recorded with the Clerk of the Circuit Court in the county or counties in which the decedent owned property. (see form 19, p.141.) For persons dying after January 1, 2000, the Florida Department of Revenue will not issue a Nontaxable Certificate if the **DR-312** has been filed and no federal IRS 706 or 706-NA is required. However, for decedents who died before January 1, 2000 owning real estate in Florida, a Nontaxable Certificate should be obtained from the Florida Department of Revenue by filing a PRELIMINARY NOTICE AND REPORT (DR-301). (see form 45, p.182.)

If a federal IRS Form 706 is filed with the Florida Department of Revenue and no Florida estate tax is due, the Department of Revenue will still provide a Nontaxable Certificate and Receipt for Estate Tax for a $5.00 fee, which is evidence that no Florida estate tax is due. This should also be recorded in the county in which the decedent owned real property.

For more information check the website:

http://sun6.dms.state.fl.us/dor

ORDER OF FAMILY ADMINISTRATION

Distribution of the assets in family administration is described in the ORDER OF FAMILY ADMINISTRATION ORDER (Form 26—WITH WILL, or Form 28—WITHOUT WILL). The ORDER describes the asset(s) to be received by each beneficiary. If the ORDER states that the estate has debts, the following information must be included as well:

- the name of the creditor;
- the type of debt, the amount and due date;
- who will pay the debt;
- how the debt will be paid; and
- the creditor's consent to any agreement regarding payment.

Summary Administration 4

Summary administration is a simplified form of probate administration that may be used if the entire value of the estate, less the amount that is exempt from creditors, is less than $25,000, *or* the decedent died more than two years prior to filing for administration. (Fla. Stat., Ch. 735, Part II.) There is no personal representative, as the heirs or beneficiaries are the petitioners. Because there is no personal representative, the court should not require that the heirs or beneficiaries hire an attorney to handle the paperwork. (Florida Probate Rule 5.030; Fla. Stat., Sec. 454.18.)

Summary administration is not allowed if the last will and testament of the decedent requires formal administration. (See the SUMMARY ADMINISTRATION CHECKLIST in Appendix B to help get you organized.)

OATH OF WITNESS

Self-proved wills (signed as required under Florida law) may be admitted to probate without any additional documentation. *Self-proved* means that the witnesses took an oath at the time the will was signed, the statement is included in the last will and testament, and the decedent's signature was notarized by a qualified notary public.

If the will was not self-proved then it may be admitted to probate only after the oath of any of the attesting witnesses is taken before a circuit judge, clerk, or court-appointed commissioner. This means that you must contact one of the witnesses and ask that they appear at the -courthouse to sign the OATH OF WITNESS TO WILL. (see form 10, p.128.)

If the witness cannot appear at the courthouse without great hardship then the court will appoint a commissioner to take the oath of the witness. See "Commission" in the next section.

If there is no competent witness available, the will may be admitted upon the oath of the personal representative or any other interested person before a circuit judge, clerk, or court-appointed commissioner, stating that he believes the will to be the true last will and testament of the decedent.

COMMISSION

If the will is not self-proved and the witness is unable to appear before the circuit court judge or clerk, the court may appoint a commissioner to take the oath of any person who witnessed the signing of the will. A commissioner is usually a notary public.

The procedure is to first locate a witness to the will and ask who the nearest notary is. Then prepare a PETITION FOR APPOINTMENT OF COMMISSIONER (form 11) and COMMISSION (form 12), naming that notary, and file them with the court clerk. After the judge signs the COMMISSION it is sent to the notary who executes it along with the witness and mails it back to the court.

If the will was prepared outside of Florida, the witnesses were probably employees of the law office which prepared the will. In such a case, call that out-of-state law office, explain the situation, and ask for the name of a notary in the law office. Then have that notary appointed as commissioner.

THE PETITION

The PETITION FOR SUMMARY ADMINISTRATION (form 29—WITH WILL, or form 31—WITHOUT WILL) may be filed by any beneficiary, legal heir, or person named in the decedent's last will and testament as personal representative.

The PETITION FOR SUMMARY ADMINISTRATION will state the interest the petitioner has in the estate (such as "son of decedent," "personal representative named in will," etc.) and include the names and addresses of all the beneficiaries, or all the known legal heirs, of the decedent. The petition must also include facts stating why the estate is entitled to summary administration, a complete list of assets and their value, including exempt assets, a statement that the estate is not indebted, or that a provision for payment of debts has been made, and a proposed schedule for distribution.

The forms included in this book cover a simple estate in which either there are no debts of the estate or the debts are barred (for example, because no claims have been filed). If there are debts that must be paid, the easiest way to handle them is for the beneficiaries to pay them before filing the PETITION FOR SUMMARY ADMINISTRATION. Otherwise the petition must include the following information:

- the name of each creditor,

- the nature of the debt,

- the amount of the debt and whether the amount is estimated or exact, and

- when the debt is due.

If provision for payment of the debt has been made other than in the proposed order of distribution, the following information must be shown:

- the name of the person who will pay the debt;

- the creditor's written consent for substitution or assumption of the debt by another person;

- the amount to be paid if the debt has been compromised; and

- if the debt is to be paid in other than one lump sum or as directed by court order, the time and method of payment.

If the debts of the estate are not paid at the time of filing the PETITION FOR SUMMARY ADMINISTRATION, you should retype the form in this book to include this information in place of paragraph 5 in form 29 or in place of paragraph 5 in form 31.

The petition must be signed and verified by the surviving spouse, if any, the heirs at law or beneficiaries, and the guardians of any heirs at law or beneficiaries. (Fla. Stat., Sec. 735.203.)

The PETITION FOR SUMMARY ADMINISTRATION is filed in the Florida county in which the decedent lived. If the decedent was a nonresident, then it should be filed in the Florida county in which the decedent owned property.

A petition may be filed at any time during formal or family administration of an estate when it appears that the estate would qualify for summary administration.

DEATH CERTIFICATE

A certified copy of the death certificate should be filed with the PETITION FOR SUMMARY ADMINISTRATION. However, it may be filed any time before the ORDER OF SUMMARY ADMINISTRATION is granted. (form 30—WITH WILL or form 32—WITHOUT WILL.)

FILING FEES

The filing fees for summary administration are generally lower than for formal administration. This amount must be submitted with the PETITION FOR SUMMARY ADMINISTRATION. Check with the court clerk to be sure of the current filing fee.

ORDER OF SUMMARY ADMINISTRATION

The ORDER OF SUMMARY ADMINISTRATION is provided to the court for signature. Use form 30 (WITH WILL) or form 32 (WITHOUT WILL). It should fully describe the assets of the estate, and provides for immediate distribution of the assets to the persons named in the petition who are entitled to them.

The ORDER OF SUMMARY ADMINISTRATION does the following:

- gives the beneficiaries or heirs the right to immediately receive the property of the estate, including any exempt property;

- requires any debtors of the estate to give specific property to those persons entitled to the property;

- provides that bona fide purchasers for value of estate property will take the property free from any claims of creditors, of the surviving spouse, or any other heirs;

- provides that property, which is subject to claims of creditors and is not purchased by third parties, continues to be subject to claims of creditors until barred by law;

- provides that petitioners for summary administration remain personally liable to creditors of the decedent to the extent of the property they received from the estate;

- provides that two years after the date of death of the decedent, neither the estate nor anyone to whom it was distributed will be responsible for any claims against the decedent, unless proceedings are already in process; and

- provides that anyone who was entitled to part of the estate but did not receive his or her share may enforce his or her rights against those to whom the estate assets were distributed.

PRELIMINARY NOTICE AND REPORT

Effective January 1, 2000, for decedents dying after January 1, 2000, estates are no longer required to file a PRELIMINARY NOTICE AND REPORT (DR-301). If Florida estate tax is not due, and no IRS Form 706 is required, the personal representative should file the form AFFIDAVIT OF NO FLORIDA ESTATE TAX DUE (DR-312). The DR-312 form must be recorded with the clerk of the Circuit Court in the county or counties in which the decedent owned property. (see form 19, p.141.) For persons dying after January 1, 2000, the Florida Department of Revenue will not issue a Nontaxable Certificate if the DR-312 has been filed and no federal IRS 706 or 706-NA is required.

NOTICE TO CREDITORS

Although not required, anyone who has received an ORDER OF SUMMARY ADMINISTRATION may publish a NOTICE TO CREDITORS SUMMARY ADMINISTRATION once a week for two consecutive weeks, giving the creditors of the estate three months from the date of first publication of the notice to file their claims with the court. This is done by contacting a newspaper that publishes legal announcements and having the paper publish a copy of the NOTICE TO CREDITORS SUMMARY ADMINISTRATION. (see form 36, p.171.) There is usually a newspaper that specializes in legal notices and is much cheaper than your local daily newspaper. You can check the newsstand at your local courthouse or the yellow pages of your phone directory to find this newspaper. Once the NOTICE TO CREDITORS has been published, the newspaper will send you a proof of publication affidavit. The newspaper may also file a copy of its affidavit with the court, or you may need to file a copy. After the *proof of publication* is received from the newspaper and filed with the court, the claims against the decedent's estate are barred unless filed within the required time period.

CONVERTING FROM FORMAL ADMINISTRATION TO SUMMARY ADMINISTRATION

If it is discovered that the estate falls within the requirements for summary administration, the court may be requested to convert from the formal administration. Once the order converting from formal to summary administration is granted, the petitioners should proceed with the steps for summary administration. There is a form in this book that may be used in requesting the court to allow conversion from formal to summary administration called PETITION TO ALLOW CONVERSION FROM FORMAL TO SUMMARY ADMINISTRATION. (see form 44, p.181.)

DISPOSITION OF PERSONAL PROPERTY WITHOUT ADMINISTRATION 5

Florida Statutes do not require administration of estates that consist only of the following assets:

- Personal property that is exempt from probate under Florida Statutes., Section 732.402 (household furniture, furnishings, and appliances in the decedent's usual place of abode up to a net value of $10,000 as of the date of death and all automobiles held in the decedent's name and regularly used by the decedent or members of the decedent's immediate family as their personal automobiles);

- Personal property that is exempt from claims of creditors under the Florida Constitution (up to $1000 in personal property);

- Nonexempt personal property of a value that does not exceed the amount of preferred funeral expenses and reasonable and necessary medical and hospital expenses incurred during the last sixty days of decedent's illness. (Fla. Stat., Sec. 735.301.)

Any interested party may submit an informal letter or affidavit explaining why the estate is exempt from administration. If the court is satisfied that this provision applies, the court will, by letter or otherwise, authorize the payment, transfer, or disposition of the personal property to those persons entitled to receive it.

This book contains forms that may be used to be sure that you include all necessary information. They are PETITION FOR DISPOSITION OF

PERSONAL PROPERTY WITHOUT ADMINISTRATION (form 33) and ORDER OF DISTRIBUTION OF PERSONAL PROPERTY WITHOUT ADMINISTRATION (form 34). In some counties the clerk may have a special form for this. If so, use the clerk's form. If you do not understand the forms the clerk at the probate court is required by Florida Probate Rule 5.420 (c) to help you fill them out.

INCOME TAX REFUNDS

If the decedent is entitled to a refund of federal income taxes in the amount of $500 or less, whether the tax return was joint or separate, the U.S. Treasury Department may pay the refund as follows:

- directly to the surviving spouse upon a sworn application; or

- if there is no surviving spouse, then to one of decedent's children named in a sworn application signed by all of decedent's children over fourteen years of age. (Fla. Stat., Sec. 735.302.)

The application must show that:

- the entire estate is exempt from claims of creditors;

- that provision has been made for the payment of decedent's debts; or

- that the decedent's estate has no debts.

The application must also show that administration of the estate has not been initiated and that, to the best of applicant's knowledge, none is planned. The APPLICATION FOR INCOME TAX REFUND in this book can be used for this purpose. (see form 35, p.170.)

If the request in the application is granted and the refund made, payment operates as a complete discharge of the United States from any action, claim, or demand. Payment by the United States Treasury Department does not establish ownership rights in the refund by the recipient.

GLOSSARY

A

administrator. *See* personal representative.

affidavit. A written declaration of facts voluntarily made and confirmed under oath before someone authorized to administer an oath (notary public).

ancillary administration. Probate of decedent's property located in a state other than the state in which the decedent lived.

ascendants. Any ancestors of an individual (either living or dead), including parents, grandparents, great-grandparents, etc.

B

beneficiary(ies). Person(s) named in a will to receive property, money, etc., from an estate.

bond. Money that backs a promise that an individual (usually the personal representative) will perform the duties required and not misuse estate funds.

C

commission. Court authorization to take the oath of a witness to will.

creditor. An individual or entity to which an estate may be indebted.

D

decedent. The person who has died.

descendants. Any offspring of an individual (either living or dead), including children, grandchildren, etc.

devisee. Person who inherits real property under a decedent's last will and testament.

domicile. The state or location in which a person has his or her principal residence, and to which he or she intends to return.

E

executor. *See* personal representative.

exempt property. Estate property that is not subject to probate proceedings.

F

family administration. Simplified probate proceeding that may be used if total value of the estate is less than $60,000.

formal administration. The procedure by which a decedent's estate is probated, usually when family or summary administration is not available.

G

guardian. A person appointed by the court to handle property and personal matters for another individual.

H

heir. An individual entitled by law to inherit from another.

homestead. Property that is set aside for the benefit of specific family members, and which cannot be transferred by the decedent to a third party.

I

interested person(s). An individual who may have a claim against the decedent's estate, or an interest in the outcome or distribution.

intestate. Dies without a will.

inventory. List of estate assets and liabilities.

J

joint tenancy. Ownership of property by two or more persons; upon the death of any one of the joint tenants the remaining joint tenants own the entire property.

jurisdiction. The authority by which courts accept and decide legal cases.

L

legatee. Persons who take real and/or personal property under a will.

letters of administration. Document signed by the court giving an individual authorization to act on behalf of the estate.

lessor. Landlord; the person who grants a lease of property to someone else (tenant).

lineal ascendant. Relationship in the direct ascending line, as in a parent.

lineal consanguinity. The relationship between persons in direct line from each other, such as father to son, grandson, great grandson.

lineal descendant. Relationship in the direct descending line, as in a son or grandson.

N

nontaxable certificate. Certificate obtained from Florida Department of Revenue confirming that there are no estate taxes due on the estate.

notary public. A public officer whose function it is to administer oaths and to take acknowledgments and certify them.

P

personal property. Having the quality of being moveable, as opposed to real property; everything that is the subject of ownership that is not classified as real property; includes tangible items such as furniture, and intangible items such as stocks and bonds.

personal representative. Individual or entity named in a will, or appointed by the court, to act on behalf of the estate during probate proceedings.

petition. Document filed in court requesting that certain action be taken, i.e. to open an estate for probate.

petitioner. Anyone who petitions, or asks the court in writing, to take a particular action.

preference. The payment to certain creditors to the exclusion of the remaining creditors; also, priority ranking of individuals or institutions who may be named as personal representative of an estate.

probate. The legal procedure of settling a decedent's estate.

pro rata. Proportionately; according to a certain percentage.

R

real property. Land, and that which is affixed to the land.

resident agent. Person in the county where estate is probated who is appointed by the court to accept any notice or service of summons in the estate proceeding.

S

self-proved will. A will in which at least two witnesses took an oath, included in the will, at the time the will was signed, and in which both the witnesses' and the decedent's signatures were notarized by a qualified notary public. (Florida Statute, Section 732.503.)

SS-4. A form that is used to apply for the federal tax identification.

statement of claim. A written statement of facts explaining on what basis a demand for payment from the decedent's estate is being made.

summary administration. A simplified probate proceeding that may be used if the total value of the estate is $25,000 or less, and there is no real property.

T

tenancy by entireties. A form of property ownership in Florida by husband and wife; each owns the entire estate, and upon the death of either the survivor is sole owner of the entire estate.

tenancy in common. Ownership by two or more individuals or entities; each owner's interest can be inherited by that owner's heirs.

testate. Dies with a will.

testator/testatrix. Male/female who signed his or her last will and testament.

trustee. Person or entity authorized by a trust document to handle certain property matters on behalf of another.

V

venue. The particular county or city in which a court with jurisdiction may hear and determine a case.

W

will. Generally a written declaration or expression of a person's wishes as to disposition of his or her property upon death.

witness. Individual who observed an individual signing his or her will, and who also signed the will as an observer.

At the time this book was published these statutes were the most current available. However, as of January 1, 2002, some sections may change. The statutes are directly available from the State of Florida website:

http://www.leg.state.fl.us/statutes.

NOTE: *The Florida Probate Rules detail procedures that must be followed in probate. The Rules should be read in conjunction with the Statutes, and can be found at:*

http://www.flabar.org/newflaba/images/
downloads/rulesofprocedure

CHAPTER 732
PROBATE CODE: INTESTATE SUCCESSION AND WILLS
PART I
INTESTATE SUCCESSION

732.101 Intestate estate.--
(1) Any part of the estate of a decedent not effectively disposed of by will passes to the decedent's heirs as prescribed in the following sections of this code.
(2) The decedent's death is the event that vests the heirs' right to intestate property.

732.102 Share of spouse.--
(1) The intestate share of the surviving spouse is:
(a) If there is no surviving lineal descendant of the decedent, the entire intestate estate.
(b) If there are surviving lineal descendants of the

decedent, all of whom are lineal descendants of the surviving spouse also, the first $20,000 of the intestate estate, plus one-half of the balance of the intestate estate. Property allocated hereunder to the surviving spouse to satisfy the $20,000 shall be valued at the fair market value on the date of the decedent's death.
(c) If there are surviving lineal descendants, one or more of whom are not lineal descendants of the surviving spouse, one-half of the intestate estate.
(2) The court shall allot the property to which the spouse is entitled, treating all beneficiaries equitably.

732.103 Share of other heirs.--The part of the intestate estate not passing to the surviving spouse under s. 732.102, or the entire intestate estate if there is no surviving spouse, descends as follows:
(1) To the lineal descendants of the decedent.
(2) If there is no lineal descendant, to the decedent's father and mother equally, or to the survivor of them.
(3) If there is none of the foregoing, to the decedent's brothers and sisters and the descendants of deceased brothers and sisters.
(4) If there is none of the foregoing, the estate shall be divided, one-half of which shall go to the decedent's paternal, and the other half to the decedent's maternal, kindred in the following order:
(a) To the grandfather and grandmother equally, or to the survivor of them.
(b) If there is no grandfather or grandmother, to uncles and aunts and descendants of deceased uncles and aunts of the decedent.

(c) If there is no paternal kindred or if there is no maternal kindred, the estate shall go to such of the kindred as shall survive in the order aforesaid.

(5) If there is no kindred of either part, the whole of such property shall go to the kindred of the last deceased spouse of the decedent as if the deceased spouse had survived the decedent and then died intestate entitled to the estate.

732.104 Inheritance per stirpes.--Descent shall be per stirpes, whether to lineal descendants or to collateral heirs.

732.105 Half blood.--When property descends to the collateral kindred of the intestate and part of the collateral kindred are of the whole blood to the intestate and the other part of the half blood, those of the half blood shall inherit only half as much as those of the whole blood; but if all are of the half blood they shall have whole parts.

732.106 Afterborn heirs.--Heirs of the decedent conceived before his or her death, but born thereafter, inherit intestate property as if they had been born in the decedent's lifetime.

732.107 Escheat.--
(1) When a person leaving an estate dies without being survived by any person entitled to it, the property shall escheat to the state.
(2) (a) In this event, or when doubt exists about the existence of any person entitled to the estate, the personal representative shall institute a proceeding for the determination of beneficiaries, as provided in this code, within 1 year after letters have been issued to him or her, and notice shall be served on the Department of Legal Affairs. If the personal representative fails to institute the proceeding within the time fixed, it may be instituted by the Department of Legal Affairs.
(b) On or before January 15 of each year, each court shall furnish to the department a list of all estates being administered in which no person appears to be entitled to the property and the personal representative has not instituted a proceeding for the determination of beneficiaries.
(3) If the court determines that there is no person entitled to the estate and that the estate escheats, the property shall be sold and the proceeds paid to the Treasurer of the state and deposited by him or her in the State School Fund within a reasonable time to be fixed by the court.
(4) At any time within 10 years after the granting of letters, a person claiming to be entitled to the estate of the decedent may petition to reopen the administration and assert his or her rights to escheated property. If the claimant is entitled to any of the estate of the decedent, the court shall fix the amount to which he or she is entitled, and it shall be repaid to him or her with interest at the legal rate by the officials charged with the disbursement of state school funds. If no claim is asserted within the time fixed, the title of the state to the property and the proceeds shall become absolute.
(5) The Department of Legal Affairs shall represent the state in all proceedings concerning escheated estates.
(6)(a) If a person entitled to the funds assigns his or her rights to receive payment to an attorney or private investigative agency which is duly licensed to do business in this state pursuant to a written agreement with such person, the Department of Banking and Finance is authorized to make distribution in accordance with such assignment.
(b) Payments made to an attorney or private investigative agency shall be promptly deposited into a trust or escrow account which is regularly maintained by the attorney or private investigative agency in a financial institution authorized to accept such deposits and located in this state.
(c) Distribution by the attorney or private investigative agency to the person entitled to the funds shall be made within 10 days following final credit of the deposit into the trust or escrow account at the financial institution, unless a party to the agreement protests in writing such distribution before it is made.
(d) The department shall not be civilly or criminally liable for any funds distributed pursuant to this subsection, provided such distribution is made in good faith.
(7) Except as herein provided, escheated estates shall be administered as other estates.

732.108 Adopted persons and persons born out of wedlock.--
(1) For the purpose of intestate succession by or from an adopted person, the adopted person is a lineal descendant of the adopting parent and is one of the natural kindred of all members of the adopting parent's family, and is not a lineal descendant of his or her natural parents, nor is he or she one of the kindred of any member of the natural parent's family or any prior adoptive parent's family, except that:
(a) Adoption of a child by the spouse of a natural parent has no effect on the relationship between the child and the natural parent or the natural parent's family.
(b) Adoption of a child by a natural parent's spouse who married the natural parent after the death of the other natural parent has no effect on the relationship between the child and the family of the deceased natural parent.
(c) Adoption of a child by a close relative, as defined in s. 63.172(2), has no effect on the relationship between the child and the families of the deceased natural parents.
(2) For the purpose of intestate succession in cases not covered by subsection (1), a person born out of wedlock is a lineal descendant of his or her mother and is one of the natural kindred of all members of the mother's family. The person is also a lineal descendant of his or her father and is one of the natural kindred of all members of the father's family, if:

(a) The natural parents participated in a marriage ceremony before or after the birth of the person born out of wedlock, even though the attempted marriage is void.

(b) The paternity of the father is established by an adjudication before or after the death of the father.

(c) The paternity of the father is acknowledged in writing by the father.

732.109 Debts to decedent.--A debt owed to the decedent shall not be charged against the intestate share of any person except the debtor. If the debtor does not survive the decedent, the debt shall not be taken into account in computing the intestate share of the debtor's heirs.

732.1101 Aliens.--No person is disqualified to take as an heir because he or she, or a person through whom he or she claims, is, or has been, an alien.

732.111 Dower and curtesy abolished.--Dower and curtesy are abolished.

PART II
ELECTIVE SHARE OF SURVIVING SPOUSE

732.201 Right to elective share.--The surviving spouse of a person who dies domiciled in Florida has the right to a share of the elective estate of the decedent as provided in this part, to be designated the elective share.

732.2025 Definitions.--As used in ss. 732.2025-732.2155, the term:

(1) "Direct recipient" means the decedent's probate estate and any other person who receives property included in the elective estate by transfer from the decedent, including transfers described in s. 732.2035(8), by right of survivorship, or by beneficiary designation under a governing instrument. For this purpose, a beneficiary of an insurance policy on the decedent's life, the net cash surrender value of which is included in the elective estate, is treated as having received property included in the elective estate. In the case of property held in trust, "direct recipient" includes the trustee but excludes the beneficiaries of the trust.

(2) "Elective share trust" means a trust where:

(a) The surviving spouse is entitled for life to the use of the property or to all of the income payable at least as often as annually;

(b) The trust is subject to the provisions of s. 738.12 or the surviving spouse has the right under the terms of the trust or state law to require the trustee either to make the property productive or to convert it within a reasonable time; and

(c) During the spouse's life, no person other than the spouse has the power to distribute income or principal to anyone other than the spouse.

(3) "General power of appointment" means a power of appointment under which the holder of the power, whether or not the holder has the capacity to exercise it, has the power to create a present or future interest in the holder, the holder's estate, or the creditors of either. The term includes a power to consume or invade the principal of a trust, but only if the power is not limited by an ascertainable standard relating to the holder's health, education, support, or maintenance.

(4) "Governing instrument" means a deed; will; trust; insurance or annuity policy; account with payable-on-death designation; security registered in beneficiary form (TOD); pension, profit-sharing, retirement, or similar benefit plan; an instrument creating or exercising a power of appointment or a power of attorney; or a dispositive, appointive, or nominative instrument of any similar type.

(5) "Payor" means an insurer, business entity, employer, government, governmental agency or subdivision, or any other person, other than the decedent's personal representative or a trustee of a trust created by the decedent, authorized or obligated by law or a governing instrument to make payments.

(6) "Person" includes an individual, trust, estate, partnership, association, company, or corporation.

(7) "Probate estate" means all property wherever

located that is subject to estate administration in any state of the United States or in the District of Columbia.

(8) "Qualifying special needs trust" or "supplemental needs trust" means a trust established for an ill or disabled surviving spouse with court approval before or after a decedent's death for such incapacitated surviving spouse, if, commencing on the decedent's death:

(a) The income and principal are distributable to or for the benefit of the spouse for life in the discretion of one or more trustees less than half of whom are ineligible family trustees. For purposes of this paragraph, ineligible family trustees include the decedent's grandparents and any descendants of the decedent's grandparents who are not also descendants of the surviving spouse; and

(b) During the spouse's life, no person other than the spouse has the power to distribute income or principal to anyone other than the spouse.

(c) The requirement for court approval and the limitation on ineligible family trustees shall not apply if the aggregate of the trust property as of the applicable valuation date in a qualifying special needs trust is less than $100,000.

(9) "Revocable trust" means a trust that is includable in the elective estate under s. 732.2035(4).

(10) "Transfer in satisfaction of the elective share" means an irrevocable transfer by the decedent to an elective share trust.

(11) "Transfer tax value" means the value the interest would have for purposes of the United States estate and gift tax laws if it passed without consideration to an unrelated person on the applicable valuation date.

732.2035 Property entering into elective estate.--

Except as provided in s. 732.2045, the elective estate consists of the sum of the values as determined under s. 732.2055 of the following property interests:

(1) The decedent's probate estate.

(2) The decedent's ownership interest in accounts or securities registered in "Pay On Death," "Transfer On Death," "In Trust For," or coownership with right of survivorship form. For this purpose, "decedent's ownership interest" means that portion of the accounts or securities which the decedent had, immediately before death, the right to withdraw or use without the duty to account to any person.

(3) The decedent's fractional interest in property, other than property described in subsection (2) or subsection (7), held by the decedent in joint tenancy with right of survivorship or in tenancy by the entirety. For this purpose, "decedent's fractional interest in property" means the value of the property divided by the number of tenants.

(4) That portion of property, other than property described in subsection (2), transferred by the decedent to the extent that at the time of the decedent's death the transfer was revocable by the decedent alone or in conjunction with any other person. This subsection does not

apply to a transfer that is revocable by the decedent only with the consent of all persons having a beneficial interest in the property.

(5)(a) That portion of property, other than property described in subsection (3), subsection (4), or subsection (7), transferred by the decedent to the extent that at the time of the decedent's death:

    1. The decedent possessed the right to, or in fact enjoyed the possession or use of, the income or principal of the property; or

    2. The principal of the property could, in the discretion of any person other than the spouse of the decedent, be distributed or appointed to or for the benefit of the decedent.

In the application of this subsection, a right to payments from an annuity or under a similar contractual arrangement shall be treated as a right to that portion of the income of the property necessary to equal the annuity or other contractual payment.

(b) The amount included under this subsection is:

    1. With respect to subparagraph (a)1., the value of the portion of the property to which the decedent's right or enjoyment related, to the extent the portion passed to or for the benefit of any person other than the decedent's probate estate; and

    2. With respect to subparagraph (a)2., the value of the portion subject to the discretion, to the extent the portion passed to or for the benefit of any person other than the decedent's probate estate.

(c) This subsection does not apply to any property if the decedent's only interests in the property are that:

    1. The property could be distributed to or for the benefit of the decedent only with the consent of all persons having a beneficial interest in the property; or

    2. The income or principal of the property could be distributed to or for the benefit of the decedent only through the exercise or in default of an exercise of a general power of appointment held by any person other than the decedent; or

    3. The income or principal of the property is or could be distributed in satisfaction of the decedent's obligation of support; or

    4. The decedent had a contingent right to receive principal, other than at the discretion of any person, which contingency was beyond the control of the decedent and which had not in fact occurred at the decedent's death.

(6) The decedent's beneficial interest in the net cash surrender value immediately before death of any policy of insurance on the decedent's life.

(7) The value of amounts payable to or for the benefit of any person by reason of surviving the decedent under any public or private pension, retirement, or deferred compensation plan, or any similar arrangement, other than benefits payable under the federal Railroad Retirement Act or the federal Social Security System. In

the case of a defined contribution plan as defined in s. 414(i) of the Internal Revenue Code of 1986, as amended, this subsection shall not apply to the excess of the proceeds of any insurance policy on the decedent's life over the net cash surrender value of the policy immediately before the decedent's death.

(8) Property that was transferred during the 1-year period preceding the decedent's death as a result of a transfer by the decedent if the transfer was either of the following types:

(a) Any property transferred as a result of the termination of a right or interest in, or power over, property that would have been included in the elective estate under subsection (4) or subsection (5) if the right, interest, or power had not terminated until the decedent's death.

(b) Any transfer of property to the extent not otherwise included in the elective estate, made to or for the benefit of any person, except:

    1. Any transfer of property for medical or educational expenses to the extent it qualifies for exclusion from the United States gift tax under s. 2503(e) of the Internal Revenue Code, as amended; and

    2. After the application of subparagraph (b)1., the first $10,000 of property transferred to or for the benefit of each donee during the 1-year period, but only to the extent the transfer qualifies for exclusion from the United States gift tax under s. 2503(b) or (c) of the Internal Revenue Code, as amended.

(c) Except as provided in paragraph (d), for purposes of this subsection:

    1. A "termination" with respect to a right or interest in property occurs when the decedent transfers or relinquishes the right or interest, and, with respect to a power over property, a termination occurs when the power terminates by exercise, release, lapse, default, or otherwise.

    2. A distribution from a trust the income or principal of which is subject to subsection (4), subsection (5), or subsection (9) shall be treated as a transfer of property by the decedent and not as a termination of a right or interest in, or a power over, property.

(d) Notwithstanding anything in paragraph (c) to the contrary:

    1. A "termination" with respect to a right or interest in property does not occur when the right or interest terminates by the terms of the governing instrument unless the termination is determined by reference to the death of the decedent and the court finds that a principal purpose for the terms of the instrument relating to the termination was avoidance of the elective share.

    2. A distribution from a trust is not subject to this subsection if the distribution is required by the terms of the governing instrument unless the event triggering the distribution is determined by reference to the death of the decedent and the court finds that a principal purpose of the terms of the governing instrument relating

to the distribution is avoidance of the elective share.

(9) Property transferred in satisfaction of the elective share.

732.2045 Exclusions and overlapping application.--
(1) EXCLUSIONS.--Section 732.2035 does not apply to:

(a) Except as provided in s. 732.2155(4), any transfer of property by the decedent to the extent the transfer is irrevocable before the effective date of this subsection or after that date but before the date of the decedent's marriage to the surviving spouse.

(b) Any transfer of property by the decedent to the extent the decedent received adequate consideration in money or money's worth for the transfer.

(c) Any transfer of property by the decedent made with the written consent of the decedent's spouse. For this purpose, spousal consent to split-gift treatment under the United States gift tax laws does not constitute written consent to the transfer by the decedent.

(d) The proceeds of any policy of insurance on the decedent's life in excess of the net cash surrender value of the policy whether payable to the decedent's estate, a trust, or in any other manner.

(e) Any policy of insurance on the decedent's life maintained pursuant to a court order.

(f) The decedent's one-half of the property to which ss. 732.216-732.228 apply and real property that is community property under the laws of the jurisdiction where it is located.

(g) Property held in a qualifying special needs trust on the date of the decedent's death.

(h) Property included in the gross estate of the decedent for federal estate tax purposes solely because the decedent possessed a general power of appointment.

(2) OVERLAPPING APPLICATION.--If s. 732.2035(1) and any other subsection of s. 732.2035 apply to the same property interest, the amount included in the elective estate under other subsections is reduced by the amount included under subsection (1). In all other cases, if more than one subsection of s. 732.2035 applies to a property interest, only the subsection resulting in the largest elective estate shall apply.

732.2055 Valuation of the elective estate.--For purposes of s. 732.2035, "value" means:

(1) In the case of any policy of insurance on the decedent's life includable under s. 732.2035(4), (5), or (6), the net cash surrender value of the policy immediately before the decedent's death.

(2) In the case of any policy of insurance on the decedent's life includable under s. 732.2035(8), the net cash surrender value of the policy on the date of the termination or transfer.

(3) In the case of amounts includable under s. 732.2035(7), the transfer tax value of the amounts on the date of the decedent's death.

(4) In the case of other property included under s. 732.2035(8), the fair market value of the property on the date of the termination or transfer, computed after deducting any mortgages, liens, or security interests on the property as of that date.

(5) In the case of all other property, the fair market value of the property on the date of the decedent's death, computed after deducting from the total value of the property:

(a) All claims, other than claims for funeral expenses, paid or payable from the elective estate; and

(b) To the extent they are not deducted under paragraph (a), all mortgages, liens, or security interests on the property.

732.2065 Amount of the elective share.--The elective share is an amount equal to 30 percent of the elective estate.

732.2075 Sources from which elective share payable; abatement.--

(1) Unless otherwise provided in the decedent's will or, in the absence of a provision in the decedent's will, in a trust referred to in the decedent's will, the following are applied first to satisfy the elective share:

(a) To the extent paid to or for the benefit of the surviving spouse, the proceeds of any term or other policy of insurance on the decedent's life if, at the time of decedent's death, the policy was owned by any person other than the surviving spouse.

(b) To the extent paid to or for the benefit of the surviving spouse, amounts payable under any plan or arrangement described in s. 732.2035(7).

(c) To the extent paid to or for the benefit of the surviving spouse, the decedent's one-half of any property described in s. 732.2045(1)(f).

(d) Property held for the benefit of the surviving spouse in a qualifying special needs trust.

(e) Property interests included in the elective estate that pass or have passed to or for the benefit of the surviving spouse.

(f) Property interests that would have satisfied the elective share under any preceding paragraph of this subsection but were disclaimed.

(2) If, after the application of subsection (1), the elective share is not fully satisfied, the unsatisfied balance shall be apportioned among the direct recipients of the remaining elective estate in the following order of priority:

(a) Class 1.--The decedent's probate estate and revocable trusts.

(b) Class 2.--Recipients of property interests included in the elective estate under s. 732.2035(2), (3), or (6) and, to the extent the decedent had at the time of death the power to designate the recipient of the property, property interests included under s. 732.2035(5) and (7).

(c) Class 3.--Recipients of all other property interests included in the elective estate except interests for which a charitable deduction with respect to the transfer of the property was allowed or allowable to the decedent or the decedent's spouse under the United States gift tax laws.

(3) The contribution required of the decedent's probate estate and revocable trusts may be made in cash or in kind. In the application of this subsection, subsections (4) and (5) are to be applied to charge contribution for the elective share to the beneficiaries of the probate estate and revocable trusts as if all beneficiaries were taking under a common governing instrument.

(4) Unless otherwise provided in the decedent's will or, in the absence of a provision in the decedent's will, in a trust referred to in the decedent's will, any amount to be satisfied from the decedent's probate estate, other than from property passing to an inter vivos trust, shall be paid from the assets of the probate estate in the order prescribed in s. 733.805.

(5) Unless otherwise provided in the trust instrument or, in the decedent's will if there is no provision in the trust instrument, any amount to be satisfied from trust property shall be paid from the assets of the trust in the order provided for claims under s. 737.3054(2) and (3). A direction in the decedent's will is effective only for revocable trusts.

732.2085 Liability of direct recipients and beneficiaries.--

(1) Only direct recipients of property included in the elective estate and the beneficiaries of the decedent's probate estate or of any trust that is a direct recipient, are liable to contribute toward satisfaction of the elective share.

(a) Within each of the classes described in s. 732.2075(2)(b) and (c), each direct recipient is liable in an amount equal to the value, as determined under s. 732.2055, of the proportional part of the liability for all members of the class.

(b) Trust and probate estate beneficiaries who receive a distribution of principal after the decedent's death are liable in an amount equal to the value of the principal distributed to them multiplied by the contribution percentage of the distributing trust or estate. For this purpose, "contribution percentage" means the remaining unsatisfied balance of the trust or estate at the time of the distribution divided by the value of the trust or estate as determined under s. 732.2055. "Remaining unsatisfied balance" means the amount of liability initially apportioned to the trust or estate reduced by amounts or property previously contributed by any person in satisfaction of that liability.

(2) In lieu of paying the amount for which they are liable, beneficiaries who have received a distribution of property included in the elective estate and direct recipients other than the decedent's probate estate or revocable trusts, may:

(a) Contribute a proportional part of all property received; or

(b) With respect to any property interest received

before the date of the court's order of contribution:

1. Contribute all of the property; or

2. If the property has been sold or exchanged prior to the date on which the spouse's election is filed, pay an amount equal to the value of the property, less reasonable costs of sale, on the date it was sold or exchanged.

In the application of paragraph (a), the "proportional part of all property received" is determined separately for each class of priority under s. 732.2075(2).

(3) If a person pays the value of the property on the date of a sale or exchange or contributes all of the property received, as provided in paragraph (2)(b):

(a) No further contribution toward satisfaction of the elective share shall be required with respect to such property.

(b) Any unsatisfied contribution is treated as additional unsatisfied balance and reapportioned to other recipients as provided in s. 732.2075 and this section.

(4) If any part of s. 732.2035 or s. 732.2075 is preempted by federal law with respect to a payment, an item of property, or any other benefit included in the elective estate, a person who, not for value, receives the payment, item of property, or any other benefit is obligated to return the payment, item of property, or benefit, or is personally liable for the amount of the payment or the value of that item of property or benefit, as provided in ss. 732.2035 and 732.2075, to the person who would have been entitled to it were that section or part of that section not preempted.

732.2095 Valuation of property used to satisfy elective share.--

(1) DEFINITIONS.--As used in this section, the term:

(a) "Applicable valuation date" means:

1. In the case of transfers in satisfaction of the elective share, the date of the decedent's death.

2. In the case of property held in a qualifying special needs trust on the date of the decedent's death, the date of the decedent's death.

3. In the case of other property irrevocably transferred to or for the benefit of the surviving spouse during the decedent's life, the date of the transfer.

4. In the case of property distributed to the surviving spouse by the personal representative, the date of distribution.

5. Except as provided in subparagraphs 1., 2., and 3., in the case of property passing in trust for the surviving spouse, the date or dates the trust is funded in satisfaction of the elective share.

6. In the case of property described in s. 732.2035(3) or (4), the date of the decedent's death.

7. In the case of proceeds of any policy of insurance payable to the surviving spouse, the date of the decedent's death.

8. In the case of amounts payable to the surviving spouse under any plan or arrangement described in s. 732.2035(7), the date of the decedent's death.

9. In all other cases, the date of the decedent's death or the date the surviving spouse first comes into possession of the property, whichever occurs later.

(b) "Qualifying power of appointment" means a general power of appointment that is exercisable alone and in all events by the decedent's spouse in favor of the spouse or the spouse's estate. For this purpose, a general power to appoint by will is a qualifying power of appointment if the power may be exercised by the spouse in favor of the spouse's estate without the consent of any other person.

(c) "Qualifying invasion power" means a power held by the surviving spouse or the trustee of an elective share trust to invade trust principal for the health, support, and maintenance of the spouse. The power may, but need not, provide that the other resources of the spouse are to be taken into account in any exercise of the power.

(2) Except as provided in this subsection, the value of property for purposes of s. 732.2075 is the fair market value of the property on the applicable valuation date.

(a) If the surviving spouse has a life interest in property not in trust that entitles the spouse to the use of the property for life, the value of the spouse's interest is one-half of the value of the property on the applicable valuation date.

(b) If the surviving spouse has an interest in a trust, or portion of a trust, which meets the requirements of an elective share trust, the value of the spouse's interest is a percentage of the value of the principal of the trust, or trust portion, on the applicable valuation date as follows:

1. One hundred percent if the trust instrument includes both a qualifying invasion power and a qualifying power of appointment.

2. Eighty percent if the trust instrument includes a qualifying invasion power but no qualifying power of appointment.

3. Fifty percent in all other cases.

(c) If the surviving spouse is a beneficiary of a trust, or portion of a trust, which meets the requirements of a qualifying special needs trust, the value of the principal of the trust, or trust portion, on the applicable valuation date.

(d) If the surviving spouse has an interest in a trust that does not meet the requirements of an elective share trust, the value of the spouse's interest is the transfer tax value of the interest on the applicable valuation date; however, the aggregate value of all of the spouse's interests in the trust shall not exceed one-half of the value of the trust principal on the applicable valuation date.

(e) In the case of any policy of insurance on the decedent's life the proceeds of which are payable outright or to a trust described in paragraph (b), paragraph (c), or paragraph (d), the value of the policy for purposes of s. 732.2075 and paragraphs (b), (c), and (d) is the net proceeds.

(f) In the case of a right to one or more payments from

an annuity or under a similar contractual arrangement or under any plan or arrangement described in s. 732.2035(7), the value of the right to payments for purposes of s. 732.2075 and paragraphs (b), (c), and (d) is the transfer tax value of the right on the applicable valuation date.

732.2105 Effect of election on other interests.--
(1) The elective share shall be in addition to homestead, exempt property, and allowances as provided in part IV.
(2) If an election is filed, the balance of the elective estate, after the application of s. 732.2145(1), shall be administered as though the surviving spouse had predeceased the decedent.

732.2115 Protection of payors and other third parties.--Although a property interest is included in the decedent's elective estate under s. 732.2035(2)-(8), a payor or other third party is not liable for paying, distributing, or transferring the property to a beneficiary designated in a governing instrument, or for taking any other action in good faith reliance on the validity of a governing instrument.

732.2125 Right of election; by whom exercisable.--
The right of election may be exercised:
(1) By the surviving spouse.
(2) By an attorney in fact or a guardian of the property of the surviving spouse, with approval of the court having jurisdiction of the probate proceeding. The court shall determine the election as the best interests of the surviving spouse, during the spouse's probable lifetime, require.

732.2135 Time of election; extensions; withdrawal.--
(1) Except as provided in subsection (2), the election must be filed within the earlier of 6 months of the date of the first publication of notice of administration or 2 years after the date of the decedent's death.
(2) Within the period provided in subsection (1), the surviving spouse or an attorney in fact or guardian of the property of the surviving spouse may petition the court for an extension of time for making an election. After notice and hearing, the court for good cause shown may extend the time for election. If the court grants the petition for an extension, the election must be filed within the time allowed by the extension.
(3) The surviving spouse or an attorney in fact, guardian of the property, or personal representative of the surviving spouse may withdraw an election at any time within 8 months of the decedent's death and before the court's order of contribution. If an election is withdrawn, the court may assess attorney's fees and costs against the surviving spouse or the spouse's estate.
(4) A petition for an extension of the time for making the election or for approval to make the election shall toll the time for making the election.

732.2145 Order of contribution; personal representative's duty to collect contribution.--
(1) The court shall determine the elective share and shall order contribution. All contributions are to bear interest at the statutory rate provided in s. 55.03(1) beginning 90 days from the date of the order. The order of contribution is prima facie correct in proceedings in any court or jurisdiction.
(2) Except as provided in subsection (3), the personal representative shall collect contribution from the recipients of the elective estate as provided in the court's order of contribution.
(a) If property within the possession or control of the personal representative is distributable to a beneficiary or trustee who is required to contribute in satisfaction of the elective share, the personal representative shall withhold from the distribution the contribution required of the beneficiary or trustee.
(b) If, after the order of contribution, the personal representative brings an action to collect contribution from property not within the personal representative's control, the judgment shall include the personal representative's costs and reasonable attorney's fees. The personal representative is not required to seek collection of any portion of the elective share from property not within the personal representative's control until after the entry of the order of contribution.
(3) A personal representative who has the duty under this section of enforcing contribution may be relieved of that duty by an order of the court finding that it is impracticable to enforce contribution in view of the improbability of obtaining a judgment or the improbability of collection under any judgment that might be obtained, or otherwise. The personal representative shall not be liable for failure to attempt collection if the attempt would have been economically impracticable.
(4) Nothing in this section limits the independent right of the surviving spouse to collect the elective share as provided in the order of contribution, and that right is hereby conferred. If the surviving spouse brings an action to enforce an order of contribution, the judgment shall include the surviving spouse's costs and reasonable attorney's fees.

732.2155 Effective date; effect of prior waivers; transition rules.--
(1) Sections 732.201-732.2155 are effective on October 1, 1999, for all decedents dying on or after October 1, 2001. The law in effect prior to October 1, 1999, applies to decedents dying before October 1, 2001.
(2) Nothing in ss. 732.201-732.2155 modifies or applies to the rights of spouses under chapter 61.
(3) A waiver of elective share rights before the effective date of this section which is otherwise in compliance with the requirements of s. 732.702 is a waiver of all rights under ss. 732.201-732.2145.
(4) Notwithstanding anything in s. 732.2045(1)(a) to the

contrary, any trust created by the decedent before the effective date of this section that meets the requirements of an elective share trust is treated as if the decedent created the trust after the effective date of this subsection and in satisfaction of the elective share.

(5) Sections 732.201-732.2155 do not affect any interest in contracts entered into for adequate consideration in money or money's worth before October 1, 1999, to the extent that the contract was irrevocable at all times from October 1, 1999, until the date of the decedent's death.

732.216 Short title.--Sections 732.216-732.228 may be cited as the "Florida Uniform Disposition of Community Property Rights at Death Act."

732.217 Application.--Sections 732.216-732.228 apply to the disposition at death of the following property acquired by a married person:

(1) Personal property, wherever located, which:

(a) Was acquired as, or became and remained, community property under the laws of another jurisdiction;

(b) Was acquired with the rents, issues, or income of, or the proceeds from, or in exchange for, community property; or

(c) Is traceable to that community property.

(2) Real property, except homestead and real property held as tenants by the entirety, which is located in this state, and which:

(a) Was acquired with the rents, issues, or income of, the proceeds from, or in exchange for, property acquired as, or which became and remained, community property under the laws of another jurisdiction; or

(b) Is traceable to that community property.

732.218 Rebuttable presumptions.--In determining whether ss. 732.216-732.228 apply to specific property, the following rebuttable presumptions apply:

(1) Property acquired during marriage by a spouse of that marriage while domiciled in a jurisdiction under whose laws property could then be acquired as community property is presumed to have been acquired as, or to have become and remained, property to which these sections apply.

(2) Real property located in this state, other than real property held as tenants by the entirety and homestead, and personal property wherever located acquired by a married person while domiciled in a jurisdiction under whose laws property could not then be acquired as community property and title to which was taken in a form which created rights of survivorship are presumed not to be property to which these sections apply.

732.219 Disposition upon death.--Upon the death of a married person, one-half of the property to which ss. 732.216-732.228 apply is the property of the surviving spouse and is not subject to testamentary disposition by the decedent or distribution under the laws of succession of this state. One-half of that property is the property of

the decedent and is subject to testamentary disposition or distribution under the laws of succession of this state. The decedent's one-half of the property is not subject to the surviving spouse's right to elect against the will.

732.221 Perfection of title of personal representative, heir, or devisee.--If the title to any property to which ss. 732.216-732.228 apply is held by the surviving spouse at the time of the decedent's death, the personal representative or an heir or devisee of the decedent may institute an action to perfect title to the property. The personal representative has no fiduciary duty to discover whether any property held by the surviving spouse is property to which these sections apply, unless a written demand is made by an heir, devisee, or creditor of the decedent within 6 months after the first publication of the notice of administration.

732.222 Purchaser for value or lender.--

(1) If a surviving spouse has apparent title to property to which ss. 732.216-732.228 apply, a purchaser for value or a lender taking a security interest in the property takes his or her interest in the property free of any rights of the personal representative or an heir or devisee of the decedent.

(2) If a personal representative or an heir or devisee of the decedent has apparent title to property to which ss. 732.216-732.228 apply, a purchaser for value or a lender taking a security interest in the property takes his or her interest in the property free of any rights of the surviving spouse.

(3) A purchaser for value or a lender need not inquire whether a vendor or borrower acted properly.

(4) The proceeds of a sale or creation of a security interest must be treated as the property transferred to the purchaser for value or a lender.

732.223 Perfection of title of surviving spouse.--If the title to any property to which ss. 732.216-732.228 apply was held by the decedent at the time of his or her death, title of the surviving spouse may be perfected by an order of the probate court or by execution of an instrument by the personal representative or the heirs or devisees of the decedent with the approval of the probate court. The probate court in which the decedent's estate is being administered has no duty to discover whether property held by the decedent is property to which ss. 732.216-732.228 apply. The personal representative has no duty to discover whether property held by the decedent is property to which ss. 732.216-732.228 apply unless a written demand is made by the surviving spouse or the spouse's successor in interest within 6 months after the first publication of the notice of administration.

732.224 Creditor's rights.--Sections 732.216-732.228 do not affect rights of creditors with respect to property to which ss. 732.216-732.228 apply.

732.225 Acts of married persons.--Sections 732.216-732.228 do not prevent married persons from severing or altering their interests in property to which these sections apply. The reinvestment of any property to which these sections apply in real property located in this state which is or becomes homestead property creates a conclusive presumption that the spouses have agreed to terminate the community property attribute of the property reinvested.

732.226 Limitations on testamentary disposition.--Sections 732.216-732.228 do not authorize a person to dispose of property by will if it is held under limitations imposed by law preventing testamentary disposition by that person.

732.227 Homestead defined.--For purposes of ss. 732.216-732.228, the term "homestead" refers only to property the descent and devise of which is restricted by s. 4(c), Art. X of the State Constitution.

732.228 Uniformity of application and construction.--Sections 732.216-732.228 are to be so applied and construed as to effectuate their general purpose to make uniform the law with respect to the subject of these sections among those states which enact them.

PART III
PRETERMITTED SPOUSE AND CHILDREN

732.301   Pretermitted spouse.
732.302   Pretermitted children.

732.301 Pretermitted spouse.--When a person marries after making a will and the spouse survives the testator, the surviving spouse shall receive a share in the estate of the testator equal in value to that which the surviving spouse would have received if the testator had died intestate, unless:
(1) Provision has been made for, or waived by, the spouse by prenuptial or postnuptial agreement;
(2) The spouse is provided for in the will; or
(3) The will discloses an intention not to make provision for the spouse.
The share of the estate that is assigned to the pretermitted spouse shall be obtained in accordance with s. 733.805.

732.302 Pretermitted children.--When a testator omits to provide in his or her will for any of his or her children born or adopted after making the will and the child has not received a part of the testator's property equivalent to a child's part by way of advancement, the child shall receive a share of the estate equal in value to that he or she would have received if the testator had died intestate, unless:
(1) It appears from the will that the omission was inten-

tional; or
(2) The testator had one or more children when the will was executed and devised substantially all the estate to the other parent of the pretermitted child.
The share of the estate that is assigned to the pretermitted child shall be obtained in accordance with s. 733.805.

PART IV
EXEMPT PROPERTY AND ALLOWANCES

732.401   Descent of homestead.
732.4015   Devise of homestead.
732.402   Exempt property.
732.403   Family allowance.

732.401 Descent of homestead.--
(1) If not devised as permitted by law and the Florida Constitution, the homestead shall descend in the same manner as other intestate property; but if the decedent is survived by a spouse and lineal descendants, the surviving spouse shall take a life estate in the homestead, with a vested remainder to the lineal descendants in being at the time of the decedent's death.
(2) If the decedent was domiciled in Florida and resided on real property that the decedent and the surviving spouse owned as tenants by the entirety, the real property shall not be homestead property.

732.4015 Devise of homestead.--
(1) As provided by the Florida Constitution, the homestead shall not be subject to devise if the owner is survived by a spouse or minor child, except that the homestead may be devised to the owner's spouse if there is no minor child.
(2) For the purposes of subsection (1), the term:
(a) "Owner" includes the settlor of a trust evidenced by a written instrument in existence at the time of the settlor's death pursuant to which the settlor retained the right either alone or in conjunction with any other person to amend or revoke the trust at any time before his or her death.
(b) "Devise" includes a disposition by trust of that portion of the trust estate which, if titled in the name of the settlor of the trust, would be the settlor's homestead.

1732.402 Exempt property.--
(1) If a decedent was domiciled in this state at the time of death, the surviving spouse, or, if there is no surviving spouse, the children of the decedent shall have the right to a share of the estate of the decedent as provided in this section, to be designated "exempt property."
(2) Exempt property shall consist of:
(a) Household furniture, furnishings, and appliances in the decedent's usual place of abode up to a net value of $10,000 as of the date of death.
(b) All automobiles held in the decedent's name and regularly used by the decedent or members of the dece-

dent's immediate family as their personal automobiles.

(c) Florida Prepaid College Program contracts purchased under s. 240.551 and Florida College Savings agreements established under s. 240.553.

(3) Exempt property shall be exempt from all claims against the estate except perfected security interests thereon.

(4) Exempt property shall be in addition to any property passing to the surviving spouse or heirs of the decedent under s. 4, Art. X of the State Constitution or the decedent's will, or by intestate succession, elective share, or family allowance.

(5) Property specifically or demonstratively devised by the decedent's will to any devisee shall not be included in exempt property. However, persons to whom property has been specifically or demonstratively devised and who would otherwise be entitled to it as exempt property under this section may have the court determine the property to be exempt from claims, except for perfected security interests thereon, after complying with the provisions of subsection (6).

(6) Persons entitled to exempt property shall be deemed to have waived their rights under this section unless a petition for determination of exempt property is filed by or on behalf of the persons entitled to the exempt property within 4 months after the date of the first publication of the notice of administration or within 40 days from the date of termination of any proceeding involving the construction, admission to probate, or validity of the will or involving any other matter affecting any part of the estate subject to this section.

732.403 Family allowance.--In addition to homestead and exempt property, if the decedent was domiciled in Florida at the time of death, the surviving spouse and the decedent's lineal heirs whom the decedent was obligated to support or who were in fact being supported by him or her are entitled to a reasonable allowance in money out of the estate for their maintenance during administration. After notice and hearing, the court may order this allowance to be paid as a lump sum or in periodic installments. The allowance shall not exceed a total of $6,000. It shall be paid to the surviving spouse, if living, for the use of the spouse and dependent lineal heirs. If the surviving spouse is not living, it shall be paid to the lineal heirs or to the persons having their care and custody. If any lineal heir is not living with the surviving spouse, the allowance may be made partly to the lineal heir or his or her guardian or other person having the lineal heir's care and custody and partly to the surviving spouse, as the needs of the dependent lineal heir and the surviving spouse appear. The family allowance shall have the priority established by s. 733.707. The family allowance is not chargeable against any benefit or share passing to the surviving spouse or to the dependent lineal heirs by intestate succession, elective share, or the will of the decedent, unless the will other-

wise provides. The death of any person entitled to a family allowance terminates his or her right to the part of the allowance not paid. For purposes of this section, the term "lineal heir" or "lineal heirs" means lineal ascendants and lineal descendants of the decedent.

PART V
WILLS

732.501 Who may make a will.--Any person 18 or more years of age who is of sound mind may make a will.

732.502 Execution of wills.--Every will must be in writing and executed as follows:

(1)   (a) Testator's signature.--

1. The testator must sign the will at the end; or

2. The testator's name must be subscribed at the end of the will by some other person in the testator's presence and by his or her direction.

(b) Witnesses.--The testator's:

1. Signing, or

2. Acknowledgment:

a. That he or she has previously signed the will, or

b. That another person has subscribed the testator's name to it,

must be in the presence of at least two attesting witnesses.

(c) Witnesses' signatures.--The attesting witnesses must sign the will in the presence of the testator and in the presence of each other.

(2) Any will, other than a holographic or nuncupative will, executed by a nonresident of Florida, either before or after this law takes effect, is valid as a will in this state if valid under the laws of the state or country

where the testator was at the time of execution. A will in the testator's handwriting that has been executed in accordance with subsection (1) shall not be considered a holographic will.

(3) No particular form of words is necessary to the validity of a will if it is executed with the formalities required by law.

(4) A codicil shall be executed with the same formalities as a will.

732.503 Self-proof of will.--A will or codicil executed in conformity with s. 732.502(1) and (2) may be made self-proved at the time of its execution or at any subsequent date by the acknowledgment of it by the testator and the affidavits of the witnesses, each made before an officer authorized to administer oaths and evidenced by the officer's certificate attached to or following the will, in substantially the following form:

STATE OF _____

COUNTY OF _____

We, _____, _____, and _____ the testator and the witnesses, respectively, whose names are signed to the attached or foregoing instrument, having been sworn, declared to the undersigned officer that the testator, in the presence of witnesses, signed the instrument as the testator's last will (codicil), that the testator (signed) (or directed another to sign for him or her), and that each of the witnesses, in the presence of the testator and in the presence of each other, signed the will as a witness.

(Testator)

(Witness)

(Witness)

Subscribed and sworn to before me by _____, the testator who is personally known to me or who has produced (type of identification) as identification, and by _____, a witness who is personally known to me or who has produced (type of identification) as identification, and by _____, a witness who is personally known to me or who has produced (type of identification) as identification, on _____, (year) .

(Signature of Notary Public)

(Print, type, or stamp commissioned name of Notary Public)

732.504 Who may witness.--

(1) Any person competent to be a witness may act as a witness to a will.

(2) A will or codicil, or any part of either, is not invalid because the will or codicil is signed by an interested witness.

732.505 Revocation by writing.--A will or codicil, or any part of either, is revoked:

(1) By a subsequent inconsistent will or codicil, even though the subsequent inconsistent will or codicil does not expressly revoke all previous wills or codicils, but the revocation extends only so far as the inconsistency exists.

(2) By a subsequent written will, codicil, or other writing declaring the revocation, if the same formalities required for the execution of wills are observed in the execution of the will, codicil, or other writing.

732.506 Revocation by act.--A will or codicil is revoked by the testator, or some other person in the testator's presence and at the testator's direction, by burning, tearing, canceling, defacing, obliterating, or destroying it with the intent, and for the purpose, of revocation.

732.507 Effect of subsequent marriage, birth, or dissolution of marriage.--

(1) Neither subsequent marriage nor subsequent marriage and birth or adoption of lineal descendants shall revoke the prior will of any person, but the pretermitted child or spouse shall inherit as set forth in ss. 732.301 and 732.302, regardless of the prior will.

(2) Any provisions of a will executed by a married person, which provision affects the spouse of that person, shall become void upon the divorce of that person or upon the dissolution or annulment of the marriage. After the dissolution, divorce, or annulment, any such will shall be administered and construed as if the former spouse had died at the time of the dissolution, divorce, or annulment of the marriage, unless the will or the dissolution or divorce judgment expressly provides otherwise.

732.508 Revival by revocation.--

(1) The revocation by the testator of a will that revokes a former will shall not revive the former will, even though the former will is in existence at the date of the revocation of the subsequent will.

(2) The revocation of a codicil to a will does not revoke the will, and, in the absence of evidence to the contrary, it shall be presumed that in revoking the codicil the testator intended to reinstate the provisions of a will or codicil that were changed or revoked by the revoked codicil, as if the revoked codicil had never been executed.

732.509 Revocation of codicil.--The revocation of a will revokes all codicils to that will.

732.5105 Republication of wills by codicil.--The execution of a codicil referring to a previous will has the effect of republishing the will as modified by the codicil.

732.511 Republication of wills by reexecution.--If a will has been revoked or if it is invalid for any other reason, it may be republished and made valid by its reexecution or the execution of a codicil republishing it with the formalities required by this law for the execution of wills.

732.512 Incorporation by reference.--

(1) A writing in existence when a will is executed may be incorporated by reference if the language of the will manifests this intent and describes the writing sufficiently to permit its identification.

(2) A will may dispose of property by reference to acts and events which have significance apart from their effect upon the dispositions made by the will, whether they occur before or after the execution of the will or before or after the testator's death. The execution or revocation of a will or trust by another person is such an event.

732.513 Devises to trustee.--

(1) A valid devise may be made to the trustee of a trust that is evidenced by a written instrument in existence at the time of making the will, or by a written instrument subscribed concurrently with making of the will, if the written instrument is identified in the will.

(2) The devise shall not be invalid for any or all of the following reasons:

(a) Because the trust is amendable or revocable, or both, by any person.

(b) Because the trust has been amended or revoked in part after execution of the will or a codicil to it.

(c) Because the trust instrument or any amendment to it was not executed in the manner required for wills.

(d) Because the only res of the trust is the possible expectancy of receiving, as a named beneficiary, a devise under a will or death benefits as described in s. 733.808, and even though the testator or other person has reserved any or all rights of ownership in such death benefit policy, contract, or plan, including the right to change the beneficiary.

(e) Because of any of the provisions of s. 689.075.

(3) The devise shall dispose of property under the terms of the instrument that created the trust as theretofore or thereafter amended.

(4) An entire revocation of the trust by an instrument in writing before the testator's death shall invalidate the devise or bequest.

(5) Unless the will provides otherwise, the property devised shall not be held under a testamentary trust of the testator but shall become a part of the principal of the trust to which it is devised.

(6) This section shall be cumulative to all laws touching upon the subject matter.

732.514 Vesting of devises.--

The death of the testator is the event that vests the right to devises unless the testator in his or her will has provided that some other event must happen before a devise shall vest.

732.515 Separate writing identifying devises of tangible property.--

A will may refer to a written statement or list to dispose of items of tangible personal property not otherwise specifically disposed of by the will, other than money and property used in trade or business. To be admissible under this section as evidence of the intended disposition, the writing must be signed by the testator and must describe the items and the devisees with reasonable certainty. The writing may be referred to as one in existence at the time of the testator's death. It may be prepared before or after the execution of the will. It may be altered by the testator after its preparation. It may be a writing that has no significance apart from its effect upon the dispositions made by the will.

732.5165 Effect of fraud, duress, mistake, and undue influence.--

A will is void if the execution is procured by fraud, duress, mistake, or undue influence. Any part of the will is void if so procured, but the remainder of the will not so procured shall be valid if it is not invalid for other reasons.

732.517 Penalty clause for contest.--

A provision in a will purporting to penalize any interested person for contesting the will or instituting other proceedings relating to the estate is unenforceable.

732.518 Will contests.--

An action to contest the validity of a will may not be commenced before the death of the testator.

PART VI
RULES OF CONSTRUCTION

732.6005	Rules of construction and intention.
732.601	Simultaneous Death Law.
732.603	Antilapse; deceased devisee; class gifts.
732.604	Failure of testamentary provision.
732.605	Change in securities; accessions; nonademption.
732.606	Nonademption of specific devises in certain cases; sale by guardian of the property; unpaid proceeds of sale, condemnation, or insurance.
732.607	Exercise of power of appointment.
732.608	Construction of generic terms.
732.609	Ademption by satisfaction.
732.611	Devises to be per stirpes.

732.6005 Rules of construction and intention.--

(1) The intention of the testator as expressed in his or her will controls the legal effect of the testator's dispositions. The rules of construction expressed in this part shall apply unless a contrary intention is indicated by the will.

(2) Subject to the foregoing, a will is construed to pass all property which the testator owns at death, including property acquired after the execution of the will.

732.601 Simultaneous Death Law.--

(1) When title to property or its devolution depends on priority of death and there is insufficient evidence that the persons have died otherwise than simultaneously, the property of each person shall be disposed of as if he or she had survived, except as provided otherwise in this law.

(2) When two or more beneficiaries are designated to take successively by reason of survivorship under another person's disposition of property and there is

insufficient evidence that the beneficiaries died otherwise than simultaneously, the property thus disposed of shall be divided into as many equal parts as there are successive beneficiaries and the parts shall be distributed to those who would have taken if each designated beneficiary had survived.

(3) When there is insufficient evidence that two joint tenants or tenants by the entirety died otherwise than simultaneously, the property so held shall be distributed one-half as if one had survived and one-half as if the other had survived. If there are more than two joint tenants and all of them so died, the property thus distributed shall be in the proportion that one bears to the whole number of joint tenants.

(4) When the insured and the beneficiary in a policy of life or accident insurance have died and there is insufficient evidence that they died otherwise than simultaneously, the proceeds of the policy shall be distributed as if the insured had survived the beneficiary.

(5) This law shall not apply in the case of wills, living trusts, deeds, or contracts of insurance in which provision has been made for distribution of property different from the provisions of this law.

732.603 Antilapse; deceased devisee; class gifts.--
Unless a contrary intention appears in the will:
(1) If a devisee who is a grandparent, or a lineal descendant of a grandparent, of the testator:
(a) Is dead at the time of the execution of the will,
(b) Fails to survive the testator, or
(c) Is required by the will to be treated as if he or she predeceased the testator,
then the descendants of the devisee take per stirpes in place of the deceased devisee. A person who would have been a devisee under a class gift if he or she had survived the testator shall be a devisee for purposes of this section whether his or her death occurred before or after the execution of the will.
(2) If a devisee who is not a grandparent, or a descendant of a grandparent, of the testator:
(a) Is dead at the time of the execution of the will,
(b) Fails to survive the testator, or
(c) Is required by the will to be treated as if he or she predeceased the testator,
then the testamentary disposition to the devisee shall lapse unless an intention to substitute another in his or her place appears in the will.

732.604 Failure of testamentary provision.--
(1) Except as provided in s. 732.603, if a devise other than a residuary devise fails for any reason, it becomes a part of the residue.
(2) Except as provided in s. 732.603, if the residue is devised to two or more persons and the share of one of the residuary devisees fails for any reason, his or her share passes to the other residuary devisee, or to the other residuary devisees in proportion to their interests in the residue.

732.605 Change in securities; accessions; non-ademption.--
(1) If the testator intended a specific devise of certain securities rather than their equivalent value, the specific devisee is entitled only to:
(a) As much of the devised securities as is a part of the estate at the time of the testator's death.
(b) Any additional or other securities of the same entity owned by the testator because of action initiated by the entity, excluding any acquired by exercise of purchase options.
(c) Securities of another entity owned by the testator as a result of a merger, consolidation, reorganization, or other similar action initiated by the entity.
(2) Distributions before death of a specifically devised security not provided for in subsection (1) are not part of the specific devise.

732.606 Nonademption of specific devises in certain cases; sale by guardian of the property; unpaid proceeds of sale, condemnation, or insurance.--
(1) If specifically devised property is sold by a guardian of the property for the care and maintenance of the ward or if a condemnation award or insurance proceeds are paid to a guardian of the property as a result of condemnation, fire, or casualty, the specific devisee has the right to a general pecuniary devise equal to the net sale price, the condemnation award, or the insurance proceeds. This subsection does not apply if, subsequent to the sale, condemnation, or casualty, it is adjudicated that the disability of the testator has ceased and the testator survives the adjudication by 1 year. The right of the specific devisee under this subsection is reduced by any right he or she has under subsection (2).
(2) A specific devisee has the right to the remaining specifically devised property and:
(a) Any balance of the purchase price owing from a purchaser to the testator at death because of sale of the property plus any security interest.
(b) Any amount of a condemnation award for the taking of the property unpaid at death.
(c) Any proceeds unpaid at death on fire or casualty insurance on the property.
(d) Property owned by the testator at his or her death as a result of foreclosure, or obtained instead of foreclosure, of the security for the specifically devised obligation.

732.607 Exercise of power of appointment.--A general residuary clause in a will, or a will making general disposition of all the testator's property, does not exercise a power of appointment held by the testator unless specific reference is made to the power or there is some other indication of intent to include the property subject to the power.

732.608 Construction of generic terms.--Adopted persons and persons born out of wedlock are included in class gift terminology and terms of relationship, in accordance with rules for determining relationships for purposes of intestate succession.

732.609 Ademption by satisfaction.--Property that a testator gave to a person in the testator's lifetime is treated as a satisfaction of a devise to that person, in whole or in part, only if the will provides for deduction of the lifetime gift, the testator declares in a contemporaneous writing that the gift is to be deducted from the devise or is in satisfaction of the devise, or the devisee acknowledges in writing that the gift is in satisfaction. For purposes of part satisfaction, property given during the testator's lifetime is valued at the time the devisee came into possession or enjoyment of the property or at the time of the death of the testator, whichever occurs first.

732.611 Devises to be per stirpes.--Unless the will provides otherwise, all devises shall be per stirpes.

PART VII
CONTRACTUAL ARRANGEMENTS
RELATING TO DEATH

732.701   Agreements concerning succession.
732.702   Waiver of right to elect and of other rights.

732.701 Agreements concerning succession.--
(1) No agreement to make a will, to give a devise, not to revoke a will, not to revoke a devise, not to make a will, or not to make a devise shall be binding or enforceable unless the agreement is in writing and signed by the agreeing party in the presence of two attesting witnesses.
(2) The execution of a joint will or mutual wills neither creates a presumption of a contract to make a will nor creates a presumption of a contract not to revoke the will or wills.

732.702 Waiver of right to elect and of other rights.--
(1) The right of election of a surviving spouse, the rights of the surviving spouse as intestate successor or as a pretermitted spouse, and the rights of the surviving spouse to homestead, exempt property, and family allowance, or any of them, may be waived, wholly or partly, before or after marriage, by a written contract, agreement, or waiver, signed by the waiving party. Unless it provides to the contrary, a waiver of "all rights," or equivalent language, in the property or estate of a present or prospective spouse, or a complete property settlement entered into after, or in anticipation of, separation, dissolution of marriage, or divorce, is a waiver of all rights to elective share, intestate share, pretermitted share, homestead property, exempt property, and family allowance by each spouse in the property of the other and a renunciation by each of all benefits that would

otherwise pass to either from the other by intestate succession or by the provisions of any will executed before the waiver or property settlement.
(2) Each spouse shall make a fair disclosure to the other of his or her estate if the agreement, contract, or waiver is executed after marriage. No disclosure shall be required for an agreement, contract, or waiver executed before marriage.
(3) No consideration other than the execution of the agreement, contract, or waiver shall be necessary to its validity, whether executed before or after marriage.

PART VIII
GENERAL PROVISIONS

732.801   Disclaimer of interests in property passing by will or intestate succession or under certain powers of appointment.
732.802   Killer not entitled to receive property or other benefits by reason of victim's death.
732.804   Provisions relating to cremation.

732.801 Disclaimer of interests in property passing by will or intestate succession or under certain powers of appointment.--
(1) DEFINITIONS.--For purposes of this section:
(a) "Beneficiary" means a person who would succeed to an interest in property in any manner described in subsection (2).
(b) "Decedent" means the person by whom an interest in property was created or from whom it would have been received by a beneficiary.
(c) "Power of appointment" means any power described in subparagraph (d)3.
(d) An "interest in property" that may be disclaimed shall include:
    1. The whole of any property, real or personal, legal or equitable, present or future interest, or any fractional part, share, or portion of property or specific assets thereof.
    2. Any estate in the property.
    3. Any power to appoint, consume, apply, or expend property, or any other right, power, privilege, or immunity relating to it.
(2) SCOPE OF RIGHT TO DISCLAIM.--
(a) A beneficiary may disclaim his or her succession to any interest in property that, unless disclaimed, would pass to the beneficiary:
    1. By intestate succession or devise.
    2. Under descent of homestead, exempt property, or family allowance or under s. 222.13.
    3. Through exercise or nonexercise of a power of appointment exercisable by will.
    4. Through testamentary exercise or nonexercise of a power of appointment exercisable by either deed or will.
    5. As beneficiary of a testamentary trust.

6. As a beneficiary of a testamentary gift to any nontestamentary trust.

7. As donee of a power of appointment created by will.

8. By succession in any manner described in this subsection to a disclaimed interest.

9. In any manner not specifically enumerated herein under a testamentary instrument.

(b) Disclaimer may be made for a minor, incompetent, incapacitated person, or deceased beneficiary by the guardian or personal representative if the court having jurisdiction of the estate of the minor, incompetent, incapacitated person, or deceased beneficiary finds that the disclaimer:

1. Is in the best interests of those interested in the estate of the beneficiary and of those who take the beneficiary's interest by virtue of the disclaimer and

2. Is not detrimental to the best interests of the beneficiary.

The determination shall be made on a petition filed for that purpose and served on all interested persons. If ordered by the court, the guardian or personal representative shall execute and record the disclaimer on behalf of the beneficiary within the time and in the manner in which the beneficiary could disclaim if he or she were living, of legal age, and competent.

(3) DISPOSITION OF DISCLAIMED INTERESTS.--

(a) Unless the decedent or a donee of a power of appointment has otherwise provided by will or other appropriate instrument with reference to the possibility of a disclaimer by the beneficiary, the interest disclaimed shall descend, be distributed, or otherwise be disposed of in the same manner as if the disclaimant had died immediately preceding the death or other event that caused him or her to become finally ascertained as a beneficiary and the disclaimant's interest to become indefeasibly fixed both in quality and quantity. The disclaimer shall relate to that date for all purposes, whether recorded before or after the death or other event. An interest in property disclaimed shall never vest in the disclaimant. If the provisions of s. 732.603 would have been applicable had the disclaimant in fact died immediately preceding the death or other event, they shall be applicable to the disclaimed interest.

(b) Unless his or her disclaimer instrument so provides, a beneficiary who disclaims any interest that would pass to him or her in any manner described in subsection (2) shall not be excluded from sharing in any other interest to which he or she may be entitled in any manner described in the subsection, including subparagraph (2)(a)8., even though the interest includes disclaimed assets by virtue of the beneficiary's disclaimer.

(4) FORM, FILING, RECORDING, AND SERVICE OF DISCLAIMER INSTRUMENTS.--

(a) To be a disclaimer, a writing shall declare the disclaimer and its extent, describe the interest in property disclaimed, and be signed, witnessed, and acknowledged in the manner provided for the conveyance of real property.

(b) A disclaimer shall be effective and irrevocable when the instrument is recorded by the clerk where the estate of the decedent is or has been administered. If no administration has been commenced, recording may be made with the clerk of any county where venue of administration is proper.

(c) The person disclaiming shall deliver or mail a copy of the disclaimer instrument to the personal representative, trustee, or other person having legal title to, or possession of, the property in which the disclaimed interest exists. No representative, trustee, or other person shall be liable for any otherwise proper distribution or other disposition made without actual notice of the disclaimer or, if the disclaimer is waived or barred as hereinafter provided, for any otherwise proper distribution or other disposition made in reliance on the disclaimer, if the distribution or disposition is made without actual notice of the facts constituting the waiver or barring the right to disclaim.

(5) TIME FOR RECORDING DISCLAIMER.--A disclaimer shall be recorded at any time after the creation of the interest, but in any event within 9 months after the event giving rise to the right to disclaim, including the death of the decedent; or, if the disclaimant is not finally ascertained as a beneficiary or the disclaimant's interest has not become indefeasibly fixed both in quality and quantity at the death of the decedent, then the disclaimer shall be recorded not later than 6 months after the event that would cause him or her to become finally ascertained and his or her interest to become indefeasibly fixed both in quality and quantity. However, a disclaimer may be recorded at any time after the creation of the interest, upon the written consent of all interested parties as provided in s. 731.302.

(6) WAIVER OR BAR TO RIGHT TO DISCLAIM.--

(a) The right to disclaim otherwise conferred by this section shall be barred if the beneficiary is insolvent at the time of the event giving rise to the right to disclaim and also by:

1. Making a voluntary assignment or transfer of, a contract to assign or transfer, or an encumbrance of, an interest in real or personal property.

2. Giving a written waiver of the right to disclaim the succession to an interest in real or personal property.

3. Making any sale or other disposition of an interest in real or personal property pursuant to judicial process by the beneficiary before he or she has recorded a disclaimer.

(b) The acceptance, assignment, transfer, encumbrance, or written waiver of the right to disclaim a part of an interest in property, or the sale pursuant to judicial process of a part of an interest in property, shall not bar the right to disclaim any other part of the interest in property.

(7) EFFECT OF RESTRAINTS.--The right to disclaim granted by this section shall exist irrespective of any limitation imposed on the interest of the disclaimant in the nature of an express or implied spendthrift provision or similar restriction.

(8) RIGHT TO DISCLAIM UNDER OTHER LAW NOT ABRIDGED.--This law shall not abridge the right of any person to disclaim, renounce, alienate, release, or otherwise transfer or dispose of any interest in property under any other existing or future law.

732.802 Killer not entitled to receive property or other benefits by reason of victim's death.--

(1) A surviving person who unlawfully and intentionally kills or participates in procuring the death of the decedent is not entitled to any benefits under the will or under the Florida Probate Code, and the estate of the decedent passes as if the killer had predeceased the decedent. Property appointed by the will of the decedent to or for the benefit of the killer passes as if the killer had predeceased the decedent.

(2) Any joint tenant who unlawfully and intentionally kills another joint tenant thereby effects a severance of the interest of the decedent so that the share of the decedent passes as the decedent's property and the killer has no rights by survivorship. This provision applies to joint tenancies with right of survivorship and tenancies by the entirety in real and personal property; joint and multiple-party accounts in banks, savings and loan associations, credit unions, and other institutions; and any other form of coownership with survivorship incidents.

(3) A named beneficiary of a bond, life insurance policy, or other contractual arrangement who unlawfully and intentionally kills the principal obligee or the person upon whose life the policy is issued is not entitled to any benefit under the bond, policy, or other contractual arrangement; and it becomes payable as though the killer had predeceased the decedent.

(4) Any other acquisition of property or interest by the killer, including a life estate in homestead property, shall be treated in accordance with the principles of this section.

(5) A final judgment of conviction of murder in any degree is conclusive for purposes of this section. In the absence of a conviction of murder in any degree, the court may determine by the greater weight of the evidence whether the killing was unlawful and intentional for purposes of this section.

(6) This section does not affect the rights of any person who, before rights under this section have been adjudicated, purchases from the killer for value and without notice property which the killer would have acquired except for this section, but the killer is liable for the amount of the proceeds or the value of the property. Any insurance company, bank, or other obligor making payment according to the terms of its policy or obligation is not liable by reason of this section unless prior to payment it has received at its home office or principal address written notice of a claim under this section.

732.804 Provisions relating to cremation.--The fact that cremation occurred pursuant to a provision of a will or any written contract signed by the decedent in which he or she expressed the intent that his or her body be cremated is a complete defense to a cause of action against the personal representative or person providing the services.

PART IX
PRODUCTION OF WILLS

732.901   Production of wills.

732.901 Production of wills.--

(1) The custodian of a will must deposit the will with the clerk of the court having venue of the estate of the decedent within 10 days after receiving information that the testator is dead. The custodian must supply the testator's date of death or social security number to the clerk upon deposit. Willful failure to deposit the will with the clerk within the time period specified shall render the custodian responsible for all costs and damages sustained by anyone if the court finds that the custodian had no just or reasonable cause for withholding the deposit of the will.

(2) By petition and notice of it served on him or her, the custodian of any will may be compelled to produce and deposit the will as provided in subsection (1). All costs, damages, and a reasonable attorney's fee shall be adjudged to petitioner against the delinquent custodian if the court finds that the custodian had no just or reasonable cause for withholding the deposit of the will.

PART X
ANATOMICAL GIFTS

and Procurement Trust Fund.

732.9216   Organ and tissue donor education panel.

732.922   Duty of certain hospital administrators; liability of hospital administrators, organ procurement organizations, eye banks, and tissue banks.

732.910 Legislative declaration.--Because of the rapid medical progress in the fields of tissue and organ preservation, transplantation of tissue, and tissue culture, and because it is in the public interest to aid the medical developments in these fields, the Legislature in enacting this part intends to encourage and aid the development of reconstructive medicine and surgery and the development of medical research by facilitating premortem and postmortem authorizations for donations of tissue and organs. It is the purpose of this part to regulate the gift of a body or parts of a body, the gift to be made after the death of a donor.

732.911 Definitions.--As used in this part, the term:

(1) "Bank" or "storage facility" means a facility licensed, accredited, or approved under the laws of any state for storage of human bodies or parts thereof.

(2) "Death" means the absence of life as determined, in accordance with currently accepted medical standards, by the irreversible cessation of all respiration and circulatory function, or as determined, in accordance with s. 382.009, by the irreversible cessation of the functions of the entire brain, including the brain stem.

(3) "Donor" means an individual who makes a gift of all or part of his or her body.

(4) "Hospital" means a hospital licensed, accredited, or approved under the laws of any state and includes a hospital operated by the United States Government or a state, or a subdivision thereof, although not required to be licensed under state laws.

(5) "Physician" or "surgeon" means a physician or surgeon licensed to practice under chapter 458 or chapter 459 or similar laws of any state. "Surgeon" includes dental or oral surgeon.

732.912 Persons who may make an anatomical gift.--

(1) Any person who may make a will may give all or part of his or her body for any purpose specified in s. 732.910, the gift to take effect upon death. An anatomical gift made by an adult donor and not revoked by the donor as provided in s. 732.916 is irrevocable and does not require the consent or concurrence of any person after the donor's death.

(2) If the decedent has executed an agreement concerning an anatomical gift, including signing an organ and tissue donor card, expressing his or her wish to donate in a living will or advance directive, or signifying his or her intent to donate on his or her driver's license or in some other written form has indicated his or her wish to make an anatomical gift, and in the absence of actual notice of contrary indications by the decedent, the surrogate designated by the decedent pursuant to part II of chapter 765 may give all or any part of the decedent's body for any purpose specified in s. 732.910.

(3) If the decedent has not executed an agreement concerning an anatomical gift or designated a surrogate pursuant to part II of chapter 765 to make an anatomical gift pursuant to the conditions of subsection (2), a member of one of the classes of persons listed below, in the order of priority stated and in the absence of actual notice of contrary indications by the decedent or actual notice of opposition by a member of the same or a prior class, may give all or any part of the decedent's body for any purpose specified in s. 732.910:

(a) The spouse of the decedent;

(b) An adult son or daughter of the decedent;

(c) Either parent of the decedent;

(d) An adult brother or sister of the decedent;

(e) A grandparent of the decedent;

(f) A guardian of the person of the decedent at the time of his or her death; or

(g) A representative ad litem who shall be appointed by a court of competent jurisdiction forthwith upon a petition heard ex parte filed by any person, which representative ad litem shall ascertain that no person of higher priority exists who objects to the gift of all or any part of the decedent's body and that no evidence exists of the decedent's having made a communication expressing a desire that his or her body or body parts not be donated upon death;

but no gift shall be made by the spouse if any adult son or daughter objects, and provided that those of higher priority, if they are reasonably available, have been contacted and made aware of the proposed gift, and further provided that a reasonable search is made to show that there would have been no objection on religious grounds by the decedent.

(4) If the donee has actual notice of contrary indications by the decedent or, in the case of a spouse making the gift, an objection of an adult son or daughter or actual notice that a gift by a member of a class is opposed by a member of the same or a prior class, the donee shall not accept the gift.

(5) The person authorized by subsection (3) may make the gift after the decedent's death or immediately before the decedent's death.

(6) A gift of all or part of a body authorizes any examination necessary to assure medical acceptability of the gift for the purposes intended.

(7) Once the gift has been made, the rights of the donee are paramount to the rights of others, except as provided by s. 732.917.

732.913 Persons and entities that may become donees; purposes for which anatomical gifts may be made.--The following persons or entities may become donees of gifts of bodies or parts of them for the purposes stated:

(1) Any hospital, surgeon, or physician for medical or dental education or research, advancement of medical or dental science, therapy, or transplantation.

(2) Any accredited medical or dental school, college, or university for education, research, advancement of medical or dental science, or therapy.

(3) Any bank or storage facility for medical or dental education, research, advancement of medical or dental science, therapy, or transplantation.

(4) Any individual specified by name for therapy or transplantation needed by him or her.

However, the Legislature declares that the public policy of this state prohibits restrictions on the possible recipients of an anatomical gift on the basis of race, color, religion, sex, national origin, age, physical handicap, health status, marital status, or economic status, and such restrictions are hereby declared void and unenforceable.

732.914 Manner of executing anatomical gifts.--

(1) A gift of all or part of the body under s. 732.912(1) may be made by will. The gift becomes effective upon the death of the testator without waiting for probate. If the will is not probated or if it is declared invalid for testamentary purposes, the gift is nevertheless valid to the extent that it has been acted upon in good faith.

(2)(a) A gift of all or part of the body under s. 732.912(1) may also be made by a document other than a will. The gift becomes effective upon the death of the donor. The document must be signed by the donor in the presence of two witnesses who shall sign the document in the donor's presence. If the donor cannot sign, the document may be signed for him or her at the donor's direction and in his or her presence and the presence of two witnesses who must sign the document in the donor's presence. Delivery of the document of gift during the donor's lifetime is not necessary to make the gift valid.

(b) The following form of written instrument shall be sufficient for any person to give all or part of his or her body for the purposes of this part:

UNIFORM DONOR CARD

The undersigned hereby makes this anatomical gift, if medically acceptable, to take effect on death. The words and marks below indicate my desires:

I give:

(a) _____ any needed organs or parts;

(b) _____ only the following organs or parts

[Specify the organ(s) or part(s)]

for the purpose of transplantation, therapy, medical research, or education;

(c) _____ my body for anatomical study if needed.

Limitations or special wishes, if any:

(If applicable, list specific donee)

Signed by the donor and the following witnesses in the presence of each other:

(Signature of donor)

(Date of birth of donor)

(Date signed)

(City and State)

(Witness)

(Witness)

(Address)

(Address)

(3) The gift may be made to a donee specified by name. If the donee is not specified by name, the gift may be accepted by the attending physician as donee upon or following the donor's death. If the gift is made to a specified donee who is not available at the time and place of death, the attending physician may accept the gift as donee upon or following death in the absence of any expressed indication that the donor desired otherwise. However, the Legislature declares that the public policy of this state prohibits restrictions on the possible recipients of an anatomical gift on the basis of race, color, religion, sex, national origin, age, physical handicap, health status, marital status, or economic status, and such restrictions are hereby declared void and unenforceable. The physician who becomes a donee under this subsection shall not participate in the procedures for removing or transplanting a part.

(4) Notwithstanding s. 732.917(2), the donor may designate in his or her will or other document of gift the surgeon or physician to carry out the appropriate procedures. In the absence of a designation or if the designee is not available, the donee or other person authorized to accept the gift may employ or authorize any surgeon or physician for the purpose.

(5) Any gift by a member of a class designated in s. 732.912(3) must be made by a document signed by that person or made by that person's witnessed telephonic discussion, telegraphic message, or other recorded message.

732.915 Delivery of document; organ and tissue donor registry.--

(1) If a gift is made through the program established by the Agency for Health Care Administration and the Department of Highway Safety and Motor Vehicles under the authority of s. 732.921, the completed donor registration card shall be delivered to the Department of Highway Safety and Motor Vehicles and processed in a manner specified in subsection (4), but delivery is not necessary to the validity of the gift. If the donor withdraws the gift, the records of the Department of Highway Safety and Motor Vehicles shall be updated to reflect such withdrawal.

(2) If a gift is not made through the program established by the Agency for Health Care Administration and the Department of Highway Safety and Motor Vehicles under the authority of s. 732.921 and is made by the donor to a specified donee, the document, other than a will, may be delivered to the donee to expedite the appropriate procedures immediately after death, but delivery is not necessary to the validity of the gift. Such

document may be deposited in any hospital, bank, storage facility, or registry office that accepts such documents for safekeeping or for facilitation of procedures after death.

(3) On the request of any interested party upon or after the donor's death, the person in possession shall produce the document for examination.

(4) The Agency for Health Care Administration and the Department of Highway Safety and Motor Vehicles shall develop and implement an organ and tissue donor registry which shall record, through electronic means, organ and tissue donation documents submitted through the driver license identification program or by other sources. The registry shall be maintained in a manner which will allow, through electronic and telephonic methods, immediate access to organ and tissue donation documents 24 hours a day, 7 days a week. Hospitals, organ and tissue procurement agencies, and other parties identified by the agency by rule shall be allowed access through coded means to the information stored in the registry. Costs for the organ and tissue donor registry shall be paid from the Florida Organ and Tissue Donor Education and Procurement Trust Fund created by s. 732.92155. Funds deposited into the Florida Organ and Tissue Donor Education and Procurement Trust Fund shall be utilized by the Agency for Health Care Administration for maintaining the organ and tissue donor registry and for organ and tissue donor education.

732.916 Amendment or revocation of the gift.--
(1) A donor may amend or revoke an anatomical gift by:
(a) The execution and delivery to the donee of a signed statement.
(b) An oral statement that is:
    1. Made to the donor's spouse; or
    2. Made in the presence of two persons and communicated to the donor's family or attorney or to the donee.
(c) A statement during a terminal illness or injury addressed to an attending physician, who must communicate the revocation of the gift to the procurement organization that is certified by the state.
(d) A signed document found on the donor's person or in the donor's effects.
(2) Any gift made by a will may also be amended or revoked in the manner provided for amendment or revocation of wills or as provided in subsection (1).

732.917 Rights and duties at death.--
(1) The donee, as specified under the provisions of s. 732.915(2), may accept or reject the gift. If the donee accepts a gift of the entire body or a part of the body to be used for scientific purposes other than a transplant, the donee may authorize embalming and the use of the body in funeral services, subject to the terms of the gift. If the gift is of a part of the body, the donee shall cause the part to be removed without unnecessary mutilation

upon the death of the donor and before or after embalming. After removal of the part, custody of the remainder of the body vests in the surviving spouse, next of kin, or other persons under obligation to dispose of the body.

(2) The time of death shall be determined by a physician who attends the donor at the donor's death or, if there is no such physician, the physician who certifies the death. After death and in the absence of other qualified personnel, this physician may participate in, but shall not obstruct, the procedures to preserve the donor's organs or tissues and shall not be paid or reimbursed by, nor be associated with or employed by, an organ procurement organization, tissue bank, or eye bank. This physician shall not participate in the procedures for removing or transplanting a part.

(3) The organ procurement organization, tissue bank, or eye bank, or hospital medical professionals under the direction thereof, may perform any and all tests to evaluate the deceased as a potential donor and any invasive procedures on the deceased body in order to preserve the potential donor's organs. These procedures do not include the surgical removal of an organ or penetrating any body cavity, specifically for the purpose of donation, until a properly executed donor card or document is located or, if a properly executed donor card or document cannot be located, a person specified in s. 732.912(3) has been located, has been notified of the death, and has granted legal permission for the donation.

(4) All reasonable additional expenses incurred in the procedures to preserve the donor's organs or tissues shall be reimbursed by the organ procurement organization, tissue bank, or eye bank.

(5) A person who acts in good faith and without negligence in accord with the terms of this part or under the anatomical gift laws of another state or a foreign country is not liable for damages in any civil action or subject to prosecution for his or her acts in any criminal proceeding.

(6) The provisions of this part are subject to the laws of this state prescribing powers and duties with respect to autopsies.

732.918 Eye banks.--
(1) Any state, county, district, or other public hospital may purchase and provide the necessary facilities and equipment to establish and maintain an eye bank for restoration of sight purposes.
(2) The Department of Education may have prepared, printed, and distributed:
(a) A form document of gift for a gift of the eyes.
(b) An eye bank register consisting of the names of persons who have executed documents for the gift of their eyes.
(c) Wallet cards reciting the document of gift.

732.9185 Corneal removal by medical examiners.--
(1) In any case in which a patient is in need of corneal tis-

sue for a transplant, a district medical examiner or an appropriately qualified designee with training in ophthalmologic techniques may, upon request of any eye bank authorized under s. 732.918, provide the cornea of a decedent whenever all of the following conditions are met:

(a) A decedent who may provide a suitable cornea for the transplant is under the jurisdiction of the medical examiner and an autopsy is required in accordance with s. 406.11.

(b) No objection by the next of kin of the decedent is known by the medical examiner.

(c) The removal of the cornea will not interfere with the subsequent course of an investigation or autopsy.

(2) Neither the district medical examiner nor the medical examiner's appropriately qualified designee nor any eye bank authorized under s. 732.918 may be held liable in any civil or criminal action for failure to obtain consent of the next of kin.

732.919 Enucleation of eyes by licensed funeral directors.--With respect to a gift of an eye as provided for in this part, a licensed funeral director as defined in chapter 470 who has completed a course in eye enucleation and has received a certificate of competence from the Department of Ophthalmology of the University of Florida School of Medicine, the University of South Florida School of Medicine, or the University of Miami School of Medicine may enucleate eyes for gift after proper certification of death by a physician and in compliance with the intent of the gift as defined in this chapter. No properly certified funeral director acting in accordance with the terms of this part shall have any civil or criminal liability for eye enucleation.

732.921 Donations as part of driver license or identification card process.--

(1) The Agency for Health Care Administration and the Department of Highway Safety and Motor Vehicles shall develop and implement a program encouraging and allowing persons to make anatomical gifts as a part of the process of issuing identification cards and issuing and renewing driver licenses. The donor registration card distributed by the Department of Highway Safety and Motor Vehicles shall include the material specified by s. 732.914(2)(b) and may require such additional information, and include such additional material, as may be deemed necessary by that department. The Department of Highway Safety and Motor Vehicles shall also develop and implement a program to identify donors, which program shall include notations on identification cards, driver licenses, and driver records or such other methods as the department may develop. This program shall include, after an individual has completed a donor registration card, making a notation on the front of the driver license or identification card that clearly indicates the individual's intent to donate the individual's organs or tissue. A notation on an individual's

driver license or identification card that the individual intends to donate organs or tissues is deemed sufficient to satisfy all requirements for consent to organ or tissue donation. The Agency for Health Care Administration shall provide the necessary supplies and forms through funds appropriated from general revenue or contributions from interested voluntary, nonprofit organizations. The Department of Highway Safety and Motor Vehicles shall provide the necessary recordkeeping system through funds appropriated from general revenue. The Department of Highway Safety and Motor Vehicles and the Agency for Health Care Administration shall incur no liability in connection with the performance of any acts authorized herein.

(2) The Department of Highway Safety and Motor Vehicles, after consultation with and concurrence by the Agency for Health Care Administration, shall adopt rules to implement the provisions of this section according to the provisions of chapter 120.

(3) Funds expended by the Agency for Health Care Administration to carry out the intent of this section shall not be taken from any funds appropriated for patient care.

732.9215 Education program relating to anatomical gifts.--The Agency for Health Care Administration, subject to the concurrence of the Department of Highway Safety and Motor Vehicles, shall develop a continuing program to educate and inform medical professionals, law enforcement agencies and officers, high school children, state and local government employees, and the public regarding the laws of this state relating to anatomical gifts and the need for anatomical gifts.

(1) The program is to be implemented with the assistance of the organ and tissue donor education panel as provided in s. 732.9216 and with the funds collected under ss. 320.08047 and 322.08(6)(b). Existing community resources, when available, must be used to support the program, and volunteers may assist the program to the maximum extent possible. The Agency for Health Care Administration may contract for the provision of all or any portion of the program. When awarding such contract, the agency shall give priority to existing nonprofit groups that are located within the community, including within the minority communities specified in subsection (2). The program aimed at educating medical professionals may be implemented by contract with one or more medical schools located in the state.

(2) The Legislature finds that particular difficulties exist in making members of the various minority communities within the state aware of laws relating to anatomical gifts and the need for anatomical gifts. Therefore, the program shall include, as a demonstration project, activities especially targeted at providing such information to the nonwhite, Hispanic, and Caribbean populations of the state.

(3) The Agency for Health Care Administration shall, no later than March 1 of each year, submit a report to the Legislature containing statistical data on the effective-

ness of the program in procuring donor organs and the effect of the program on state spending for health care.

(4) The Agency for Health Care Administration, in furtherance of its educational responsibilities regarding organ and tissue donation, shall have access to the buildings and workplace areas of all state agencies and political subdivisions of the state.

732.92155 Florida Organ and Tissue Donor Education and Procurement Trust Fund.--The Florida Organ and Tissue Donor Education and Procurement Trust Fund is hereby created, to be administered by the Agency for Health Care Administration. Funds shall be credited to the trust fund as provided for in general law.

732.9216 Organ and tissue donor education panel.--

(1) The Legislature recognizes that there exists in the state a shortage of organ and tissue donors to provide the organs and tissue that could save lives or enhance the quality of life for many Floridians. The Legislature further recognizes the need to encourage the various minority populations of Florida to donate organs and tissue. It is the intent of the Legislature that the funds collected pursuant to ss. 320.08047 and 322.08(6)(b) be used for educational purposes aimed at increasing the number of organ and tissue donors, thus affording more Floridians who are awaiting organ or tissue transplants the opportunity for a full and productive life.

(2) There is created within the Agency for Health Care Administration a statewide organ and tissue donor education panel, consisting of 12 members, to represent the interests of the public with regard to increasing the number of organ and tissue donors within the state. The panel and the Organ and Tissue Procurement and Transplantation Advisory Board established in s. 381.6023 shall jointly develop, subject to the approval of the Agency for Health Care Administration, education initiatives pursuant to s. 732.9215, which the agency shall implement. The membership must be balanced with respect to gender, ethnicity, and other demographic characteristics so that the appointees reflect the diversity of the population of this state. The panel members must include:

(a) A representative from the Agency for Health Care Administration, who shall serve as chairperson of the panel.

(b) A representative from a Florida licensed organ procurement organization.

(c) A representative from a Florida licensed tissue bank.

(d) A representative from a Florida licensed eye bank.

(e) A representative from a Florida licensed hospital.

(f) A representative from the Division of Driver Licenses of the Department of Highway Safety and Motor Vehicles, who possesses experience and knowledge in dealing with the public.

(g) A representative from the family of an organ, tissue, or eye donor.

(h) A representative who has been the recipient of a transplanted organ, tissue, or eye, or is a family member of a recipient.

(i) A representative who is a minority person as defined in 1s. 381.81.

(j) A representative from a professional association or public relations or advertising organization.

(k) A representative from a community service club or organization.

(l) A representative from the Department of Education.

(3) All members of the panel shall be appointed by the Secretary of Health Care Administration to serve a term of 2 years, except that, initially, six members shall be appointed for 1-year terms and six members shall be appointed for 2-year terms.

(4) Members of the panel shall receive no compensation but shall be reimbursed for per diem and travel expenses by the agency in accordance with the provisions of s. 112.061, while engaged in the performance of their duties.

(5) The panel shall meet at least semiannually or upon the call of the chairperson or the Secretary of Health Care Administration.

732.922 Duty of certain hospital administrators; liability of hospital administrators, organ procurement organizations, eye banks, and tissue banks.--

(1) When used in this section, "hospital" means any establishment licensed under chapter 395 except psychiatric and rehabilitation hospitals.

(2) Where, based on accepted medical standards, a hospital patient is a suitable candidate for organ or tissue donation, the hospital administrator or the hospital administrator's designee shall, at or near the time of death, access the organ and tissue donor registry created by s. 732.915(4) to ascertain the existence of a donor card or document executed by the decedent. In the absence of a donor card, organ donation sticker or organ donation imprint on a driver's license, or other properly executed document, the hospital administrator or designee shall request:

(a) The patient's health care surrogate, as permitted in s. 732.912(2); or

(b) If the patient does not have a surrogate, or the surrogate is not reasonably available, any of the persons specified in s. 732.912(3), in the order and manner of priority stated in s. 732.912(3),

to consent to the gift of all or any part of the decedent's body for any purpose specified in this part. Except as provided in s. 732.912, in the absence of actual notice of opposition, consent need only be obtained from the person or persons in the highest priority class reasonably available.

(3) A gift made pursuant to a request required by this section shall be executed pursuant to s. 732.914.

(4) The Agency for Health Care Administration shall

establish rules and guidelines concerning the education of individuals who may be designated to perform the request and the procedures to be used in making the request. The agency is authorized to adopt rules concerning the documentation of the request, where such request is made.

(5) There shall be no civil or criminal liability against any organ procurement organization, eye bank, or tissue bank certified under s. 381.6022, or against any hospital or hospital administrator or designee, when complying with the provisions of this part and the rules of the Agency for Health Care Administration or when, in the exercise of reasonable care, a request for organ donation is inappropriate and the gift is not made according to this part and the rules of the Agency for Health Care Administration.

(6) The hospital administrator or a designee shall, at or near the time of death of a potential organ donor, directly notify the affiliated Health Care Financing Administration designated organ procurement organization of the potential organ donor. This organ procurement organization must offer any organ from such a donor first to patients on a Florida-based local or state organ sharing transplant list. For the purpose of this subsection, the term "transplant list" includes certain categories of national or regional organ sharing for patients of exceptional need or exceptional match, as approved or mandated by the United Network for Organ Sharing. This notification must not be made to a tissue bank or eye bank in lieu of the organ procurement organization unless the tissue bank or eye bank is also a Health Care Financing Administration designated organ procurement organization.

CHAPTER 733
PART I
GENERAL PROVISIONS

733.101 Venue of probate proceedings.--

(1) The venue of probate of all wills and granting of letters shall be:

(a) In the county in this state where the decedent had his or her domicile.

(b) If the decedent had no domicile in this state, then in any county where the decedent was possessed of any property.

(c) If the decedent had no domicile in this state and possessed no property in this state, then in the county where any debtor of the decedent resides.

(2) For the purpose of this section, a married woman whose husband is an alien or a nonresident of Florida may establish or designate a separate domicile in this state.

(3) When any proceeding is filed laying venue in the wrong county, the court may transfer the action in the same manner as provided in the Florida Rules of Civil Procedure. Any action taken by the court or the parties before the transfer is not affected because of the improper venue.

733.103 Effect of probate.--

(1) Until admitted to probate in this state or in the state where the decedent was domiciled, the will shall be ineffective to prove title to, or the right to possession of, property of the testator.

(2) In any collateral action or proceeding relating to devised property, the probate of a will in Florida shall be conclusive of its due execution; that it was executed by a competent testator, free of fraud, duress, mistake, and undue influence; and of the fact that the will was unrevoked on the testator's death.

733.104 Suspension of statutes of limitation in favor of the personal representative.--

(1) If a person entitled to bring an action dies before the expiration of the time limited for the commencement of the action and the cause of action survives, the action may be commenced by his or her personal representative after the expiration and within 12 months from the date of the decedent's death.

(2) If a person against whom a cause of action exists dies before the expiration of the time limited for commencement of the action and the cause of action survives, claim shall be filed on the cause of action, and it shall then proceed as other claims against the estate, notwithstanding the expiration of the time limited for commencement of the action.

733.105 Determination of beneficiaries.--

(1) When property passes by intestate succession or under a will to a person not sufficiently identified in the will and the personal representative is in doubt about:

(a) Who is entitled to receive it or part of it, or

(b) The shares and amounts that any person is entitled to receive, the personal representative may file a petition setting forth the names, residences, and post office addresses of all persons in interest, except creditors of the decedent, so far as known or ascertainable by diligent search and inquiry, and the nature of their respective interests, designating those who are believed by the personal representative to be minors or incompetents and stating whether those so designated are under legal guardianship in this state. If the personal representative believes that there are, or may be, persons whose names are not known to him or her who have claims against, or interest in, the estate as heirs or devisees, the petition shall so state.

(2) After formal notice and hearing, the court shall enter an order determining the heirs or devisees or the shares and amounts they are entitled to receive, or both. Any personal representative who makes distribution or takes any other action pursuant to the order shall be fully protected.

(3) When it is necessary to determine who are or were the heirs or devisees, the court may make a determination, on the petition of any interested person, in like proceedings and after formal notice, irrespective of whether the estate of the deceased person is administered or, if administered, whether the administration of the estate has been closed or the personal representative discharged. A separate civil action may be brought under this subsection when an estate is not being administered.

733.106 Costs and attorney fees.--

(1) In all probate proceedings costs may be awarded as in chancery actions.

(2) A person nominated as personal representative of the last known will, or any proponent of the will if the person so nominated does not act within a reasonable time, if in good faith justified in offering the will in due form for probate, shall receive his or her costs and attorney fees out of the estate even though he or she is unsuccessful.

(3) Any attorney who has rendered services to an estate may apply for an order awarding attorney fees, and after informal notice to the personal representative and all persons bearing the impact of the payment the court shall enter its order on the petition.

(4) When costs and attorney fees are to be paid out of the estate, the court may, in its discretion, direct from what part of the estate they shall be paid.

733.107 Burden of proof in contests.--In all proceedings contesting the validity of a will, the burden shall be upon the proponent of the will to establish prima facie its formal execution and attestation. Thereafter, the contestant shall have the burden of establishing the grounds on which the probate of the will is opposed or revocation sought.

733.109 Revocation of probate.--

(1) Any interested person, including a beneficiary under a prior will, except those barred under s. 733.212 or s. 733.2123, may, before final discharge of the personal representative, petition the court in which the will was admitted to probate for revocation of probate.

(a) The petition shall state the interest of the petitioner and the grounds for revocation.

(b) The petition shall be served upon the personal representative and all interested persons by formal notice, and thereafter proceedings shall be conducted as an adversary proceeding under the rules of civil procedure.

(2) Pending the determination of any petition for revocation of probate, the personal representative shall pro-

ceed with the administration of the estate as if no revocation proceeding had been commenced, except that no distribution may be made to devisees in contravention of the rights of those who, but for the will, would be entitled to the property disposed of.

(3) Revocation of probate of a will shall not affect or impair the title to the property theretofore purchased in good faith for value from the personal representative.

**PART II
COMMENCING ADMINISTRATION**

733.201	Proof of wills.
733.202	Petition.
733.203	Notice; when required.
733.204	Probate of a will written in a foreign language.
733.205	Probate of notarial will.
733.206	Probate of will of resident after foreign probate.
733.207	Establishment and probate of lost or destroyed will.
733.208	Discovery of later will.
733.209	Estates of missing persons.
733.212	Notice of administration; filing of objections and claims.
733.2123	Adjudication before issuance of letters.
733.213	Probate as prerequisite to petition for construction of will.

733.201 Proof of wills.--

(1) Self-proved wills executed in accordance with this code may be admitted to probate without further proof.

(2) A will may be admitted to probate upon the oath of any attesting witness taken before any circuit judge, commissioner appointed by the court, or clerk.

(3) If it appears to the court that the attesting witnesses cannot be found or that they have become incompetent after the execution of the will or their testimony cannot be obtained within a reasonable time, a will may be admitted to probate upon the oath of the personal representative nominated by the will as provided in subsection (2), whether or not he or she is interested in the estate, or of any person having no interest in the estate under the will, that he or she believes the writing exhibited to be the true last will of the decedent.

733.202 Petition.--

(1) A verified petition for administration may be filed by any interested person.

(2) The petition for administration shall contain:

(a) A statement of the interest of the petitioner, the petitioner's name and address, and the name and office address of his or her attorney.

(b) The name, last known address, social security number, and date and place of death of the decedent and the state and county of the decedent's domicile.

(c) So far as is known, the names and addresses of the beneficiaries and the dates of birth of any who are minors.

(d) A statement showing venue.

(e) The priority under part III of the person whose appointment as the personal representative is sought.

(f) A statement of the approximate value and nature of the assets so the clerk can ascertain the amount of the filing fee and the court can determine the amount of any bond authorized by this code.

(3) If the decedent was a nonresident of this state, the petition shall state whether domiciliary proceedings are pending in another state or country, if known, and, if so, the name and address of the foreign personal representative and the court issuing letters.

(4) In an intestate estate, the petition shall:

(a) State that after the exercise of reasonable diligence the petitioner is unaware of any unrevoked wills or codicils or, if the petitioner is aware of any unrevoked wills or codicils, why the wills or codicils are not being probated, or

(b) Otherwise give the facts concerning the will or codicil.

(5) In a testate estate, the petition shall:

(a) Identify all unrevoked wills and codicils being presented for probate.

(b) State that the petitioner is unaware of any other unrevoked will or codicil or, if the petitioner is aware of any other unrevoked will or codicil, why the other will or codicil is not being probated.

(c) State that the original of the decedent's last will is in the possession of the court or accompanies the petition or that an authenticated copy of a will probated in another jurisdiction accompanies the petition.

733.203 Notice; when required.--

(1) If a caveat has been filed by an heir or a devisee under a will other than that being offered for probate, the procedure provided for in s. 733.2123 shall be followed.

(2) Except as may otherwise be provided in this part, no notice need be given of the petition for administration or of the order granting letters when it appears that the petitioner is entitled to preference of appointment. Before letters shall be granted to any person who is not entitled to preference, formal notice shall be served on all known persons qualified to act as personal representative and entitled to preference equal to or greater than the applicant, unless those entitled to preference waive it in writing.

733.204 Probate of a will written in a foreign language.--

(1) No will written in a foreign language shall be admitted to probate unless it is accompanied by a true and complete English translation.

(2) In admitting the will to probate, the court shall estab-lish its correct English translation. If the original will is not or cannot be filed, a photographic copy of the original will shall be filed. At any time during the administration any interested person may have the correctness of the trans-lation, or any part, redetermined after formal notice to all other interested persons. No personal representative who complies in good faith with the English translation of the will as may then be established by the court shall thereafter be held liable as a result of having done so.

733.205 Probate of notarial will.--

(1) When a copy of a notarial will in the possession of a notary entitled to its custody in a foreign state or coun-try, the laws of which state or country require that the will remain in the custody of such notary, duly authenti-cated by the notary, whose official position, signature, and seal of office are further authenticated by an American consul, vice consul, or other American con-sular officer within whose jurisdiction the notary is a resi-dent, is presented to the court, it may be admitted to probate if the original could have been admitted to pro-bate in this state.

(2) The duly authenticated copy shall be prima facie evidence of its purported execution and of the facts stated in the certificate in compliance with subsection (1).

(3) Any interested person notified may oppose the pro-bate of such notarial will or may petition for revocation of probate of such notarial will, as in the case of original probate of a will in this state.

733.206 Probate of will of resident after foreign pro-bate.--

(1) If a will of any person who dies a resident of this state is admitted to probate in any other state or country through inadvertence, error, or omission before probate in this state, the will may be admitted to probate in this state if the original could have been admitted to probate in this state.

(2) An authenticated copy of the will, foreign proof of the will, the foreign order of probate, and any letters issued shall be filed instead of the original will and shall be prima facie evidence of its execution and admission to foreign probate.

(3) Any interested person may oppose the probate of the will, or may petition for revocation of the probate of the will, as in the case of the original probate of a will in this state.

733.207 Establishment and probate of lost or destroyed will.--

(1) The establishment and probate of a lost or destroyed will shall be in one proceeding. The court shall recite, and thereby establish and preserve, the full

and precise terms and provisions of the will in the order admitting it to probate.

(2) The petition for probate of a lost or destroyed will shall contain a copy of the will or its substance. The testimony of each witness must be reduced to writing and filed and shall be evidence in any contest of the will if the witness has died or moved from the state.

(3) No lost or destroyed will shall be admitted to probate unless formal notice has been given to those who, but for the will, would be entitled to the property thereby devised. The content of the will must be clearly and distinctly proved by the testimony of two disinterested witnesses, or, if a correct copy is provided, it shall be proved by one disinterested witness.

733.208 Discovery of later will.--On the discovery of a later will or codicil expressly or impliedly revoking the probated will in whole or in part, pending or during administration, any interested person may offer the later will for probate. The proceedings shall be similar to those for revocation of probate. No later will or codicil may be offered after the closing of the estate.

733.209 Estates of missing persons.--The estates of missing persons shall be administered in the same manner as other estates. A petition for administration of the estate shall request entry of an order declaring the death of a missing person prior to appointing a personal representative and commencing administration.

733.212 Notice of administration; filing of objections and claims.--

(1) The personal representative shall promptly publish a notice of administration. The notice shall contain the name of the decedent, the file number of the estate, the designation and address of the court in which the proceedings are pending, the name and address of the personal representative, and the name and address of the personal representative's attorney and state the date of first publication. The notice shall require all interested persons to file with the court:

(a) All claims against the estate within the time periods set forth in s. 733.702, or be forever barred.

(b) Any objection by an interested person on whom notice was served that challenges the validity of the will, the qualifications of the personal representative, venue, or jurisdiction of the court within the later of 3 months after the date of the first publication of the notice or 30 days after the date of service of a copy of the notice on the objecting person.

(2) Publication shall be once a week for 2 consecutive weeks, two publications being sufficient, in a newspaper published in the county where the estate is administered or, if there is no newspaper published in the county, in a newspaper of general circulation in that county.

(3) The personal representative shall serve a copy of the notice on the following persons who are known to the personal representative:

(a) The decedent's surviving spouse;

(b) Beneficiaries; and

(c) The trustee of any trust described in s. 733.707(3), of which the decedent was grantor

in the manner provided for service of formal notice, unless served under s. 733.2123. The personal representative may similarly serve a copy of the notice on any devisees under a known prior will or heirs.

(4)(a) The personal representative shall promptly make a diligent search to determine the names and addresses of creditors of the decedent who are reasonably ascertainable and shall serve on those creditors a copy of the notice within 3 months after the first publication of the notice. Under s. 409.9101, the Agency for Health Care Administration is considered a reasonably ascertainable creditor in instances where the decedent had received Medicaid assistance for medical care after reaching 55 years of age. Impracticable and extended searches are not required. Service is not required on any creditor who has filed a claim as provided in this part; a creditor whose claim has been paid in full; or a creditor whose claim is listed in a personal representative's timely proof of claim if the personal representative notified the creditor of that listing.

(b) The personal representative is not individually liable to any person for giving notice under this subsection, regardless of whether it is later determined that such notice was not required by this section. The service of notice in accordance with this subsection shall not be construed as admitting the validity or enforceability of a claim.

(c) If the personal representative in good faith fails to give notice required by this subsection, the personal representative is not liable to any person for the failure. Liability, if any, for the failure in such a case is on the estate.

(5) Objections under paragraph (1)(b), by persons on whom notice was served, that are not filed within the later of 3 months after the date of first publication of the notice or 30 days after the date of service of a copy of the notice on the objecting person are forever barred.

(6) Claims under paragraph (1)(a) are barred as provided in s. 733.702.

733.2123 Adjudication before issuance of letters.--A petitioner may serve formal notice of his or her petition for administration on interested persons. A copy of the will proposed to be admitted to probate shall be attached to the notice. No person who is served with formal notice of the petition for administration prior to the issuance of letters or who has waived notice may challenge the validity of the will, testacy of the decedent, qualifications of the personal representative, venue, or jurisdiction of the court, except in connection with the proceedings before issuance of letters.

733.213 Probate as prerequisite to petition for construction of will.--No pleading seeking construction of a will may be maintained until the will has first been probated.

PART III
PRIORITY TO ADMINISTER AND QUALIFICATIONS OF PERSONAL REPRESENTATIVE

733.301 Preference in appointment of personal representative.--In the granting of letters, the following preferences shall be observed:

(1) In testate estates:

(a) The personal representative, or his or her successor, nominated by the will or pursuant to a power conferred in the will.

(b) The person selected by a majority in interest of the persons entitled to the estate.

(c) A devisee under the will. If more than one devisee applies, the court may exercise its discretion in selecting the one best qualified.

(2) In intestate estates:

(a) The surviving spouse.

(b) The person selected by a majority in interest of the heirs.

(c) The heir nearest in degree. If more than one applies, the court may exercise its discretion in selecting the one best qualified for the office.

(3) A guardian of the property of a ward who if competent would be entitled to appointment as, or to select, a personal representative may exercise the right to select the personal representative.

(4) In either a testate or an intestate estate, if no application is made by any of the persons named in subsection (1) or subsection (2), the court shall appoint a capable person; but no person may be appointed under this subsection:

(a) Who works for, or holds public office under, the court.

(b) Who is employed by, or holds office under, any judge exercising probate jurisdiction.

(5) After letters have been granted in either a testate or an intestate estate, if a person who was entitled to, and has not waived, preference over the person appointed at the time of his or her appointment and on whom formal notice was not served seeks the appointment, the letters granted may be revoked and the person entitled to preference may have letters granted to him or her after formal notice and hearing.

(6) After letters have been granted in either a testate or an intestate estate, if any will is subsequently admitted to probate the letters shall be revoked and new letters granted as provided in subsection (1).

733.302 Who may be appointed personal representative.--Subject to the limitations in this part, any person sui juris who is a resident of Florida at the time of the death of the person whose estate he or she seeks to administer is qualified to act as personal representative in Florida. A person who has been convicted of a felony or who, from sickness, intemperance, or want of understanding, is incompetent to discharge the duties of a personal representative is not qualified.

733.303 Persons not qualified.--

(1) A person is not qualified to act as a personal representative if the person:

(a) Has been convicted of a felony.

(b) Is mentally or physically unable to perform the duties.

(c) Is under the age of 18 years.

(2) If the person named as personal representative in the will is not qualified, letters shall be granted as provided in s. 733.301.

733.304 Nonresidents.--A person who is not domiciled in the state cannot qualify as personal representative unless the person is:

(1) A legally adopted child or adoptive parent of the decedent;

(2) Related by lineal consanguinity to the decedent;

(3) A spouse or a brother, sister, uncle, aunt, nephew, or niece of the decedent, or someone related by lineal consanguinity to any such person; or

(4) The spouse of a person otherwise qualified under this section.

733.305 Trust companies and other corporations and associations.--

(1) All trust companies incorporated under the laws of the state, all state banking corporations and state savings associations authorized and qualified to exercise fiduciary powers in Florida, and all national banking associations and federal savings and loan associations authorized and qualified to exercise fiduciary powers in Florida shall be entitled to act as personal representatives and curators of estates.

(2) When a qualified corporation has been named as a personal representative in a will and thereafter transfers its business and assets to, consolidates or merges with, or is in any manner provided by law succeeded by, another qualified corporation, on the death of the testator, the successor corporation may qualify, and the court may issue letters to the successor corporation unless the will provides otherwise.

(3) A corporation authorized and qualified to act as a

personal representative as a result of merger or consolidation shall succeed to the rights and duties of all predecessor corporations as the personal representative of estates upon filing proof in the court, and without a new appointment. A purchase of substantially all the assets and the assumption of substantially all the liabilities shall be deemed a merger for the purpose of this section.

733.306 Effect of appointment of debtor.--The appointment of a debtor as personal representative shall not extinguish the debt due to the decedent. This section shall not prevent a testator from releasing a debtor by will.

733.307 Succession of administration.--No personal representative of a personal representative as such shall be authorized to administer the estate of the first decedent. On the death of the sole or surviving personal representative, the court shall appoint a successor personal representative to complete the administration of the estate.

733.308 Administrator ad litem.--When it is necessary that an estate be represented and there is no personal representative of the estate, the court shall appoint an administrator ad litem without bond for that particular proceeding. The fact that the personal representative is seeking reimbursement for claims against the decedent paid by the personal representative does not require appointment of an administrator ad litem.

733.309 Executor de son tort.--No person shall be liable to a creditor of a decedent as executor de son tort, but any person taking, converting, or intermeddling with the property of a decedent shall be liable to the personal representative or curator, when appointed, for the value of all the property so taken or converted and for all damages to the estate caused by his or her wrongful action. This section shall not be construed to prevent a creditor of a decedent from suing anyone in possession of property fraudulently conveyed by the decedent to set aside the fraudulent conveyance.

PART IV
APPOINTMENT OF PERSONAL
REPRESENTATIVE; BONDS

733.401   Issuance of letters.
733.402   Bond of personal representative; when required; form.
733.403   Amount of bond.
733.404   Liability of surety.
733.405   Release of surety.
733.406   Bond premium allowable as expense or costs.

733.401 Issuance of letters.--
(1) After the petition for administration is filed:

(a) The will, if any, shall be proved as provided elsewhere in this code and shall be admitted to probate.
(b) The court shall appoint the person entitled and qualified to be personal representative.
(c) The court shall determine the amount of any bond required under this part. The clerk may approve the bond in the amount determined by the court and shall not charge a service fee.
(d) Any required oath or designation of, and acceptance by, a resident agent shall be filed.
(2) Upon compliance with all of the foregoing, letters shall be issued to the personal representative.
(3) Mistaken noncompliance with any of the requirements of subsection (1) shall not be jurisdictional.

733.402 Bond of personal representative; when required; form.--
(1) Unless the testator waived the requirement, every person to whom letters are granted shall execute and file a bond with surety, as defined in s. 45.011, to be approved by the clerk. The bond shall be payable to the Governor and the Governor's successors in office, conditioned on the performance of all duties as personal representative according to law. The bond must be joint and several.
(2) No bond executed by a personal representative or curator shall be void or invalid because of an informality in it or an informality or illegality in the appointment of the fiduciary. The bond shall have the same force as if the appointment had been legally made and the bond executed in proper form.
(3) The requirements of this section shall not apply to banks and trust companies authorized by law to act as personal representative.

733.403 Amount of bond.--
(1) All bonds required by this part shall be in the penal sum that the court deems sufficient after consideration of the gross value of the estate, the relationship of the personal representative to the beneficiaries, exempt property and any family allowance, the type and nature of assets, and liens and encumbrances on the assets.
(2) On petition by any interested person or on the court's own motion, the court may waive the requirement of filing a bond, require a personal representative or curator to give bond, increase or decrease the bond, or require additional surety.

733.404 Liability of surety.--No surety for any personal representative or curator shall be charged beyond the assets of an estate because of any omission or mistake in pleading or of false pleading of the personal representative or curator.

733.405 Release of surety.--
(1) On petitioning the surety, or the personal representative of a surety, on the bond of any personal represen-

tative or curator shall be entitled as a matter of right to be released from future liability upon the bond.

(2) Pending the hearing of the petition, the court may restrain the principal from acting in his or her representative capacity, except to preserve the estate.

(3) On hearing, the court shall enter an order prescribing the amount of the new bond for the personal representative or curator and the date when the bond shall be filed. If the principal fails to give the new bond, he or she shall be removed at once, and further proceedings shall be had as in cases of removal.

(4) The original surety or sureties shall be liable for all acts of the personal representative or surety until he or she has given the new bond and, after the giving of the new bond, shall remain liable for all the principal's acts to the time of the filing and approval of the new bond. The new surety shall be liable for the principal's acts only after the filing and approval of the new bond.

733.406 Bond premium allowable as expense or costs.--Any receiver, assignee, trustee, committee, guardian, executor or administrator, or other fiduciary required by law to give bond as such, may include as part of his or her lawful expense such reasonable sum paid such an insurer for such suretyship not exceeding 1 percent per annum on the amount of the bond, as the head of department, board, court, judge or officer by whom, or the court or body in which, he or she was appointed allows; and in all actions or proceedings the party entitled to recover costs may include therein such reasonable sum as may have been paid such an insurer executing or guaranteeing any bond or undertaking therein.

PART V
CURATORS; SUCCESSOR PERSONAL REPRESENTATIVES; REMOVAL

733.501 Curators.--

(1) When it is necessary, the court may appoint a curator and issue letters of curatorship to take charge of the estate of a decedent until letters are granted. If the person entitled to letters is a resident of the county where the property is situated, no curator shall be appointed until formal notice is given to the person so entitled to letters. On appointment, the court shall direct the person in possession of the effects of the decedent to deliver them to the curator. The order may be enforced by contempt.

(2) If there is great danger that the property or any part of it is likely to be wasted, destroyed, or removed beyond the jurisdiction of the court and if the appointment of a curator would be delayed by giving notice, the court may appoint a curator without giving notice.

(3) On special order of the court, the curator may be authorized to perform any duty or function of a personal representative.

(4) Bond shall be required of the curator as the court deems necessary to secure the property. No bond shall be required of banks and trust companies as curators.

(5) The curator shall file an inventory of the property within 20 days. When the personal representative qualifies, the curator shall immediately account and deliver all assets of the estate in his or her hands to the personal representative within 20 days, and in default shall be subject to the provisions of this code relating to removal of personal representatives.

(6) Curators shall be allowed reasonable compensation for their services.

733.502 Resignation of personal representative.--A

personal representative may resign and be relieved of his or her office. Notice of the petition shall be given to all interested persons. Before relieving the personal representative from his or her duties and obligations, the court shall require the personal representative to file a true and correct account of his or her administration and deliver to his or her successor or to his or her joint personal representative all of the property of the decedent and all records concerning the estate. The acceptance of the resignation, after compliance with this section, shall not exonerate any personal representative or his or her surety from liability previously incurred.

733.503 Appointment of successor upon resignation.--If there is no joint personal representative, a successor must be appointed and qualified before a personal representative may be relieved of his or her duties and obligations as provided in s. 733.502.

733.504 Causes of removal of personal representative.--A personal representative may be removed and his or her letters revoked for any of the following causes, and the removal shall be in addition to any penalties prescribed by law:

(1) Adjudication of incompetency.

(2) Physical or mental incapacity rendering the personal representative incapable of the discharge of his or her duties.

(3) Failure to comply with any order of the court, unless the order has been superseded on appeal.

(4) Failure to account for the sale of property or to produce and exhibit the assets of the estate when so required.

(5) The wasting or maladministration of the estate.

(6) Failure to give bond or security for any purpose.

(7) Conviction of a felony.

(8) Insolvency of, or the appointment of a receiver or liquidator for, any corporate personal representative.

(9) The holding or acquiring by the personal representative of conflicting or adverse interests against the estate that will or may adversely interfere with the administration of the estate as a whole. This cause of removal shall not apply to the surviving spouse because of the exercise of the right to the elective share, family allowance, or exemptions, as provided elsewhere in this code.

(10) Revocation of the probate of the decedent's will that authorized or designated the appointment of such personal representative.

(11) Removal of domicile from Florida, if the personal representative is no longer qualified under part III of this chapter.

733.505 Jurisdiction in removal proceedings.--A petition for removal shall be filed in the court issuing the letters.

733.506 Proceedings for removal.--Proceedings for removal may be commenced by the court or by any interested person or joint personal representative.

733.507 Administration following resignation or removal.--When a personal representative has resigned or is removed and there is a remaining personal representative, no other personal representative shall be appointed unless the will otherwise requires. The remaining personal representative, together with any successor personal representative, if appointed, shall complete the administration of the estate. If the resigned or removed personal representative is a sole personal representative, the court shall appoint a successor personal representative as provided in s. 733.301.

733.508 Accounting upon removal.--A removed personal representative shall file a full, true, and correct account of his or her administration within 30 days after removal.

733.509 Surrender of assets upon removal.--The removed personal representative shall deliver to the remaining or successor personal representative all of the property of the decedent and all records, documents, papers, and other property of or concerning the estate.

PART VI
DUTIES AND POWERS OF PERSONAL REPRESENTATIVE

733.601 Time of accrual of duties and powers.--The duties and powers of a personal representative commence upon his or her appointment. The powers of a personal representative relate back in time to give acts by the person appointed, occurring before appointment and beneficial to the estate, the same effect as those occurring thereafter. Before issuance of letters, a person named executor in a will may carry out written instructions of the decedent relating to the decedent's body and funeral and burial arrangements. A personal representative may ratify and accept acts on behalf of the estate done by others when the acts would have been proper for a personal representative.

733.602 General duties.--

(1) A personal representative is a fiduciary who shall observe the standards of care applicable to trustees as described by s. 737.302. A personal representative is under a duty to settle and distribute the estate of the decedent in accordance with the terms of the decedent's will and this code as expeditiously and efficiently as is consistent with the best interests of the estate. A personal representative shall use the authority conferred upon him

or her by this code, the authority in the will, if any, and the authority of any order in proceedings to which he or she is party, for the best interests of interested persons, including creditors as well as beneficiaries.

(2) A personal representative shall not be liable for any act of administration or distribution if the act was authorized at the time. Subject to other obligations of administration, a probated will is authority to administer and distribute the estate according to its terms. An order of appointment of a personal representative is authority to distribute apparently intestate assets to the heirs of the decedent if, at the time of distribution, the personal representative is not aware of a proceeding challenging intestacy or a proceeding questioning his or her appointment or fitness to continue. Nothing in this section affects the duty of the personal representative to administer and distribute the estate in accordance with the rights of interested persons.

733.603 Personal representative to proceed without court order.--A personal representative shall proceed expeditiously with the settlement and distribution of a decedent's estate and, except as otherwise specified by this code or ordered by the court, shall do so without adjudication, order, or direction of the court. A personal representative may invoke the jurisdiction of the court to resolve judicial questions concerning the estate or its administration.

733.604 Inventory.--

(1)(a) Within 60 days after issuance of letters, a personal representative who is not a curator or a successor to another personal representative who has previously discharged the duty shall file an inventory of property of the estate, listing it with reasonable detail and including for each listed item its estimated fair market value at the date of the decedent's death. Unless otherwise ordered by the court for good cause shown, any such inventory or amended or supplementary inventory is subject to inspection only by the clerk of the court or the clerk's representative, the personal representative and the personal representative's attorney, and other interested persons.

(b) The initial opening of any safe-deposit box of the decedent must be conducted in the presence of an employee of the institution where the box is located and the personal representative. The inventory of the contents of the box also must be conducted in the presence of the employee and the personal representative, each of whom must verify the contents of the box by signing a copy of the inventory. The personal representative shall file the safe-deposit box inventory with the court within 10 days after the box is opened.

(2) The personal representative shall serve a copy of the inventory on the Department of Revenue, as provided in s. 199.062(4), the surviving spouse, each heir at law in an intestate estate, each residuary beneficiary in a testate estate, and any other interested person who

may request it; and the personal representative shall file proof of such service. The inventory shall be verified by the personal representative.

(3) If the personal representative learns of any property not included in the original inventory, or learns that the estimated value or description indicated in the original inventory for any item is erroneous or misleading, he or she shall prepare an amended or supplementary inventory showing the estimated value of the new item at the date of the decedent's death, or the revised estimated value or description; and the personal representative shall serve a copy of the amended or supplementary inventory on each person on whom a copy of the inventory was served and shall file proof of such service. The amended or supplementary inventory shall be verified by the personal representative.

(4) Upon the written request of a beneficiary for any asset specifically devised to that beneficiary, a beneficiary for any asset received by that beneficiary in satisfaction of a general devise, or a residuary beneficiary of a testate estate or an heir of an intestate estate, for any asset not specifically devised, the personal representative shall promptly furnish a written explanation of how the inventory value for the asset was determined, including whether the personal representative obtained an independent appraisal for that asset and from whom the appraisal was obtained. The personal representative must notify each beneficiary of the right to request information regarding determination of the inventory value of an asset. Neither a request nor the failure to request information under this subsection affects any rights of a beneficiary in subsequent proceedings concerning any accounting of the personal representative or the propriety of any action of the personal representative.

733.605 Appraisers.--The personal representative may employ a qualified and disinterested appraiser to assist him or her in ascertaining the fair market value of any asset at the date of the decedent's death or any other date that may be appropriate, the value of which may be subject to reasonable doubt. Different persons may be employed to appraise different kinds of assets included in the estate.

733.607 Possession of estate.--

(1) Except as otherwise provided by a decedent's will, every personal representative has a right to, and shall take possession or control of, the decedent's property, except the homestead, but any real property or tangible personal property may be left with, or surrendered to, the person presumptively entitled to it unless possession of the property by the personal representative will be necessary for purposes of administration. The request by a personal representative for delivery of any property possessed by a beneficiary is conclusive evidence that the possession of the property by the personal representative is necessary for the purposes of administra-

tion, in any action against the beneficiary for possession of it. The personal representative shall take all steps reasonably necessary for the management, protection, and preservation of the estate until distribution. He or she may maintain an action to recover possession of property or to determine the title to it.

(2) If, after providing for statutory entitlements and all devises other than residuary devises, the assets of the decedent's estate are insufficient to pay the expenses of administration of the decedent's estate and enforceable claims of the decedent's creditors, the personal representative is entitled to payment from the trustee of a trust described in s. 733.707(3), in the amount the personal representative certifies in writing to be required to satisfy such insufficiency.

733.608 General power of the personal representative.--All real and personal property of the decedent, except the homestead, within this state and the rents, income, issues, and profits from it shall be assets in the hands of the personal representative:

(1) For the payment of devises, debts, family allowance, estate and inheritance taxes, claims, charges, and expenses of administration.

(2) To enforce contribution and equalize advancement.

(3) For distribution.

733.609 Improper exercise of power; breach of fiduciary duty.--If the exercise of power concerning the estate is improper or in bad faith, the personal representative is liable to interested persons for damage or loss resulting from a breach of his or her fiduciary duty to the same extent as a trustee of an express trust. In all actions challenging the proper exercise of a personal representative's powers, the court shall award taxable costs as in chancery actions, including attorney's fees.

733.610 Sale, encumbrance or transaction involving conflict of interest.--Any sale or encumbrance to the personal representative or his or her spouse, agent, or attorney, or any corporation or trust in which the personal representative has a substantial beneficial interest, or any transaction that is affected by a conflict of interest on the part of the personal representative, is voidable by any interested person except one who has consented after fair disclosure, unless:

(1) The will or a contract entered into by the decedent expressly authorized the transaction; or

(2) The transaction is approved by the court after notice to interested persons.

733.611 Persons dealing with the personal representative; protection.--Except as provided in s. 733.613(1), a person who in good faith either assists a personal representative or deals with him or her for value is protected as if the personal representative properly exercised his or her power. The fact that a person

knowingly deals with the personal representative does not alone require the person to inquire into the existence of his or her power, the limits on the power, or the propriety of its exercise. A person is not bound to see to the proper application of estate assets paid or delivered to the personal representative. The protection here expressed extends to instances in which a procedural irregularity or jurisdictional defect occurred in proceedings leading to the issuance of letters, including a case in which the alleged decedent is alive. The protection here expressed is not by substitution for that provided in comparable provisions of the laws relating to commercial transactions and laws simplifying transfers of securities by fiduciaries.

733.612 Transactions authorized for the personal representative; exceptions.--Except as otherwise provided by the will or by order of court, and subject to the priorities stated in s. 733.805, without order of court, a personal representative, acting reasonably for the benefit of the interested persons, may properly:

(1) Retain assets owned by the decedent, pending distribution or liquidation, including those in which the personal representative is personally interested or that are otherwise improper for trust investments.

(2) Perform or compromise, or, when proper, refuse performance of, the decedent's contracts. In performing enforceable contracts by the decedent to convey or lease real property, among other possible courses of action, the personal representative may:

(a) Convey the real property for cash payment of all sums remaining due or for the purchaser's note for the sum remaining due, secured by a mortgage on the land.

(b) Deliver a deed in escrow, with directions that the proceeds, when paid in accordance with the escrow agreement, be paid to the distributees of the decedent, as designated in the escrow agreement.

(3) Receive assets from fiduciaries or other sources.

(4) If funds are not needed to meet debts and expenses currently payable and are not immediately distributable, deposit or invest liquid assets of the estate, including moneys received from the sale of other assets, in federally insured interest-bearing accounts, readily marketable secured loan arrangements, or other prudent investments that would be reasonable for use by trustees.

(5) Acquire or dispose of an asset, excluding real property in this or another state, for cash or on credit and at public or private sale, and manage, develop, improve, exchange, partition, or change the character of an estate asset.

(6) Make ordinary or extraordinary repairs or alterations in buildings or other structures; demolish improvements; or erect new party walls or buildings.

(7) Enter into a lease, as lessor or lessee, for a term within, or extending beyond, the period of administration, with or without an option to renew.

(8) Enter into a lease or arrangement for exploration

and removal of minerals or other natural resources or enter into a pooling or unitization agreement.

(9) Abandon property when it is valueless or so encumbered, or in such condition, that it is of no benefit to the estate.

(10) Vote, or refrain from voting, stocks or other securities in person or by general or limited proxy.

(11) Pay calls, assessments, and other sums chargeable or accruing against, or on account of, securities, unless barred by the provisions relating to claims.

(12) Hold property in the name of a nominee or in other form without disclosure of the interest of the estate, but the personal representative is liable for any act of the nominee in connection with the property so held.

(13) Insure the assets of the estate against damage, loss, and liability and insure himself or herself against liability to third persons.

(14) Borrow money, with or without security, to be repaid from the estate assets or otherwise, other than real property, and advance money for the protection of the estate.

(15) Extend, renew, or in any manner modify any obligation owing to the estate. If the personal representative holds a mortgage, security interest, or other lien upon property of another person, he or she may accept a conveyance or transfer of encumbered assets from the owner in satisfaction of the indebtedness secured by its lien instead of foreclosure.

(16) Pay taxes, assessments, and other expenses incident to the administration of the estate.

(17) Sell or exercise stock subscription or conversion rights or consent, directly or through a committee or other agent, to the reorganization, consolidation, merger, dissolution, or liquidation of a corporation or other business enterprise.

(18) Allocate items of income or expense to either estate income or principal, as permitted or provided by law.

(19) Employ persons, including attorneys, accountants, auditors, investment advisers, and others, even if they are one and the same as the personal representative or are associated with the personal representative, to advise or assist the personal representative in the performance of his or her administrative duties; act upon the recommendations of such employed persons without independent investigation; and, instead of acting personally, employ one or more agents to perform any act of administration, whether or not discretionary. Any fees and compensation paid to any such person who is the same as, associated with, or employed by, the personal representative shall be taken into consideration in determining the personal representative's compensation.

(20) Prosecute or defend claims or proceedings in any jurisdiction for the protection of the estate and of the personal representative in the performance of his or her duties.

(21) Sell, mortgage, or lease any personal property of the estate or any interest in it for cash, credit, or for part cash or part credit, and with or without security for the unpaid balance.

(22) Continue any unincorporated business or venture in which the decedent was engaged at the time of his or her death:

(a) In the same business form for a period of not more than 4 months from the date of his or her appointment, if continuation is a reasonable means of preserving the value of the business, including good will.

(b) In the same business form for any additional period of time that may be approved by order of court.

(23) Provide for exoneration of the personal representative from personal liability in any contract entered into on behalf of the estate.

(24) Satisfy and settle claims and distribute the estate as provided in this code.

(25) Enter into agreements with the proper officer or department head, commissioner, or agent of any department of the government of the United States, waiving the statute of limitations concerning the assessment and collection of any federal tax or any deficiency in a federal tax.

(26) Make part distribution to the beneficiaries of any part of the estate not necessary to satisfy claims, expenses of administration, taxes, family allowance, exempt property, and an elective share, in accordance with the decedent's will or as authorized by operation of law.

(27) Execute any instruments necessary in the exercise of the personal representative's powers.

733.6121 Powers of personal representatives conferred by this part in relation to environmental or human health laws affecting property subject to administration or to property subject to administration contaminated with hazardous or toxic substances; liability.--

(1) Except as otherwise provided by the will or by order of court, and subject to s. 733.805, the personal representative has, without court authorization, the powers specified in subsection (2).

(2) A personal representative has the power, acting reasonably and for the benefit of the interested parties:

(a) To inspect or investigate, or cause to be inspected or investigated, property subject to administration, including interests in sole proprietorships, partnerships, or corporations and any assets owned by any such business entity for the purpose of determining compliance with an environmental law affecting that property or to respond to an actual or threatened violation of an environmental law affecting that property;

(b) To take, on behalf of the estate, any action necessary to prevent, abate, or otherwise remedy an actual or potential violation of an environmental law affecting property subject to administration, either before or after initiation of an enforcement action by a governmental body;

(c) To settle or compromise at any time any claim against the estate or the personal representative that may be asserted by a governmental body or private party which involves the alleged violation of an environmental law affecting property subject to administration over which the personal representative has responsibility;

(d) To disclaim any power granted by any document, statute, or rule of law which, in the sole judgment of the personal representative, could cause the personal representative to incur personal liability, or the estate to incur liability, under any environmental law;

(e) To decline to serve as a personal representative, or having undertaken to serve as a personal representative, to resign at any time, if the personal representative believes that there is or could be a conflict of interest in his or her fiduciary capacity and in his or her individual capacity because of potential claims or liabilities that could be asserted against it on behalf of the estate by reason of the type or condition of the assets held; or

(f) To charge against the assets of the estate the cost of any inspection, investigation, review, abatement, response, cleanup, or remedial action that this section authorizes the personal representative to take; and, in the event of the closing or termination of the estate or the transfer of the estate property to another personal representative, to hold moneys sufficient to cover the cost of cleaning up any known environmental problem.

(3) A personal representative is not personally liable to any beneficiary or any other party for a decrease in value of assets in an estate by reason of the personal representative's compliance or efforts to comply with an environmental law, specifically including any reporting requirement under that law.

(4) A personal representative who acquires ownership or control of a vessel or other property without having owned, operated, or materially participated in the management of that vessel or property before assuming ownership or control as personal representative is not considered an owner or operator for purposes of liability under chapter 376, chapter 403, or any other environmental law. A personal representative who willfully, knowingly, or recklessly causes or exacerbates a release or threatened release of a hazardous substance is personally liable for the cost of the response, to the extent that the release or threatened release is attributable to the personal representative's activities. This subsection does not preclude the filing of claims against the assets that constitute the estate held by the personal representative or the filing of actions against the personal representative in his or her representative capacity. In any such action, an award or judgment against the personal representative must be satisfied only from the assets of the estate.

(5) Neither the acceptance by the personal representative of the property or a failure by the personal representative to inspect or investigate the property creates any inference as to whether there is liability under an environmental law with respect to that property.

(6) For the purposes of this section, the term "environmental law" means a federal, state, or local law, rule, regulation, or ordinance that relates to protection of the environment or human health, and the term "hazardous substance" means a substance, material, or waste defined as hazardous or toxic, or any contaminant, pollutant, or constituent thereof, or otherwise regulated by an environmental law.

(7) This section applies to any estate admitted to probate on or after July 1, 1995.

733.613 Personal representative's right to sell real property.--

(1) When a personal representative of a decedent dying intestate, or whose testator has not conferred upon him or her a power of sale or whose testator has granted a power of sale but his or her power is so limited by the will or by operation of law that it cannot be conveniently exercised, shall consider that it is for the best interest of the estate and of those interested in it that real property be sold, the personal representative may sell it at public or private sale. No title shall pass until the sale is authorized or confirmed by the court. Petition for authorization or confirmation of sale shall set forth the reasons for the sale, a description of the property sold or to be sold, and the price and terms of the sale. Except when interested persons have joined in the petition for sale of real property or have consented to the sale, notice of the petition shall be given. No bona fide purchaser shall be required to examine any proceedings before the order of sale.

(2) When a decedent's will confers specific power to sell or mortgage real property or a general power to sell any asset of the estate, the personal representative may sell, mortgage, or lease, without authorization or confirmation of court, any real property of the estate or any interest therein for cash or credit, or for part cash and part credit, and with or without security for unpaid balances. The sale, mortgage, or lease need not be justified by a showing of necessity, and the sale pursuant to power of sale shall be valid.

733.614 Powers and duties of successor personal representative.--A successor personal representative has the same power and duty as the original personal representative to complete the administration and distribution of the estate as expeditiously as possible, but he or she shall not exercise any power made personal to the personal representative named in the will.

733.615 Joint personal representatives; when joint action required.--

(1) If two or more persons are appointed joint personal representatives, and unless the will provides otherwise, the concurrence of all joint personal representatives appointed pursuant to a will or codicil executed prior to October 1, 1987, or appointed to administer an intestate

estate of a decedent who died prior to October 1, 1987, or of a majority of joint personal representatives appointed pursuant to a will or codicil executed on or after October 1, 1987, or appointed to administer the intestate estate of a decedent dying on or after October 1, 1987, is required on all acts connected with the administration and distribution of the estate. This restriction does not apply when any joint personal representative receives and receipts for property due the estate, when the concurrence required under this subsection cannot readily be obtained in the time reasonably available for emergency action necessary to preserve the estate, or when a joint personal representative has been delegated to act for the others.

(2) Where action by a majority of the joint personal representatives appointed is authorized, a joint personal representative who has not joined in exercising a power is not liable to the beneficiaries or to others for the consequences of the exercise, and a dissenting joint personal representative is not liable for the consequences of an act in which he or she joins at the direction of the majority of the joint personal representatives, if he or she expressed his or her dissent in writing to any of his or her joint personal representatives at or before the time of the joinder.

(3) A person dealing with a joint personal representative without actual knowledge that joint personal representatives have been appointed or if advised by the joint personal representative with whom he or she deals that the joint personal representative has authority to act alone for any of the reasons mentioned in subsection (1) is as fully protected in dealing with that joint personal representative as if that joint personal representative possessed and properly exercised the power he or she purports to exercise.

733.616 Powers of surviving personal representatives.--Unless the terms of the will otherwise provide, every power exercisable by joint personal representatives may be exercised by the one or more remaining after the appointment of one or more is terminated, and if one or more, but not all, nominated as joint personal representatives are not appointed, those appointed may exercise all the powers incident to the office.

733.617 Compensation of personal representative.--
(1) As compensation for its ordinary services, a personal representative shall be entitled, without order of court unless otherwise stated, to a commission payable from the estate assets. Such commission shall be based upon the probate estate's value as determined finally for probate inventory purposes and as accounted for by the personal representative, which value shall include all property, real or personal, tangible or intangible, and all income earned thereon.

(2) Upon the probate estate's value as defined in subsection (1), such commission shall be computed as follows:

(a) At the rate of 3 percent for the first $1 million.
(b) At the rate of 2.5 percent for all above $1 million and not exceeding $5 million.
(c) At the rate of 2 percent for all above $5 million and not exceeding $10 million.
(d) At the rate of 1.5 percent for all above $10 million.

(3) In addition to the aforesaid commission, a personal representative shall be allowed such further compensation as the court may deem just and reasonable for any extraordinary services including, but not limited to:
(a) The sale of real or personal property.
(b) The conduct of litigation on behalf of or against the estate.
(c) Involvement in proceedings for the adjustment or payment of any taxes.
(d) The carrying on of the decedent's business.
(e) Any other special services which may be necessary for the personal representative to perform.

(4) If a decedent's will provides that a personal representative's compensation shall be based upon specific criteria, other than a general reference to commissions allowed by law or words or similar import, including, but not limited to, rates, amounts, commissions, or reference to the personal representative's regularly published schedule of fees in effect at the decedent's date of death, or words of similar import, then a personal representative shall be entitled to compensation in accordance with such provision. However, except for such references in a decedent's will to the personal representative's regularly published schedule of fees in effect at the decedent's date of death, or words of similar import, if there is no written contract with the decedent regarding compensation, a personal representative may renounce the provisions contained in the will and be entitled to compensation hereunder. A personal representative may also renounce its right to all or any part of the compensation.

(5) If the probate estate's value as defined in subsection (1) is $100,000 or more, and there are two representatives, each personal representative is entitled to the full commission allowed to a sole personal representative. If there are more than two personal representatives and the probate estate's value is more than $100,000, the compensation to which two would be entitled must be apportioned among the personal representatives. The basis for such apportionment shall be one full commission allowed to the personal representative who has possession of and primary responsibility for administration of the assets and one full commission among the remaining personal representatives according to the services rendered by each of them respectively. If the probate estate's value is less than $100,000 and there is more than one personal representative, then one full commission allowed herein to a sole personal representative must be apportioned among the personal representatives according to the services ren-

dered by each of them respectively.

(6) If the personal representative is a member of The Florida Bar and has rendered legal services in connection with the administration of the estate, then in addition to a fee as personal representative, there also shall be allowed a fee for the legal services rendered.

(7) The compensation for a personal representative as set forth in subsections (2) and (3) may, upon petition of any interested person, be increased or decreased by the court. In determining whether to increase or decrease the compensation for ordinary services, the court must consider each of the following factors, giving each such weight as it determines to be appropriate:

(a) The promptness, efficiency, and skill with which the administration was handled by the personal representative;

(b) The responsibilities assumed by and the potential liabilities of the personal representative;

(c) The nature and value of the assets that are affected by the decedent's death;

(d) The benefits or detriments resulting to the estate or its beneficiaries from the personal representative's services;

(e) The complexity or simplicity of the administration and the novelties of the issues presented;

(f) The personal representative's participation in tax planning for the estate and the estate's beneficiaries and in tax return preparation, review, or approval;

(g) The nature of the probate, nonprobate, and exempt assets; the expenses of administration; the liabilities of the decedent; and the compensation paid to other professionals and fiduciaries;

(h) Any delay in payment of the compensation after the services were furnished; and

(i) Any other relevant factors.

733.6171 Compensation of attorney for the personal representative.--

(1) Attorneys for personal representatives shall be entitled to reasonable compensation for their services payable from the assets of the estate without court order.

(2) The attorney, the personal representative, and persons bearing the impact of the compensation may agree to compensation determined in a different manner than provided in this section. Compensation may also be determined in a different manner than provided in this section if the manner is disclosed to the parties bearing the impact of the compensation in the petition for discharge or final accounting and there is no objection filed pursuant to s. 733.901.

(3) Compensation provided in the following schedule for ordinary services based upon the inventory value of the estate assets and the income earned by the estate during the administration is presumed to be reasonable compensation for attorneys in formal estate administration:

(a) One thousand five hundred dollars for estates having a value of $40,000 or less.

(b) An additional $750 for estates having a value of more than $40,000 and not exceeding $70,000.

(c) An additional $750 for estates having a value of more than $70,000 and not exceeding $100,000.

(d) For estates having a value in excess of $100,000, at the rate of 3 percent on the next $900,000.

(e) At the rate of 2.5 percent for all above $1 million and not exceeding $3 million.

(f) At the rate of 2 percent for all above $3 million and not exceeding $5 million.

(g) At the rate of 1.5 percent for all above $5 million and not exceeding $10 million.

(h) At the rate of 1 percent for all above $10 million.

(4) In addition to the attorney's fees for ordinary services, the attorney for the personal representative shall be allowed further reasonable compensation for any extraordinary service. What is an extraordinary service may vary depending on many factors, including the size of the estate. Extraordinary services may include, but are not limited to:

(a) Involvement in a will contest, will construction, a proceeding for determination of beneficiaries, a contested claim, elective share proceeding, apportionment of estate taxes, or any other adversarial proceeding or litigation by or against the estate.

(b) Representation of the personal representative in audit or any proceeding for adjustment, determination, or collection of any taxes.

(c) Tax advice on postmortem tax planning, including, but not limited to, disclaimer, renunciation of fiduciary commission, alternate valuation date, allocation of administrative expenses between tax returns, the QTIP or reverse QTIP election, allocation of GST exemption, qualification for Internal Revenue Code ss. 6166 and 303 privileges, deduction of last illness expenses, fiscal year planning, distribution planning, asset basis considerations, handling income or deductions in respect of a decedent, valuation discounts, special use and other valuation, handling employee benefit or retirement proceeds, prompt assessment request, or request for release of personal liability for payment of tax.

(d) Review of estate tax return and preparation or review of other tax returns required to be filed by the personal representative.

(e) Preparation of the estate's federal estate tax return. If this return is prepared by the attorney, a fee of one-half of 1 percent up to a value of $10 million and one-fourth of 1 percent on the value in excess of $10 million of the gross estate as finally determined for federal estate tax purposes, is presumed to be reasonable compensation for the attorney for this service. These fees shall include services for routine audit of the return, not beyond the examining agent level, if required.

(f) Purchase, sale, lease, or encumbrance of real property by the personal representative or involvement in zoning, land use, environmental, or other similar matters.

(g) Legal advice regarding carrying on of decedent's business or conducting other commercial activity by the personal representative.

(h) Legal advice regarding claims for damage to the environment or related procedures.

(i) Legal advice regarding homestead status of real property or proceedings involving that status.

(j) Involvement in fiduciary, employee, or attorney compensation disputes.

(k) Proceedings involving ancillary administration of assets not subject to administration in this state.

(5) Upon petition of any interested person, the court may increase or decrease the compensation for ordinary services of the attorney or award compensation for extraordinary services if the facts and circumstances of the particular administration warrant. In determining reasonable compensation, the court shall consider all of the following factors giving such weight to each as it may determine to be appropriate:

(a) The promptness, efficiency, and skill with which the administration was handled by the attorney.

(b) The responsibilities assumed by, and potential liabilities of, the attorney.

(c) The nature and value of the assets that are affected by the decedent's death.

(d) The benefits or detriments resulting to the estate or its beneficiaries from the attorney's services.

(e) The complexity or simplicity of the administration and the novelty of issues presented.

(f) The attorney's participation in tax planning for the estate and the estate's beneficiaries and tax return preparation or review and approval.

(g) The nature of the probate, nonprobate, and exempt assets, the expenses of administration and liabilities of the decedent, and the compensation paid to other professionals and fiduciaries.

(h) Any delay in payment of the compensation after the services were furnished.

(i) Any other relevant factors.

(6) The court may determine reasonable attorney's compensation without receiving expert testimony. Any party may offer expert testimony after notice to interested persons. If expert testimony is offered, an expert witness fee may be awarded by the court and paid from the assets of the estate. The court may, in its discretion, direct from what part of the estate it shall be paid.

(7) If a separate written agreement regarding compensation exists between the attorney and the decedent, the attorney shall furnish a copy to the personal representative prior to commencement of employment, and, if employed, shall promptly file and serve a copy on all interested persons. Neither a separate agreement nor a provision in the will suggesting or directing the personal representative to retain a specific attorney will obligate the personal representative to employ the attorney or obligate the attorney to accept the representation, but if the attorney who is a party to the agreement or who drafted the will is employed, the compensation paid shall not exceed the compensation provided in the agreement.

(8) Court proceedings to determine compensation, if required, are a part of the estate administration process, and the costs, including fees for the personal representative's attorney, shall be determined by the court and paid from the assets of the estate unless the court finds the request for attorney's fees to be substantially unreasonable. The court shall direct from which part of the estate they shall be paid.

(9) The amount and manner of determining compensation for attorneys for personal representatives must be disclosed in the final accounting, unless the disclosure is waived in writing signed by the parties bearing the impact of the compensation and filed with the court. No such waiver shall be valid unless it contains language declaring that the waiving party has actual knowledge of the amount and manner of determining such compensation and, in addition, expressly acknowledging either one of the following two elements:

(a) That the waiving party has agreed to the amount and manner of determining such compensation and is waiving any objections to payment of such compensation; or

(b) That the waiving party has the right under subsection (5) to petition the court to decrease such compensation and is waiving that right.

The requirements of this subsection shall not apply if the full amount of such compensation has previously been determined by order of the court after notice. A waiver of the final accounting shall not be effective if it does not meet the requirements of this subsection.

(10) This section shall apply to estates in which an order of discharge has not been entered prior to its effective date but not to those estates in which attorney's fees have previously been determined by order of court after notice.

733.6175 Proceedings for review of employment of agents and compensation of personal representatives and employees of estate.--After notice to all affected interested persons and upon petition of an interested person bearing all or part of the impact of the payment of compensation to the personal representative or any person employed by him or her, the propriety of such employment and the reasonableness of such compensation or payment may be reviewed by the court. The burden of proof of propriety of such employment and the reasonableness of the compensation shall be upon the personal representative and the person employed by him or her. Any person who is determined to have received excessive compensation from an estate for services rendered may be ordered to make appropriate refunds.

733.619 Individual liability of personal representative.--

(1) Unless otherwise provided in the contract, a personal representative is not individually liable on a contract, except a contract for attorney's fee, properly entered into in his or her fiduciary capacity in the administration of the estate unless the personal representative fails to reveal his or her representative capacity and identify the estate in the contract.

(2) A personal representative is individually liable for obligations arising from ownership or control of the estate or for torts committed in the course of administration of the estate only if he or she is personally at fault.

(3) Claims based on contracts, except a contract for attorney's fee, entered into by a personal representative in his or her fiduciary capacity, on obligations arising from ownership or control of the estate, or on torts committed in the course of estate administration, may be asserted against the estate by proceeding against the personal representative in his or her fiduciary capacity, whether or not the personal representative is individually liable therefor.

(4) Issues of liability as between the estate and the personal representative individually may be determined in a proceeding for accounting, surcharge, or indemnification, or other appropriate proceeding.

PART VII
CREDITORS' CLAIMS

733.701	Notifying creditors.
733.702	Limitations on presentation of claims.
733.703	Form and manner of presenting claim.
733.704	Amendment of claims.
733.705	Payment of and objection to claims.
733.706	Executions and levies.
733.707	Order of payment of expenses and obligations.
733.708	Compromise.
733.710	Limitations on claims against estates.

733.701 Notifying creditors.--Unless the proceedings are under chapter 734 or chapter 735, every personal representative shall cause notice of administration to be published and served under s. 733.212.

733.702 Limitations on presentation of claims.--

(1) If not barred by s. 733.710, no claim or demand against the decedent's estate that arose before the death of the decedent, including claims of the state and any of its subdivisions, whether due or not, direct or contingent, or liquidated or unliquidated; no claim for funeral or burial expenses; no claim for personal property in the possession of the personal representative; and no claim for damages, including, but not limited to, an action founded on fraud or another wrongful act or omission of the decedent, is binding on the estate, on the personal representative, or on any beneficiary unless filed within the later of 3 months after the time of the first publication of the notice of administration or, as to any creditor required to be served with a copy of the notice of administration, 30 days after the date of service of such copy of the notice on the creditor, even though the personal representative has recognized the claim or demand by paying a part of it or interest on it or otherwise. The personal representative may settle in full any claim without the necessity of the claim being filed when the settlement has been approved by the beneficiaries adversely affected according to the priorities provided in this code and when the settlement is made within the statutory time for filing claims; or, within 3 months after the first publication of the notice of administration, he or she may file a proof of claim of all claims he or she has paid or intends to pay.

(2) No cause of action heretofore or hereafter accruing, including, but not limited to, an action founded upon fraud or other wrongful act or omission, shall survive the death of the person against whom the claim may be made, whether an action is pending at the death of the person or not, unless the claim is filed within the time periods set forth in this part.

(3) Any claim not timely filed as provided in this section is barred even though no objection to the claim is filed on the grounds of timeliness or otherwise unless the court extends the time in which the claim may be filed. Such an extension may be granted only upon grounds of fraud, estoppel, or insufficient notice of the claims period. No independent action or declaratory action may be brought upon a claim which was not timely filed unless such an extension has been granted. If the personal representative or any other interested person serves on the creditor a notice to file a petition for an extension or be forever barred, the creditor shall be limited to a period of 30 days from the date of service of the notice in which to file a petition for extension.

(4) Nothing in this section affects or prevents:

(a) A proceeding to enforce any mortgage, security interest, or other lien on property of the decedent.

(b) To the limits of casualty insurance protection only, any proceeding to establish liability of the decedent or the personal representative for which he or she is protected by the casualty insurance.

(c) The filing of a claim by the Department of Revenue subsequent to the expiration of the time for filing claims provided in subsection (1), provided it does so file within 30 days after the service of the inventory by the personal representative on the department or, in the event an amended or supplementary inventory has been prepared, within 30 days after the service of the amended or supplementary inventory by the personal representative on the department.

(d) The filing of a cross-claim or counterclaim against the estate in an action instituted by the estate; however, no recovery on such a cross-claim or counterclaim shall exceed the estate's recovery in such an action.

(5) Nothing in this section shall extend the limitations period set forth in s. 733.710.

733.703 Form and manner of presenting claim.--

(1) A creditor shall file a written statement of the claim. No additional charge may be imposed by a claimant who files a claim against the estate.

(2) A claimant whose claim is listed in a personal representative's proof of claim filed within 3 months after the first publication of the notice of administration shall be deemed to have filed a statement of the claim listed. Except as provided otherwise in this part, the claim shall be treated for all other purposes as if it had been filed by the claimant.

733.704 Amendment of claims.--If a bona fide attempt

to file a claim is made by a creditor but the claim is defective as to form, the court may permit the amendment of the claim at any time.

733.705 Payment of and objection to claims.--

(1) The personal representative shall pay all claims within 1 year from the date of first publication of notice of administration, provided that the time shall be extended with respect to claims in litigation, unmatured claims, and contingent claims for the period necessary to dispose of such claims pursuant to subsections (4), (5), (6), and (7). The court may extend the time for payment of any claim upon a showing of good cause. No personal representative shall be compelled to pay the debts of the decedent until after the expiration of 5 months from the first publication of notice of administration. If any person brings an action against a personal representative within the 5 months on any claim to which the personal representative has filed no objection, the plaintiff shall not receive any costs or attorneys' fees if he or she prevails, nor shall the judgment change the class of the claim for payment under this code.

(2) On or before the expiration of 4 months from the first publication of notice of administration or within 30 days from the timely filing of a claim, whichever occurs later, a personal representative or other interested person may file a written objection to a claim. An objection to a claim shall contain a statement that the claimant is limited to a period of 30 days from the date of service of the objection within which to bring an action on the claim as provided in subsection (4). The failure to include such a statement in the objection shall not affect the validity of the objection but may be considered as good cause for extending the time for filing an action or proceeding after the objection is filed. If an objection is filed, the person filing it shall serve a copy of the objection by registered or certified mail to the address of the claimant or the claimant's attorney as shown on the claim or by delivery to the claimant to whose claim the

person objects or the claimant's attorney of record, if any, not later than 10 days after the objection has been filed, and also on the personal representative if the objection is filed by any interested person other than the personal representative. The failure to serve a copy of the objection constitutes an abandonment of the objection. For good cause, the court may extend the time for filing an objection to any claim or may extend the time for serving the objection. The extension of time shall be granted only after notice.

(3) An objection by an interested person to a personal representative's proof of claim shall state the particular item or items to which the interested person objects and shall be filed and served as provided in subsection (2). Issues of liability as between the estate and the personal representative individually for items paid by the personal representative and thereafter listed in a personal representative's proof of claim shall be determined in the estate administration proceeding, in a proceeding for accounting, surcharge, or other appropriate proceeding, whether or not an objection has been filed. If an objection to an item listed as to be paid in a personal representative's proof of claim is filed and served, and the personal representative has not paid the item, the other subsections of this section shall apply as if a claim for the item had been filed by the claimant; but if the personal representative has paid the claim after listing it as to be paid, issues of liability as between the estate and the personal representative individually shall be determined in the manner provided for an item listed as paid.

(4) The claimant is limited to a period of 30 days from the date of service of an objection within which to bring an independent action upon the claim, or a declaratory action to establish the validity and amount of an unmatured claim which is not yet due but which is certain to become due in the future, or a declaratory action to establish the validity of a contingent claim upon which no cause of action has accrued on the date of service of an objection and that may or may not become due in the future. For good cause, the court may extend the time for filing an action or proceeding after objection is filed. The extension of time shall be granted only after notice. No action or proceeding on the claim shall be brought against the personal representative after the time limited above, and any such claim is thereafter forever barred without any court order. If an objection is filed to the claim of any creditor and an action is brought by the creditor to establish his or her claim, a judgment establishing the claim shall give it no priority over claims of the same class to which it belongs.

(5) A claimant may bring an independent action or declaratory action upon a claim which was not timely filed pursuant to s. 733.702(1) only if the claimant has been granted an extension of time to file the claim pursuant to s. 733.702(3).

(6) If an unmatured claim has not become due before the time for distribution of an estate, the personal representative may prepay the full amount of principal plus accrued interest due on the claim, without discount and without penalty, regardless of any prohibition against prepayment or provision for penalty in any instrument on which the claim is founded. If the claim is not prepaid, no order of discharge may be entered until the creditor and personal representative have filed an agreement disposing of the claim, or in the absence of an agreement until the court provides for payment by one of the following methods:

(a) Requiring the personal representative to reserve such assets as the court determines to be adequate to pay the claim when it becomes due; in fixing the amount to be reserved, the court may determine the value of any security or collateral to which the creditor may resort for payment of the claim and may direct the reservation, if necessary, of sufficient assets to pay the claim or to pay the difference between the value of any security or collateral and the amount necessary to pay the claim. If the estate is insolvent, the court may direct a proportionate amount to be reserved. The court shall direct that the amount reserved be retained by the personal representative until the time that the claim becomes due, and that so much of the reserved amount as is not used for payment be distributed thereafter according to law;

(b) Requiring that the claim be adequately secured by a mortgage, pledge, bond, trust, guaranty, or other security, as may be determined by the court, the security to remain in effect until the time that the claim becomes due, and that so much of the security or collateral as is not needed for payment be distributed thereafter according to law; or

(c) Making such other provision for the disposition or satisfaction of the claim as is equitable, and in a manner so as not to delay unreasonably the closing of the estate.

(7) If no cause of action has accrued on a contingent claim before the time for distribution of an estate, no order of discharge may be entered until the creditor and the personal representative have filed an agreement disposing of the claim or, in the absence of such agreement, until:

(a) The court determines that the claim is adequately secured or that it has no value,

(b) Three months from the date on which a cause of action accrues upon the claim, provided that no action on the claim is then pending,

(c) Five years from the date of first publication of notice of administration, or

(d) The court provides for payment of the claim upon the happening of the contingency by one of the methods described in paragraph (a), paragraph (b), or paragraph (c) of subsection (6), whichever occurs first. No action or proceeding may be brought against the personal representative on the claim after the time limited above, and any such claim shall thereafter be forever barred without order of court. If an action is brought within the time limited above, a judgment establishing the claim shall give it no priority over claims of the same class to which it belongs.

(8) No interest shall be paid by the personal representative or allowed by the court on a claim until the expiration of 5 calendar months from the first publication of the notice of administration, unless the claim is founded on a written obligation of the decedent providing for the payment of interest. Interest shall be paid by the personal representative on written obligations of the decedent providing for the payment of interest. On all other claims, interest shall be allowed and paid beginning 5 months from the first publication of the notice of administration.

(9) The court may determine all issues concerning claims or matters not requiring trial by jury.

(10) An order for extension of time authorized under this section may be entered only in the estate administration proceeding.

733.706 Executions and levies.--Except upon approval by the court, no execution or other process shall issue on or be levied against property of the estate. An order approving execution or other process to be levied against property of the estate may be entered only in the estate administration proceeding. Claims on all judgments against a decedent shall be filed in the same manner as other claims against estates of decedents. This section shall not be construed to prevent the enforcement of mortgages, security interests, or liens encumbering specific property.

733.707 Order of payment of expenses and obligations.--

(1) The personal representative shall pay the expenses of the administration and obligations of the estate in the following order:

(a) Class 1.--Costs, expenses of administration, and compensation of personal representatives and their attorneys' fees.

(b) Class 2.--Reasonable funeral, interment, and grave marker expenses, whether paid by a guardian under s. 744.441(16), the personal representative, or any other person, not to exceed the aggregate of $6,000.

(c) Class 3.--Debts and taxes with preference under federal law.

(d) Class 4.--Reasonable and necessary medical and hospital expenses of the last 60 days of the last illness of the decedent, including compensation of persons attending him or her.

(e) Class 5.--Family allowance.

(f) Class 6.--Arrearage from court-ordered child support.

(g) Class 7.--Debts acquired after death by the continuation of the decedent's business, in accordance with s. 733.612(22), but only to the extent of the assets of that business.

(h) Class 8.--All other claims, including those founded on judgments or decrees rendered against the decedent during the decedent's lifetime, and any excess over the sums allowed in paragraphs (b) and (d).

(2) After paying any preceding class, if the estate is insufficient to pay all of the next succeeding class, the creditors of the latter class shall be paid ratably in proportion to their respective claims.

(3) Any portion of a trust with respect to which a decedent who is the grantor has at the decedent's death a right of revocation, as defined in paragraph (e), either alone or in conjunction with any other person, is liable for the expenses of the administration of the decedent's estate and enforceable claims of the decedent's creditors to the extent the decedent's estate is insufficient to pay them as provided in s. 733.607(2).

(a) For purposes of this subsection, any trusts established as part of, and all payments from, either an employee annuity described in s. 403 of the Internal Revenue Code of 1986, as amended, an Individual Retirement Account, as described in s. 408 of the Internal Revenue Code of 1986, as amended, a Keogh (HR-10) Plan, or a retirement or other plan established by a corporation which is qualified under s. 401 of the Internal Revenue Code of 1986, as amended, shall not be considered a trust over which the decedent has a right of revocation.

(b) For purposes of this subsection, any trust described in s. 664 of the Internal Revenue Code of 1986, as amended, shall not be considered a trust over which the decedent has a right of revocation.

(c) This subsection shall not impair any rights an individual has under a qualified domestic relations order as that term is defined in s. 414(p) of the Internal Revenue Code of 1986, as amended.

(d) For purposes of this subsection, property held or received by a trust to the extent that the property would not have been subject to claims against the decedent's estate if it had been paid directly to a trust created under the decedent's will or other than to the decedent's estate, or assets received from any trust other than a trust described in this subsection, shall not be deemed assets of the trust available for the payment of the expenses of administration of and enforceable claims against the decedent's estate.

(e) For purposes of this subsection, a "right of revocation" is a power retained by the decedent, held in any capacity, to:

    1. Amend or revoke the trust and revest the principal of the trust in the decedent; or

    2. Withdraw or appoint the principal of the trust to or for the decedent's benefit.

733.708 Compromise.--When a proposal is made to compromise any claim, whether in suit or not, by or against the estate of a decedent or to compromise any

question concerning the distribution of a decedent's estate, the court may enter an order authorizing the compromise if satisfied that the compromise will be for the best interest of the beneficiaries. The order shall relieve the personal representative of liability or responsibility for the compromise. Claims against the estate may not be compromised until after the time for filing objections to claims has expired. Notice must be given to those who have filed objection to the claim proposed to be compromised.

733.710 Limitations on claims against estates.--

(1) Notwithstanding any other provision of the code, 2 years after the death of a person, neither the decedent's estate, the personal representative (if any), nor the beneficiaries shall be liable for any claim or cause of action against the decedent, whether or not letters of administration have been issued, except as provided in this section.

(2) This section shall not apply to a creditor who has filed a claim pursuant to s. 733.702 within 2 years after the person's death, and whose claim has not been paid or otherwise disposed of pursuant to s. 733.705.

(3) This section shall not affect the lien of any duly recorded mortgage or security interest or the lien of any person in possession of personal property or the right to foreclose and enforce the mortgage or lien.

PART VIII
SPECIAL PROVISIONS FOR DISTRIBUTION

733.801	Delivery of devises and distributive shares.
733.802	Proceedings for compulsory payment of devises or distributive interest.
733.803	Encumbered property; liability for payment.
733.805	Order in which assets are appropriated.
733.806	Advancement.
733.808	Death benefits; disposition of proceeds.
733.809	Right of retainer.
733.810	Distribution in kind; valuation.
733.811	Distribution; right or title of distributee.
733.812	Improper distribution; liability of distributee.
733.813	Purchasers from distributees protected.
733.814	Partition for purpose of distribution.
733.815	Private agreements among distributees.
733.816	Disposition of unclaimed property held by personal representatives.
733.817	Apportionment of estate taxes.

733.801 Delivery of devises and distributive shares.--No personal representative shall be required to pay or deliver any devise or distributive share or to surrender possession of any land to any beneficiary until the expiration of 5 months from the granting of letters.

733.802 Proceedings for compulsory payment of devises or distributive interest.--

(1) Before final distribution, no personal representative

shall be compelled:

(a) To pay a devise in money before the final settlement of his or her accounts,

(b) To deliver specific personal property devised that may have come into his or her hands, unless the personal property is exempt personal property,

(c) To pay all or any part of a distributive share in the personal estate of a decedent, or

(d) To surrender land to any beneficiary,

unless the beneficiary files a petition setting forth the facts that entitle him or her to relief and stating that the property will not be required for the payment of debts, family allowance, estate and inheritance taxes, claims, elective share of the surviving spouse, charges, or expenses of administration or for providing funds for contribution or enforcing equalization in case of advancements.

(2) An order directing the surrender of real property or the delivery of personal property shall describe the property to be surrendered or delivered. The order shall be conclusive in favor of bona fide purchasers for value from the beneficiary or distributee as against the personal representative and all other persons claiming by, through, under, or against the decedent or the decedent's estate.

(3) If the administration of the estate has not been completed before the entry of an order of partial distribution, the court may require the person entitled to distribution to give a bond with sureties as prescribed in s. 45.011, conditioned on the making of due contribution for the payment of devises, family allowance, estate and inheritance taxes, claims, elective share of the spouse, charges, expenses of administration, and equalization in case of advancements, plus any interest on them.

733.803 Encumbered property; liability for payment.

The specific devisee of any encumbered property shall be entitled to have the encumbrance on devised property paid at the expense of the residue of the estate only when the will shows such an intent. A general direction in the will to pay debts does not show such an intent.

733.805 Order in which assets are appropriated.

(1) If a testator makes provision by his or her will, or designates the funds or property to be used, for the payment of debts, estate and inheritance taxes, family allowance, exempt property, elective share charges, expenses of administration, and devises, they shall be paid out of the funds or from the property or proceeds as provided by the will so far as sufficient. If no provision is made or any fund designated, or if it is insufficient, the property of the estate shall be used for such purposes, except as otherwise provided in s. 733.817 with respect to estate, inheritance, and other death taxes, and to raise the shares of a pretermitted spouse and children, in the following order:

(a) Property not disposed of by the will.

(b) Property devised to the residuary devisee or devisees.

(c) Property not specifically or demonstratively devised.

(d) Property specifically or demonstratively devised.

(2) Demonstrative devises shall be classed as general devises upon the failure or insufficiency of funds or property out of which payment should be made, to the extent of the insufficiency. Devises to the decedent's surviving spouse, given in satisfaction of, or instead of, the surviving spouse's statutory rights in the estate, shall not abate until other devises of the same class are exhausted. Devises given for a valuable consideration shall abate with other devises of the same class only to the extent of the excess over the amount of value of the consideration until all others of the same class are exhausted. Except as herein provided, devises shall abate equally and ratably and without preference or priority as between real and personal property. When property that has been specifically devised or charged with a devise is sold or taken by the personal representative, other devisees shall contribute according to their respective interests to the devisee whose devise has been sold or taken, and before distribution the court shall determine the amounts of the respective contributions, and they shall be paid or withheld before distribution is made.

733.806 Advancement.

If a person dies intestate as to all his or her estate, property that the decedent gave in his or her lifetime to an heir is treated as an advancement against the latter's share of the estate only if declared in a contemporaneous writing by the decedent or acknowledged in writing by the heir. The property advanced shall be valued at the time the heir came into possession or enjoyment of the property or at the time of the death of the decedent, whichever first occurs. If the recipient of the property does not survive the decedent, the property shall not be taken into account in computing the intestate share to be received by the recipient's descendants unless the declaration or acknowledgment provides otherwise.

733.808 Death benefits; disposition of proceeds.

(1) Death benefits of any kind, including, but not limited to, proceeds of:

(a) An individual life insurance policy;

(b) A group life insurance policy;

(c) An employees' trust or under a contract purchased by an employees' trust forming part of a pension, stock bonus, or profit-sharing plan;

(d) An annuity or endowment contract; and

(e) A health and accident policy,

may be made payable to the trustee under a trust agreement or declaration of trust in existence at the time of the death of the insured, employee, or annuitant. The death benefits shall be held and disposed of by the trustee in accordance with the terms of the trust as they appear in writing on the date of the death of the insured, employee, or annuitant. It shall not be necessary to the validity of the trust agreement or declaration of trust, whether revocable or irrevocable, that it have a trust corpus other than the right of the trustee to receive death benefits.

(2) Death benefits of any kind, including, but not limited to, proceeds of:

(a) An individual life insurance policy;

(b) A group life insurance policy;

(c) An employees' trust, or under a contract purchased by an employees' trust, forming part of a pension, stock bonus, or profit-sharing plan;

(d) An annuity or endowment contract; and

(e) A health and accident policy,

may be made payable to the trustee named, or to be named, in a written instrument that is admitted to probate as the last will of the insured, the owner of the policy, the employee covered by the plan or contract, or any other person, whether or not the will is in existence at the time of designation. Upon the admission of the will to probate, the death benefits shall be paid to the trustee, to be held, administered, and disposed of in accordance with the terms of the trust or trusts created by the will.

(3) In the event no trustee makes proper claim to the proceeds from the insurance company or other obligor within a period of 6 months after the date of the death of the insured, employee, or annuitant, or if satisfactory evidence is furnished to the insurance company or such obligor within that period that there is, or will be, no trustee to receive the proceeds, payment shall be made by the insurance company or obligor to the personal representative of the person making such designation, unless otherwise provided by agreement with the insurer or other obligor during the lifetime of the insured, employee, or annuitant.

(4) Death benefits payable as provided in subsection (1), subsection (2), or subsection (3), unless paid to a personal representative under the provisions of subsection (3), shall not be deemed to be part of the estate of the testator or an intestate estate, and shall not be subject to any obligation to pay transfer or estate taxes, debts, or other charges enforceable against the estate to any greater extent than if such proceeds were payable directly to the beneficiaries named in the trust.

(5) The death benefits so held in trust may be commingled with any other assets that may properly come into the trust.

(6) Nothing in this section shall affect the validity of any designation of a beneficiary of proceeds heretofore made that designates as beneficiary the trustee of any trust established under a trust agreement or declaration of trust or by will.

733.809 Right of retainer.--The amount of a noncontingent indebtedness of a beneficiary to the estate, if due,

or its present value, if not due, may be offset against the beneficiary's interest, but the beneficiary has the benefit of any defense that would be available to him or her in a direct proceeding for recovery of the debt.

733.810 Distribution in kind; valuation.--

(1) Unless a general power of sale is conferred or a contrary intention is indicated by the will or unless assets are otherwise disposed of under the provisions of this code, the distributable assets of a decedent's estate shall be distributed in kind through application of the following provisions:

(a) Any family allowance or devise payable in money may be satisfied by value in kind if:

1. The person entitled to the payment has not demanded cash;

2. The property distributed in kind is valued at fair market value as of the date of its distribution; and

3. No residuary devisee has requested that the asset remain a part of the residue of the estate.

(b) When it is not practicable to distribute undivided interests in a residuary property, the property shall be converted into cash for distribution.

(2) When the personal representative, trustee, or other fiduciary under a will or trust instrument is required to, or has an option to, satisfy a devise or transfer in trust to, or for the benefit of, the surviving spouse with assets of the estate or trust in kind, at values as finally determined for federal estate tax purposes, the personal representative, trustee, or other fiduciary shall, unless the will or trust instrument otherwise provides, satisfy the devise or transfer in trust by distribution of assets, including cash, fairly representative of the appreciated or depreciated value of all property available for distribution in satisfaction of the devise or transfer in trust, taking into consideration any gains and losses realized from the sale, prior to distribution of the marital interest, of any property not specifically, generally, or demonstratively devised.

(3) With the consent of all beneficiaries affected, a personal representative or a trustee is authorized to distribute any distributable assets, non-pro rata among the beneficiaries entitled thereto.

733.811 Distribution; right or title of distributee.--
Proof that a distributee has received an instrument transferring assets in kind or payment in distribution or possession of specific property from a personal representative is conclusive evidence that the distributee has succeeded to the interest of the estate in the distributed assets, as against all persons interested in the estate, but the personal representative may recover the assets or their value if the distribution was improper.

733.812 Improper distribution; liability of distributee.--Unless the distribution or payment no longer can be questioned because of adjudication, estoppel, or limitations, a distributee of property improperly distributed or paid or a claimant who was improperly paid, if he or she has the property, is liable to return the property improperly received and its income since distribution to the personal representative or to the beneficiaries entitled to it. If he or she does not have the property, then he or she is liable to return the value of the property improperly received at the date of disposition and its income and gain received by him or her.

733.813 Purchasers from distributees protected.--If property distributed in kind, or a security interest therein, is acquired by a purchaser or lender for value from a distributee who has received an instrument of distribution or possession from the personal representative, the purchaser or lender takes title free of any claims of the estate and incurs no personal liability to the estate, whether or not the distribution was proper. To be protected under this provision a purchaser or lender need not inquire whether a personal representative acted properly in making the distribution in kind.

733.814 Partition for purpose of distribution.--When two or more heirs or devisees are entitled to distribution of undivided interests in any property, the personal representative or one or more of the beneficiaries may petition the court before closing the estate to make partition. After formal notice to the interested beneficiaries, the court shall partition the property in the same manner as provided by law for civil actions of partition. The court may direct the personal representative to sell any property that cannot be partitioned without prejudice to the owners and that cannot conveniently be allotted to any one party.

733.815 Private agreements among distributees.-- Subject to the rights of creditors and taxing authorities, competent interested persons may agree among themselves to alter the interests, shares, or amounts to which they are entitled under the will or under the laws of intestacy in a written contract executed by all who are affected. The personal representative shall abide by the terms of the agreement, subject to his or her obligation to administer the estate for the benefit of creditors, to pay all taxes and costs of administration, and to carry out the responsibilities of his or her office for the benefit of any beneficiaries of the decedent who are not parties to the agreement. Personal representatives are not required to see to the performance of trusts if the trustee is another person who is willing to accept the trust. Trustees of a testamentary trust are beneficiaries for the purposes of this section. Nothing herein relieves trustees of any duties owed to beneficiaries of trusts.

733.816 Disposition of unclaimed property held by personal representatives.--
(1) In all cases in which there is unclaimed property in the hands of a personal representative that cannot be distributed or paid to the lawful owner because of inability to find him or her or because no lawful owner is known, the court shall order the personal representative to sell the property and deposit the proceeds and cash already in hand, after retaining those amounts provided for in subsection (4), with the clerk and receive a receipt, and the clerk shall deposit the funds in the registry of the court to be disposed of as follows:
(a) If the value of the funds is $500 or less, the clerk shall post a notice for 30 days at the courthouse door giving the amount involved, the name of the personal representative, and the other pertinent information that will put interested persons on notice.
(b) If the value of the funds is over $500, the clerk shall publish the notice once a month for 2 consecutive months in a newspaper of general circulation in the county.
After the expiration of 6 months from the posting or first publication, the clerk shall deposit the funds with the State Treasurer after deducting his or her fees and the costs of publication.
(2) Upon receipt of the funds, the State Treasurer shall deposit them to the credit of the State School Fund, to become a part of the school fund. All interest and all income that may accrue from the money while so deposited shall belong to the fund. The funds so deposited shall constitute and be a permanent appropriation for payments by the State Treasurer in obedience to court orders entered as provided by subsection (3).
(3) Within 10 years from the date of deposit with the State Treasurer, on written petition to the court that directed the deposit of the funds and informal notice to the Department of Legal Affairs, and after proof of his or her right to them, any person entitled to the funds before or after payment to the State Treasurer and deposit as provided by subsection (1) may obtain an order of court directing the payment of the funds to him or her. All funds deposited with the State Treasurer and not claimed within 10 years from the date of deposit shall escheat to the state for the benefit of the State School Fund.
(4) The personal representative depositing assets with the clerk is permitted to retain from the funds in his or her possession a sufficient amount to pay final costs of administration, including fees allowed pursuant to s. 733.617 accruing between the deposit of the funds with the clerk of the court and the order of discharge. Any funds so retained which are surplus shall be deposited with the clerk prior to discharge of the personal representative.
(5)(a) If a person entitled to the funds assigns his or her rights to receive payment to an attorney or private investigative agency which is duly licensed to do business in this state pursuant to a written agreement with such person, the Department of Banking and Finance is autho-

rized to make distribution in accordance with such assignment.

(b) Payments made to an attorney or private investigative agency shall be promptly deposited into a trust or escrow account which is regularly maintained by the attorney or private investigative agency in a financial institution authorized to accept such deposits and located in this state.

(c) Distribution by the attorney or private investigative agency to the person entitled to the funds shall be made within 10 days following final credit of the deposit into the trust or escrow account at the financial institution, unless a party to the agreement protests in writing such distribution before it is made.

(d) The department shall not be civilly or criminally liable for any funds distributed pursuant to this subsection, provided such distribution is made in good faith.

733.817 Apportionment of estate taxes.--

(1) For purposes of this section:

(a) "Fiduciary" means a person other than the personal representative in possession of property included in the measure of the tax who is liable to the applicable taxing authority for payment of the entire tax to the extent of the value of the property in his or her possession.

(b) "Governing instrument" means a will, trust agreement, or any other document that controls the transfer of an asset on the occurrence of the event with respect to which the tax is being levied.

(c) "Gross estate" means the gross estate, as determined by the Internal Revenue Code with respect to the federal estate tax and the Florida estate tax, and as such concept is otherwise determined by the estate, inheritance, or death tax laws of the particular state, country, or political subdivision whose tax is being apportioned.

(d) "Included in the measure of the tax" means that for each separate tax that an interest may incur, only interests included in the measure of that particular tax are considered. The term "included in the measure of the tax" does not include any interest, whether passing under the will or not, to the extent the interest is initially deductible from the gross estate, without regard to any subsequent diminution of the deduction by reason of the charge of any part of the applicable tax to the interest. The term "included in the measure of the tax" does not include interests or amounts that are not included in the gross estate but are included in the amount upon which the applicable tax is computed, such as adjusted taxable gifts with respect to the federal estate tax. If an election is required for deductibility, an interest is not "initially deductible" unless the election for deductibility is allowed.

(e) "Internal Revenue Code" means the Internal Revenue Code of 1986, as amended from time to time.

(f) "Net tax" means the net tax payable to the particular state, country, or political subdivision whose tax is being apportioned, after taking into account all credits against the applicable tax except as provided in this section. With respect to the federal estate tax, "net tax" is determined after taking into account all credits against the tax except for the credit for foreign death taxes.

(g) "Nonresiduary devise" means any devise that is not a residuary devise.

(h) "Nonresiduary interest" in connection with a trust means any interest in a trust which is not a residuary interest.

(i) "Recipient" means, with respect to property or an interest in property included in the gross estate, an heir at law in an intestate estate, devisee in a testate estate, beneficiary of a trust, beneficiary of an insurance policy, annuity, or other contractual right, surviving tenant, taker as a result of the exercise or in default of the exercise of a general power of appointment, person who receives or is to receive the property or an interest in the property, or person in possession of the property.

(j) "Residuary devise" has the meaning set forth in s. 731.201(30).

(k) "Residuary interest," in connection with a trust, means an interest in the assets of a trust which remain after provision for any distribution that is to be satisfied by reference to a specific property or type of property, fund, sum, or statutory amount.

(l) "Revocable trust" means a trust as defined in s. 731.201(33) created by the decedent to the extent that the decedent had at his or her death the power to alter, amend, or revoke the trust either alone or in conjunction with any other person.

(m) "State" means any state, territory, or possession of the United States, the District of Columbia, and the Commonwealth of Puerto Rico.

(n) "Tax" means any estate tax, inheritance tax, generation skipping transfer tax, or other tax levied or assessed under the laws of this or any other state, the United States, any other country, or any political subdivision of the foregoing, as finally determined, which is imposed as a result of the death of the decedent, including, without limitation, the tax assessed pursuant to s. 4980A of the Internal Revenue Code. The term also includes any interest and penalties imposed in addition to the tax. Unless the context indicates otherwise, the term "tax" means each separate tax.

(o) "Temporary interest" means an interest in income or an estate for a specific period of time or for life or for some other period controlled by reference to extrinsic events, whether or not in trust.

(p) "Tentative Florida tax" with respect to any property means the net Florida estate tax that would have been attributable to that property if no tax were payable to any other state in respect of that property.

(q) "Value" means the pecuniary worth of the interest involved as finally determined for purposes of the applicable tax after deducting any debt, expense, or other deduction chargeable to it for which a deduction was allowed in determining the amount of the applicable tax. A lien or other encumbrance is not regarded as chargeable to a particular interest to the extent that it will be paid from other interests. The value of an interest shall not be reduced by reason of the charge against it of any part of the tax.

(2) An interest in homestead property shall be exempt from the apportionment of taxes if such interest passes to a person to whom inures the decedent's exemption from forced sale under the State Constitution.

(3) The net tax attributable to the interests included in the measure of each tax shall be determined by the proportion that the value of each interest included in the measure of the tax bears to the total value of all interests included in the measure of the tax. Notwithstanding the foregoing:

(a) The net tax attributable to interests included in the measure of the tax by reason of s. 2044 of the Internal Revenue Code shall be determined in the manner provided for the federal estate tax in s. 2207A of the Internal Revenue Code, and the amount so determined shall be deducted from the tax to determine the net tax attributable to all remaining interests included in the measure of the tax.

(b) The foreign tax credit allowed with respect to the federal estate tax shall be allocated among the recipients of interests finally charged with the payment of the foreign tax in reduction of any federal estate tax chargeable to the recipients of the foreign interests, whether or not any federal estate tax is attributable to the foreign interests. Any excess of the foreign tax credit shall be applied to reduce proportionately the net amount of federal estate tax chargeable to the remaining recipients of the interests included in the measure of the federal estate tax.

(c) The reduction in the Florida tax on the estate of a Florida resident for tax paid to other states shall be allocated as follows:

1. If the net tax paid to another state is greater than or equal to the tentative Florida tax attributable to the property subject to tax in the other state, none of the Florida tax shall be attributable to that property.

2. If the net tax paid to another state is less than the tentative Florida tax attributable to the property subject to tax in the other state, the net Florida tax attributable to the property subject to tax in the other state shall be the excess of the amount of the tentative Florida tax attributable to the property over the net tax payable to the other state with respect to the property.

3. Any remaining net Florida tax shall be attributable to property included in the measure of the Florida tax exclusive of property subject to tax in other states.

4. The net federal tax attributable to the property subject to tax in the other state shall be determined as if it were located in the state.

(d) The net tax attributable to a temporary interest, if any, shall be regarded as attributable to the principal that supports the temporary interest.

(4)(a) Except as otherwise effectively directed by the governing instrument, if the Internal Revenue Code including, but not limited to, ss. 2032A(c)(5), 2206, 2207, 2207A, 2207B, and 2603 of the Internal Revenue Code applies to apportion federal tax against recipients of certain interests, all net taxes, including taxes levied by the state attributable to each type of interest, shall be apportioned against the recipients of all interests of that type in the proportion that the value of each interest of that type included in the measure of the tax bears to the total of all interests of that type included in the measure of the tax.

(b) The provisions of this subsection do not affect allocation of the reduction in the Florida tax as provided in this section with respect to estates of Florida residents which are also subject to tax in other states.

(5) Except as provided above or as otherwise directed by the governing instrument, the net tax attributable to each interest shall be apportioned as follows:

(a) For property passing under the decedent's will:

1. The net tax attributable to nonresiduary devises shall be charged to and paid from the residuary estate whether or not all interests in the residuary estate are included in the measure of the tax. If the residuary estate is insufficient to pay the net tax attributable to all nonresiduary devises, the balance of the net tax attributable to nonresiduary devises shall be apportioned among the recipients of the nonresiduary devises in the proportion that the value of each nonresiduary devise included in the measure of the tax bears to the total of all nonresiduary devises included in the measure of the tax.

2. The net tax attributable to residuary devises shall be apportioned among the recipients of the residuary devises included in the measure of tax in the proportion that the value of each residuary devise included in the measure of the tax bears to the total of all residuary devises included in the measure of the tax.

(b) For property passing under the terms of any trust other than a trust created in the decedent's will:

1. The net tax attributable to nonresiduary interests shall be charged to and paid from the residuary portion of the trust, whether or not all interests in the residuary portion are included in the measure of the tax. If the residuary portion of the trust is insufficient to pay the net tax attributable to all nonresiduary interests, the balance of the net tax attributable to nonresiduary interests shall be apportioned among the recipients of the nonresiduary interests in the proportion that the value of each nonresiduary interest included in the measure of the tax bears to the total of all nonresiduary interests included in the measure of the tax.

2. The net tax attributable to residuary interests shall be apportioned among the recipients of the

residuary interests included in the measure of the tax in the proportion that the value of each residuary interest included in the measure of the tax bears to the total of all residuary interests included in the measure of the tax.

(c) The net tax attributable to an interest in homestead property which is exempt from apportionment pursuant to subsection (2) shall be apportioned against the recipients of other interests in the estate or passing under any revocable trust in the following order:

1. Class I: Recipients of interests not disposed of by the decedent's will or revocable trust which are included in the measure of the federal estate tax.

2. Class II: Recipients of residuary devises and residuary interests that are included in the measure of the federal estate tax.

3. Class III: Recipients of nonresiduary devises and nonresiduary interests that are included in the measure of the federal estate tax. The net tax apportioned to a class, if any, pursuant to this paragraph shall be apportioned among the recipients in the class in the proportion that the value of the interest of each bears to the total value of all interests included in that class.

(d) In the application of this subsection, paragraphs (a), (b), and (c) shall be applied to apportion the net tax to the recipients of the estate and the recipients of the decedent's revocable trust as if all recipients, other than the estate or trusts themselves, were taking under a common instrument.

(e) The net tax imposed under s. 4980A of the Internal Revenue Code shall be apportioned among the recipients of the interests included in the measure of that tax in the proportion that the value of the interest of each bears to the total value of all interests included in the measure of that tax.

(f) The net tax that is not apportioned under paragraphs (a), (b), and (c), including, but not limited to, the net tax attributable to interests passing by intestacy, jointly held interests passing by survivorship, insurance, properties in which the decedent held a reversionary or revocable interest, and annuities, shall be apportioned among the recipients of the remaining interests that are included in the measure of the tax in the proportion that the value of each such interest bears to the total value of all the remaining interests included in the measure of the tax.

(g) If the court finds that it is inequitable to apportion interest, penalties, or both, in the manner provided in paragraphs (a)-(f), the court may assess liability for the payment thereof in the manner it finds equitable.

(h) 1. To be effective as a direction for payment of tax in a manner different from that provided in this section, the governing instrument must direct that the tax be paid from assets that pass pursuant to that governing instrument, except as provided in this section.

2. If the decedent's will provides that the tax shall be apportioned as provided in the decedent's revocable trust by specific reference to the trust, the direction in the revocable trust shall be deemed to be a direction contained in the will and shall control with respect to payment of taxes from assets passing under both the will and the revocable trust.

3. A direction in the decedent's will to pay tax from the decedent's revocable trust is effective if a contrary direction is not contained in the trust agreement.

4. For a direction in a governing instrument to be effective to direct payment of taxes attributable to property not passing under the governing instrument from property passing under the governing instrument, the governing instrument must expressly refer to this section, or expressly indicate that the property passing under the governing instrument is to bear the burden of taxation for property not passing under the governing instrument. A direction in the governing instrument to the effect that all taxes are to be paid from property passing under the governing instrument whether attributable to property passing under the governing instrument or otherwise shall be effective to direct the payment from property passing under the governing instrument of taxes attributable to property not passing under the governing instrument.

5. If there is a conflict as to payment of taxes between the decedent's will and the governing instrument, the decedent's will controls, except as follows:

a. The governing instrument shall be given effect with respect to any tax remaining unpaid after the application of the decedent's will.

b. A direction in a governing instrument to pay the tax attributable to assets that pass pursuant to the governing instrument from assets that pass pursuant to that governing instrument shall be effective notwithstanding any conflict with the decedent's will, unless the tax provision in the decedent's will expressly overrides the conflicting provision in the governing instrument.

(6) The personal representative or fiduciary shall not be required to transfer to a recipient any property in possession of the personal representative or fiduciary which he or she reasonably anticipates may be necessary for the payment of taxes. Further, the personal representative or fiduciary shall not be required to transfer any property in possession of the personal representative or fiduciary to the recipient until the amount of the tax due from the recipient is paid by the recipient. If property is transferred before final apportionment of the tax, the recipient shall provide a bond or other security for his or her apportioned liability in the amount and form prescribed by the personal representative or fiduciary.

(7)(a) The personal representative may petition at any time for an order of apportionment. If no administration has been commenced at any time after 90 days from the decedent's death any fiduciary may petition for an order of apportionment in the court in which venue would be proper for administration of the decedent's estate. Formal notice of the petition for order of apportionment shall be given to all interested persons. At any time after 6 months from the decedent's death, any recipient may petition such court for an order of apportionment.

(b) The court shall determine all issues concerning apportionment. If the tax to be apportioned has not been finally determined, the court shall determine the probable tax due or to become due from all interested persons, apportion the probable tax, and retain jurisdiction over the parties and issues to modify the order of apportionment as appropriate until after the tax is finally determined.

(8)(a) If the personal representative or fiduciary does not have possession of sufficient property otherwise distributable to the recipient to pay the tax apportioned to the recipient, whether under this section, the Internal Revenue Code, or the governing instrument, if applicable, the personal representative or fiduciary shall recover the deficiency in tax so apportioned to the recipient:

1. From the fiduciary in possession of the property to which the tax is apportioned, if any; and

2. To the extent of any deficiency in collection from the fiduciary, or to the extent collection from the fiduciary is excused pursuant to subsection (9) and in all other cases, from the recipient of the property to which the tax is apportioned, unless relieved of this duty as provided in subsection (9).

(b) In any action to recover the tax apportioned, the order of apportionment shall be prima facie correct.

(c) In any action for the enforcement of an order of apportionment, the court shall award taxable costs as in chancery actions, including reasonable attorney's fees, and may award penalties and interest on the unpaid tax in accordance with equitable principles.

(d) This subsection shall not authorize the recovery of any tax from any company issuing insurance included in the gross estate, or from any bank, trust company, savings and loan association, or similar institution with respect to any account in the name of the decedent and any other person which passed by operation of law on the decedent's death.

(9)(a) A personal representative or fiduciary who has the duty under this section of collecting the apportioned tax from recipients may be relieved of the duty to collect the tax by an order of the court finding:

1. That the estimated court costs and attorney's fees in collecting the apportioned tax from a person against whom the tax has been apportioned will approximate or exceed the amount of the recovery;

2. That the person against whom the tax has been apportioned is a resident of a foreign country other than Canada and refuses to pay the apportioned tax on demand; or

3. That it is impracticable to enforce contribution of the apportioned tax against a person against whom the tax has been apportioned in view of the improbability of obtaining a judgment or the improbability of collection under any judgment that might be obtained, or otherwise.

(b) A personal representative or fiduciary shall not be liable for failure to attempt to enforce collection if the personal representative or fiduciary reasonably believes it would have been economically impracticable.

(10) Any apportioned tax that is not collected shall be reapportioned in accordance with this section as if the portion of the property to which the uncollected tax had been apportioned had been exempt.

(11) Nothing in this section shall limit the right of any person who has paid more than the amount of the tax apportionable to such person, calculated as if all apportioned amounts would be collected, to obtain contribution from those who have not paid the full amount of the tax apportionable to them, calculated as if all apportioned amounts would be collected, and that right is hereby conferred. In any action to enforce contribution, the court shall award taxable costs as in chancery actions, including reasonable attorney's fees.

(12) Nothing herein contained shall be construed to require the personal representative or fiduciary to pay any tax levied or assessed by any foreign country, unless specific directions to that effect are contained in the will or other instrument under which the personal representative or fiduciary is acting.

PART IX
CLOSING ESTATES

733.901   Distribution; final discharge.
733.903   Subsequent administration.

733.901 Distribution; final discharge.--

(1) When a personal representative has completed administration except for distribution, he or she shall file a final accounting and a petition for discharge that shall contain:

(a) A complete report of all receipts and disbursements since the date of the last annual accounting or, if none, from the commencement of administration.

(b) A statement that he or she has fully administered the estate by making payment, settlement, or other disposition of all claims and debts that were presented and the expenses of administration.

(c) The proposed distribution of the assets of the estate.

(d) Any prior distributions that have been made.

(e) A statement that objections to this report or proposed distribution of assets be filed within 30 days.

The final accounting and petition for discharge shall be filed and served on all interested persons within 12 months after issuance of letters for estates not required to file a federal estate tax return, otherwise 12 months from the date the return is due, unless the time is extended by the court for cause shown after notice to interested persons. The petition shall state the status of the estate and the reasons for the extension.

(2) If no objection to the accounting or petition for discharge has been filed within 30 days from the date of service of copies on interested persons, or if service has been waived, the personal representative may distribute the estate according to the plan of distribution set forth in the petition without a court order. The assets shall be distributed free from the claims of any interested person and, upon receipt of evidence that the estate has been properly distributed and that claims of creditors have been paid or otherwise disposed of, the court shall enter an order discharging the personal representative and releasing the surety on any bond.

(3) If an objection to the petition for discharge has been filed within the time allowed, the court shall determine the plan of distribution and, upon receipt of evidence that the estate has been properly distributed and that claims of creditors have been paid or otherwise disposed of, the court shall enter an order discharging the personal representative and releasing the surety on any bond.

(4) The final accounting required under subsection (1) may be waived upon a filing of a consent waiver with the court, by all interested persons, acknowledging that they are aware of their rights and that they waive the right to have a final accounting.

(5) The 30-day period contained in subsection (2) may be waived upon written consent of all interested persons.

(6) The discharge of the personal representative shall release the personal representative of the estate and shall bar any action against the personal representative, as such or individually, and his or her surety.

733.903 Subsequent administration.--The final settlement of an estate and the discharge of the personal representative shall not prevent a revocation of the order of discharge or the subsequent issuance of letters if other property of the estate is discovered or if it becomes necessary that further administration of the estate be had for any cause. However, the order of discharge may not be revoked under this section based upon the discovery of a will or later will.

CHAPTER 735
PROBATE CODE: FAMILY ADMINISTRATION AND SMALL ESTATES
PART I
FAMILY ADMINISTRATION

735.101 Family administration; nature of proceedings.--Family administration may be had in the administration of a decedent's estate when it appears:

(1) In an intestate estate, that the heirs at law of the decedent consist solely of a surviving spouse, lineal descendants, and lineal ascendants, or any of them.

(2) In a testate estate, that the beneficiaries under the will consist of a surviving spouse, lineal descendants, and lineal ascendants, or any of them, and that any specific or general devise to others constitutes a minor part of the decedent's estate.

(3) In a testate estate, that the decedent's will does not direct administration as required by chapter 733.

(4) That the value of the gross estate, as of the date of death, for federal estate tax purposes is less than $60,000.

(5) That the entire estate consists of personal property or, if real property forms part of the estate, that administration under chapter 733 has proceeded to the point that all claims of creditors have been processed or barred.

735.103 Petition for family administration.--A verified petition for family administration shall contain, in addition to the statements required by s. 733.202, the following:

(1) Facts showing that petitioners are entitled to family administration, as provided in s. 735.101.

(2) A complete list of the assets of the gross estate for federal estate tax purposes and their estimated value.

(3) An appropriate statement that the estate is not indebted or that provision for payment of debts has been made or the claims are barred.

(4) A proposed schedule of distribution of all assets to those entitled thereto as surviving spouse, heirs, beneficiaries, or creditors.

The petition shall be signed and verified by all beneficiaries and the surviving spouse, if any. The petition may be signed on behalf of a minor or an incompetent by her or his legal guardian or, if none, by her or his natural guardian.

735.107 Family administration distribution.--

(1) Upon filing the petition for family administration, the will, if any, shall be proved in accordance with chapter 733 and be admitted to probate.

(2) If the estate consists of personal property only, then, after such hearing as the court may require, an order of family administration may be entered allowing immediate distribution of the assets to the persons entitled to them.

(3) The order of family administration and the distribution so entered shall have the following effect:

(a) Those to whom specified parts of the decedent's estate are assigned by the order shall be entitled to receive and collect the parts and to have the parts transferred to them. They may maintain actions to enforce the right.

(b) Debtors of the decedent, those holding property of the decedent, and those with whom securities or other property of the decedent are registered are authorized and empowered to comply with the order by paying, delivering, or transferring to those specified in the order the parts of the decedent's estate assigned to them by the order, and the persons so paying, delivering, or transferring shall not be accountable to anyone else for the property.

(c) After the entry of the order, bona fide purchasers for value from those to whom property of the decedent may be assigned by the order shall take the property free of all claims of creditors of the decedent and all rights of the surviving spouse and all other heirs and devisees.

(d) Property of the decedent that is not exempt from claims of creditors and that remains in the hands of those to whom it may be assigned by the order shall continue to be liable for claims against the decedent until barred as provided in this law.

(e) The petitioners for the order of family administration shall be personally liable for all lawful claims against the estate of the decedent, but only to the extent of the value of the estate of the decedent actually received by each petitioner, exclusive of the property exempt from claims of creditors under the constitution and statutes of Florida.

(f) After 2 years from the death of the decedent, neither her nor his estate nor those to whom it may be assigned shall be liable for any claim against the decedent, unless proceedings have been taken for the enforcement of the claim.

(g) Any heir or devisee of the decedent who was lawfully entitled to share in the estate but was not included in the order of family administration and distribution may enforce her or his rights against those who procured the order in appropriate proceedings and, when successful, shall be awarded reasonable attorney's fees as an element of costs.

(4)(a) If the estate of the decedent includes real property and administration under chapter 733 has proceeded to the point that all claims of creditors have been processed or barred, or upon the satisfaction of all claims of creditors, if any, and after such hearing as the court may require, an order of family administration may be entered and the personal representative authorized to make distribution of the assets to the persons entitled to them. Upon evidence satisfactory to the court that distribution has been made, the court shall enter an order discharging the personal representative.

(b) Any heir or devisee of the decedent who was lawfully entitled to share in the estate but who was not included in the order of family administration and distribution may enforce her or his rights against those who procured the order in appropriate proceedings and, when successful, shall be awarded reasonable attorney's fees as an element of costs.

PART II
SUMMARY ADMINISTRATION

735.201 Summary administration; nature of proceedings.--Summary administration may be had in the administration of either a resident or nonresident decedent's estate, when it appears:

(1) In a testate estate, that the decedent's will does not direct administration as required by chapter 733.

(2) That the value of the entire estate subject to administration in this state, less the value of property exempt from the claims of creditors, does not exceed $25,000 or that the decedent has been dead for more than 2 years.

735.202 May be administered in the same manner as other estates.--The estate may be administered in the same manner as the administration of any other estate, or it may be administered as provided in this part.

735.203 Petition for summary administration.--

(1) A petition for summary administration may be filed by any beneficiary, heir at law, or person nominated as personal representative in the decedent's will offered for probate and shall be signed and verified by:

(a) The surviving spouse, if any; the heirs at law or beneficiaries who are sui juris; and the guardians of any heirs at law or beneficiaries who are not sui juris; or

(b) The persons described by s. 735.209.

(2) A petition for summary administration shall contain, in addition to the statements required by s. 733.202(2)(b) and (c), the following:

(a) Facts showing that petitioners are entitled to summary administration as provided in s. 735.201.

(b) A complete list of the assets of the estate and their estimated value, together with those assets claimed to be exempt.

(c) A statement that the estate is not indebted or that provision for payment of debts has been made.

(d) A proposed schedule of distribution of all assets to those entitled thereto as surviving spouse, beneficiaries, or creditors.

735.2055 Filing of petition.--The petition for summary administration may be filed at any stage of the administration of an estate if it appears that at the time of filing the estate would qualify.

735.206 Summary administration distribution.--

(1) Upon the filing of the petition for summary administration, the will, if any, shall be proved in accordance with chapter 733 and be admitted to probate.

(2) After such hearing as the court may require, an order of summary administration may be entered allowing immediate distribution of the assets to the persons entitled to them.

(3) The order of summary administration and distribution so entered shall have the following effect:

(a) Those to whom specified parts of the decedent's estate, including exempt property, are assigned by the order shall be entitled to receive and collect the parts and to have the parts transferred to them. They may maintain actions to enforce the right.

(b) Debtors of the decedent, those holding property of the decedent, and those with whom securities or other property of the decedent are registered are authorized and empowered to comply with the order by paying, delivering, or transferring to those specified in the order the parts of the decedent's estate assigned to them by the order, and the persons so paying, delivering, or transferring shall not be accountable to anyone else for the property.

(c) After the entry of the order, bona fide purchasers for value from those to whom property of the decedent may be assigned by the order shall take the property free of all claims of creditors of the decedent and all rights of the surviving spouse and all other heirs and devisees.

(d) Property of the decedent that is not exempt from claims of creditors and that remains in the hands of those to whom it may be assigned by the order shall continue to be liable for claims against the decedent until barred as provided in this law.

(e) The petitioners for the order of summary administration shall be personally liable for all lawful claims against the estate of the decedent, but only to the extent of the value of the estate of the decedent actually received by each petitioner, exclusive of the property exempt from claims of creditors under the constitution and statutes of Florida.

(f) After 2 years from the death of the decedent, neither the decedent's estate nor those to whom it may be assigned shall be liable for any claim against the decedent, unless proceedings have been taken for the enforcement of the claim.

(g) Any heir or devisee of the decedent who was lawfully entitled to share in the estate but who was not included in the order of summary administration and distribution may enforce his or her rights in appropriate proceedings against those who procured the order and, when successful, shall be awarded reasonable attorney's fees as an element of costs.

735.2063 Notice to creditors.--

(1) Any person who has received an order of summary administration may publish a notice to creditors according to the requirements of s. 731.111, notifying all persons having claims or demands against the estate of the decedent that an order of summary administration has been entered by the court. Such notice will specify the total cash value of the estate and the names and addresses of those to whom it has been assigned by such order. Such notice, if published, shall be published once a week for 2 consecutive weeks in a newspaper published in the county where such order was entered, and proof of publication of such notice shall be filed with the court.

(2) If proof of publication of such notice is filed with the court, all claims and demands of creditors against the estate of the decedent shall be forever barred unless such claims and demands are filed with the court within 3 months from the first publication of such notice.

735.209 Joinder of heirs, devisees, or surviving spouse in summary administration.--

(1) When any heir, devisee, or surviving spouse is authorized or required under this part to join in any agreement or petition and any such person has died, become incompetent or is a minor, or has conveyed or transferred all of his or her interest in the property of the estate, then:

(a) The heirs, devisees, and surviving spouse, if any, of a deceased person,

(b) The personal representative, if any, of the estate of a deceased person,

(c) The guardian of an incompetent or minor, or

(d) The grantee or transferee of any of them

shall be authorized to join in such agreement or petition instead of the heir, devisee, or surviving spouse.

(2) The joinder in, or consent to, a petition for summary administration is not required of an heir or beneficiary who will receive his or her full distributive share under the proposed distribution. Any beneficiary not joining or consenting shall receive formal notice of the petition.

PART III
DISPOSITION OF PERSONAL PROPERTY WITHOUT ADMINISTRATION

735.301   Disposition without administration.
735.302   Income tax refunds in certain cases.

735.301 Disposition without administration.--

(1) No administration shall be required or formal proceedings instituted upon the estate of a decedent leaving only personal property exempt under the provisions of s. 732.402, personal property exempt from the claims of creditors under the Constitution of Florida, and nonexempt personal property the value of which does not exceed the sum of the amount of preferred funeral expenses and reasonable and necessary medical and

hospital expenses of the last 60 days of the last illness.

(2) Upon informal application by affidavit, letter, or otherwise by any interested party, and if the court is satisfied that subsection (1) is applicable, the court, by letter or other writing under the seal of the court, may authorize the payment, transfer, or disposition of the personal property, tangible or intangible, belonging to the decedent to those persons entitled.

(3) Any person, firm, or corporation paying, delivering, or transferring property under the authorization shall be forever discharged from any liability thereon.

735.302 Income tax refunds in certain cases.--

(1) In any case when the United States Treasury Department determines that an overpayment of federal income tax exists and the person in whose favor the overpayment is determined is dead at the time the overpayment of tax is to be refunded, and irrespective of whether the decedent had filed a joint and several or separate income tax return, the amount of the overpayment, if not in excess of $500, may be refunded as follows:

(a) Directly to the surviving spouse on his or her verified application; or

(b) If there is no surviving spouse, to one of decedent's children who is designated in a verified application purporting to be executed by all of the decedent's children over the age of 14 years.

In either event, the application must show that the decedent was not indebted, that provision has been made for the payment of the decedent's debts, or that the entire estate is exempt from the claims of creditors under the constitution and statutes of the state, and that no administration of the estate, including summary administration, has been initiated and that none is planned, to the knowledge of the applicant.

(2) If a refund is made to the surviving spouse or designated child pursuant to the application, the refund shall operate as a complete discharge to the United States from liability from any action, claim, or demand by any beneficiary of the decedent or other person. Nothing in this section shall be construed as establishing the ownership or rights of any person in the refund so distributed

TITLE XXXII   REGULATION OF PROFESSIONS AND OCCUPATIONS CHAPTER 454   ATTORNEYS AT LAW

Section 454.18 Officers not allowed to practice.
No sheriff or clerk of any court, or deputy thereof, shall

practice in this state, nor shall any person not of good moral character, or who has been convicted of an infamous crime be entitled to practice. But no person shall be denied the right to practice on account of sex, race, or color. And any person, whether an attorney or not, or whether within the exceptions mentioned above or not, may conduct his or her own cause in any court of this state, or before any public board, committee, or officer, subject to the lawful rules and discipline of such court, board, committee, or officer. The provisions of this section restricting the practice of law by a sheriff or clerk, or deputy thereof, shall not apply in a case where such person is representing the office or agency in the course of duties as an attorney.

CONSTITUTION OF THE STATE OF FLORIDA ARTICLE X   MISCELLANEOUS

SECTION 4. Homestead; exemptions.

(a) There shall be exempt from forced sale under process of any court, and no judgment, decree or execution shall be a lien thereon, except for the payment of taxes and assessments thereon, obligations contracted for the purchase, improvement or repair thereof, or obligations contracted for house, field or other labor performed on the realty, the following property owned by a natural person:

(1) a homestead, if located outside a municipality, to the extent of one hundred sixty acres of contiguous land and improvements thereon, which shall not be reduced without the owner's consent by reason of subsequent inclusion in a municipality; or if located within a municipality, to the extent of one-half acre of contiguous land, upon which the exemption shall be limited to the residence of the owner or the owner's family;

(2) personal property to the value of one thousand dollars.

(b) These exemptions shall inure to the surviving spouse or heirs of the owner.

(c) The homestead shall not be subject to devise if the owner is survived by spouse or minor child, except the homestead may be devised to the owner's spouse if there be no minor child. The owner of homestead real estate, joined by the spouse if married, may alienate the homestead by mortgage, sale or gift and, if married, may by deed transfer the title to an estate by the entirety with the spouse. If the owner or spouse is incompetent, the method of alienation or encumbrance shall be as provided by law

APPENDIX B
FLORIDA PROBATE
CHECKLISTS

Florida Probate Checklist—Formal Administration with Will

❏ Gather information needed for petition:

> Original will and any codicils
> Decedent's social security number
> Names and addresses of beneficiaries (ages if under 18)
> Address of at least one witness to the will
> List of assets and how they are titled
> Amount of bond if any
> Have any claims or caveats against the estate been filed at courthouse?

❏ Prepare the following documents (forms included in this book):

> PETITION (form 3)
> OATH OF PERSONAL REPRESENTATIVE (form 5)
> DESIGNATION OF RESIDENT AGENT (form 6)
> ORDER ADMITTING WILL AND APPOINTING PERSONAL REPRESENTATIVE (form 7)
> LETTERS OF ADMINISTRATION (form 9)
> If will is not self-proved, prepare OATH OF WITNESS TO WILL (form 10)
> If will is not self-proved and witness cannot come to a Florida courthouse, prepare
> > COMMISSION (form 12)
> If bond is required, obtain it from bonding agency or insurance company

❏ File these documents along with original will, death certificate and filing fee

❏ If there is homestead property, prepare and file PETITION TO DETERMINE HOMESTEAD REAL PROPERTY (form 42) and ORDER DETERMINING HOMESTEAD REAL PROPERTY (form 43)

❏ Wait for LETTERS OF ADMINISTRATION to be issued by court

❏ Publish NOTICE OF ADMINISTRATION and mail to necessary parties (form 15)

❏ Prepare and file IRS forms:

> NOTICE OF FIDUCIARY RELATIONSHIP (IRS Form 56) (form 17)
> APPLICATION FOR EMPLOYER IDENTIFICATION NUMBER (IRS Form SS-4) (form 18)

❏ Open checking account for estate

❏ File change of address notice at post office

❏ Gather the assets and asset records of the estate, such as:

deeds	mortgages owned	savings bonds	coins
stocks	bank books	car titles	stamps
bonds	promissory notes	boat titles	antiques
mutual funds	contracts	insurance policies	personal property

❏ File DR-312 (if date of death is after January 1, 2000.) (form 19) with Florida Department of Revenue or, file the PRELIMINARY NOTICE AND REPORT (form 45) (if date of death is before January 1, 2000)

❏ Prepare INVENTORY (form 20):

> File original with court
> Mail copies to beneficiaries and Florida Department of Revenue

❏ Sell any assets which are necessary to settle the estate (may need court order)

❏ Distribute assets to beneficiaries, leaving enough for taxes, if any

> Obtain receipts from beneficiaries (form 21)

❏ Prepare FINAL ACCOUNTING (form 22) and ORDER OF DISCHARGE (form 24)

> File with court

❏ Close checking account

❏ File final IRS Form 1041 (obtain form from IRS)

❏ Cancel bond

❏ File NOTICE CONCERNING FIDUCIARY RELATIONSHIP (IRS Form 56) (form 17, with check box for "termination" checked)

FLORIDA PROBATE CHECKLIST—FORMAL ADMINISTRATION WITHOUT WILL

❏ Gather information needed for petition:

     List of heirs entitled to the estate

     Decedent's social security number

     Names and addresses of beneficiaries (ages if under 18)

     List of assets and how they are titled

     Amount of bond if any

     Have any claims or caveats been filed at courthouse?

❏ Prepare the following documents (forms included in this book):

     PETITION (form 4)

     OATH OF PERSONAL REPRESENTATIVE (form 5)

     DESIGNATION OF RESIDENT AGENT (form 6)

     ORDER APPOINTING PERSONAL REPRESENTATIVE (form 8)

     LETTERS OF ADMINISTRATION (form 9)

     If bond is required, obtain it from bonding agency or insurance company

❏ File these documents along with original death certificate and filing fee

❏ If there is homestead property, prepare and file PETITION TO DETERMINE HOMESTEAD REAL PROPERTY (form 42) and ORDER DETERMINING HOMESTEAD REAL PROPERTY (form 43)

❏ Wait for LETTERS OF ADMINISTRATION to be issued by court

❏ Publish NOTICE OF ADMINISTRATION (form 15) and mail to necessary parties

❏ Prepare and file IRS forms:

     NOTICE CONCERNING FIDUCIARY RELATIONSHIP (IRS Form 56) (form 17)

     APPLICATION FOR EMPLOYER IDENTIFICATION NUMBER (IRS FORM SS-4) (form 18)

❏ Open checking account for estate

❏ File change of address notice at post office

❏ Gather the assets and asset records of the estate, such as:

deeds	mortgages owned	savings bonds	coins
stocks	bank books	car titles	stamps
bonds	promissory notes	boat titles	antiques
mutual funds	contracts	insurance policies	personal property

❏ File DR-312 (if date of death is after January 1, 2000.) (Form 19) with Florida Department of Revenue or, file the PRELIMINARY NOTICE AND REPORT (form 45) (if date of death is before January 1, 2000)

❏ Prepare inventory:

     File with court

     Mail to beneficiaries and Florida Department of Revenue

❏ Sell any assets which are necessary to settle the estate

❏ Distribute assets to beneficiaries leaving enough for taxes, if any

     Obtain receipts from beneficiaries (form 21)

❏ Prepare FINAL ACCOUNTING (form 22) and ORDER OF DISCHARGE (form 24)

     File with court

❏ Close checking account

❏ File final IRS Form 1041

❏ Cancel bond

❏ File NOTICE CONCERNING FIDUCIARY RELATIONSHIP (IRS Form 56) (Form 17 with box for "termination" checked)

FLORIDA PROBATE CHECKLIST—FAMILY ADMINISTRATION

❑ Gather information needed for petition:

Original will and any codicils, if any
Decedent's social security number
Names and addresses of beneficiaries (ages if under 18)
Address of at least one witness

❑ Gather the assets and asset records of the estate, such as:

deeds	mortgages owned	savings bonds	coins
stocks	bank books	car titles	stamps
bonds	promissory notes	boat titles	antiques
mutual funds	contracts	insurance policies	personal property

Have any claims or caveats been filed at courthouse?

❑ Prepare the following documents (forms included in this book):

PETITION FOR FAMILY ADMINISTRATION [form 25 (WITH WILL) or form 27 (WITHOUT WILL)]
    If will is not self-proved, prepare OATH OF WITNESS (form 10)
        If will is not self-proved and witness cannot come to a Florida courthouse, prepare PETITION FOR APPOINTMENT (form 11) and COMMISSION (form 12)
ORDER OF FAMILY ADMINISTRATION [form 26 (WITH WILL) or form 28 (WITHOUT WILL)]

❑ File these documents along with original will (if any), death certificate, certified copy of out-of-state proceedings, if any, and filing fee

❑ File change of address notice at post office

❑ File DR-312 (if date of death is after January 1, 2000.) (form 19) with Florida Department of Revenue or, file the PRELIMINARY NOTICE AND REPORT (form 45) (if date of death is before January 1, 2000)

❑ Sell any assets which are necessary to settle the estate

❑ Distribute assets to beneficiaries leaving enough for taxes, if any

Florida Probate Checklist—Summary Administration

❏ Gather information needed for petition:

> Original will and any codicils, if any
> Decedent's social security number
> Names and addresses of beneficiaries (ages if under 18)
> Have any claims or caveats been filed at courthouse?

❏ Gather the assets and asset records of the estate, such as:

deeds	mortgages owned	savings bonds	coins
stocks	bank books	car titles	stamps
bonds	promissory notes	boat titles	antiques
mutual funds	contracts	insurance policies	personal property

❏ Prepare the following documents (forms included in this book):

> PETITION [form 29 (with will) or form 31 (without will)]
> If will is not self-proved prepare OATH OF WITNESS (form 10)
> If will is not self-proved and witness cannot come to a Florida courthouse, prepare PETITION FOR APPOINTMENT OF COMMISSIONER (form 11) and COMMISSION (form 12)

❏ File these documents along with original will (if any), death certificate and filing fee

❏ If there is homestead property, prepare and file PETITION TO DETERMINE HOMESTEAD REAL PROPERTY (form 42) and ORDER DETERMINING HOMESTEAD REAL PROPERTY (form 43)

❏ Publish NOTICE TO CREDITORS (Form 36) and mail to necessary parties

❏ File change of address notice at post office

❏ If real estate is involved file DR-312 (form 19) with Florida Department of Revenue or, file the PRELIMINARY NOTICE AND REPORT (form 45) (if date of death is before January 1, 2000)

❏ Sell any assets which are necessary to settle the estate

❏ File final IRS Form 1041 (obtain form from the IRS)

APPENDIX C
BLANK FORMS

On the following pages are the forms described in this book. You can tear them out and use them, but you may want to copy them first in case you make a mistake. Be sure to read this book carefully before using them. Further guidance is given in the statutes in Appendix A and in the Florida Probate Rules, which can be found in any law library and some public libraries. If there is anything you do not understand be sure to consult an attorney.

NOTE: *These forms are current at the time of this publication. As of January 1, 2002, some may have changed, so check your resources to ensure you are using the proper form.*

IN THE CIRCUIT COURT FOR

_____

COUNTY, FLORIDA

PROBATE DIVISION

FILE NO.: _____

IN RE: ESTATE OF

**PETITION TO OPEN
SAFE DEPOSIT BOX**

Deceased

Petitioner,_____ requests this court for an order authorizing petitioner to open a safe deposit box and in support would show:

1. Petitioner's name and address are:_____
_____, and his/her interest this estate is as follows: _____
_____.

2. Decedent,_____, died on _____. Decedent's last known address was _____; at the time death decedent was domiciled in _____; his/her age at the time of death was _____; his/her social security number is _____.

3. Prior to the date of death, decedent leased a safe deposit box number _____ from _____.

4. Petitioner believes decedent's safe deposit box may contain a will, deed to a burial plot, burial instructions and/or insurance policies.

5. Petitioner requests this Court for an Order authorizing Petitioner to examine the contents of the aforesaid safe deposit box in the presence of an officer of lessor, and ordering the lessor to deliver the following:
   a. Any writing purporting to be a will of the decedent, to the court having probate jurisdiction in the county wherein the lessee is located
   b. Any writing purported to be a deed to a burial plot or to give burial instructions, to the petitioner
   c. Any document purporting to be an insurance policy on the life of the decedent, to the beneficiary named in the policy

Under penalties of perjury, I declare that I have read the foregoing, and the facts alleged therein are true, to the best of my knowledge and belief.

Date:_____

_____
Petitioner

IN THE CIRCUIT COURT FOR

_____

COUNTY, FLORIDA

PROBATE DIVISION

FILE NO.: _____

IN RE: ESTATE OF

**ORDER TO OPEN
SAFE DEPOSIT BOX**

Deceased

On the Petition to Open Safe Deposit Box filed by _____the Court finds that sufficient proof of decedent's death has been provided, and that Petitioner is entitled to an Order to Open Safe Deposit Box as provided by Florida Statutes. It is, therefore,

ADJUDGED that upon presentment of proof of death, _____ _____, lessor of said safe deposit box, is authorized to allow Petitioner to open and examine the contents of said safe deposit box, in the presence of an officer of lessor, and lessor is ordered to deliver the following:

    a. Any writing purporting to be a will of the decedent, to the court having probate juris-diction in the county wherein the lessee is located

    b. Any writing purported to be a deed to a burial plot or to give burial instructions, to the petitioner

    c. Any document purporting to be an insurance policy on the life of the decedent, to the beneficiary named in the policy

No other items may be removed from said safe deposit box.

ORDERED this _____.

_____
Circuit Court Judge

IN THE CIRCUIT COURT FOR

_____

COUNTY, FLORIDA

PROBATE DIVISION

FILE NO.: _____

IN RE: ESTATE OF

**PETITION FOR ADMINISTRATION
WITH WILL**

Deceased

Petitioner alleges:

1. The interest of the Petitioner in this estate is _____.
Petitioner's name and address are: _____
_____. The name and office address of petitioner's
attorney (if any) is as follows:_____
_____.

2. The name, last known address and social security number of decedent are:
_____
_____. The date and place of death are
_____. Decedent was domiciled in
_____ County, State of _____.

3. So far as is known, the names and addresses of the beneficiaries and decedent's spouse (if any),
their relationship and the date of birth of any minors are as follows:

Name and Address:	Relationship	Birth date if under 18

4. Venue for this proceeding is in this county because _____
_____.

5. Petitioner, _____, is qualified to serve as personal representative
under the laws of the state of Florida and is entitled to preference to appointment because
_____.

6. The approximate value and nature of the assets in this estate are as follows:
_____ and the
estate ☐ will ☐ will not be required to file an estate tax return with the Internal Revenue Service.

7. The unrevoked will of decedent is dated _____ and the unrevoked codicils of
decedent are dated _____.

8. Petitioner is not aware of any other unrevoked wills or codicils.

9. The original of decedent's last will is in the possession of the court or accompanies this petition.

Under penalties of perjury, I declare that I have read the foregoing, and the facts alleged therein are true, to the best of my knowledge and belief.

Executed this date _____.

_____
Petitioner

_____
Attorney for Petitioner

Attorney's address:

IN THE CIRCUIT COURT FOR

_____

COUNTY, FLORIDA

PROBATE DIVISION

FILE NO.: _____

IN RE: ESTATE OF

**PETITION FOR ADMINISTRATION
WITHOUT WILL**

Deceased

Petitioner alleges:

1. The interest of the Petitioner in this estate is _____.
Petitioner's name and address are: _____
_____. The name and office address of petitioner's attorney (if any) is as follows:_____
_____.

2. The name, last known address and social security number of decedent are:
_____
_____. The date and place of death are
_____. Decedent was domiciled in
_____ County, State of _____.

3. So far as is known, the names and addresses of the beneficiaries and decedent's spouse (if any), their relationship and the date of birth of any minors are as follows:

Name and Address:	Relationship	Birth date if under 18

4. Venue for this proceeding is in this county because _____
_____.

5. Petitioner, _____, is qualified to serve as personal representative under the laws of the state of Florida and is entitled to preference to appointment because
_____.

6. The approximate value and nature of the assets in this estate are as follows:
_____ and the estate ☐ will ☐ will not be required to file an estate tax return with the Internal Revenue Service.

7. After the exercise of reasonable diligence the petitioner is unaware of any unrevoked wills or codicils of the decedent.

Under penalties of perjury, I declare that I have read the foregoing, and the facts alleged therein are true, to the best of my knowledge and belief.

Dated _____.

_____
Petitioner

_____
Attorney for Petitioner

Attorney's address:

IN THE CIRCUIT COURT FOR

_____

COUNTY, FLORIDA

PROBATE DIVISION

FILE NO.: _____

IN RE: ESTATE OF

OATH OF PERSONAL REPRESENTATIVE

Deceased

STATE OF FLORIDA

COUNTY OF _____

Before me, the undersigned authority, this day personally appeared _____ _____, who being by me first duly sworn, says:

1. That __he has applied for appointment as Personal Representative of the above-captioned estate.

2. That __he will faithfully administer the estate of the decedent according to law.

3. That __he resides at _____ _____ County, _____.

_____
(sign)

_____
(print)

The foregoing instrument was acknowledged before me this ___ day of _____, _____ by _____ who is personally known to me or who produced _____ as identification and who did take an oath.

Notary Public:

_____
(sign)

_____
(print)
State of Florida at Large
My Commission expires:

IN THE CIRCUIT COURT FOR

_____

COUNTY, FLORIDA

PROBATE DIVISION

FILE NO.: _____

IN RE: ESTATE OF

**DESIGNATION OF
RESIDENT AGENT
AND ACCEPTANCE**

Deceased

_____, Personal Representative, hereby designates
_____whose place of residence is _____
_____and whose post office address is
_____, as his/her agent for the service of process
or notice in either representative or personal capacity in all actions regarding the administration of the
estate.

_____
Personal Representative

ACCEPTANCE

I CERTIFY that I am a permanent resident of _____County, Florida, and
hereby accept the foregoing designation as resident agent.

Dated _____

_____
Resident Agent

IN THE CIRCUIT COURT FOR

_____

COUNTY, FLORIDA

PROBATE DIVISION

FILE NO.: _____

IN RE: ESTATE OF

**ORDER ADMITTING WILL TO PROBATE
AND APPOINTING
PERSONAL REPRESENTATIVE**

Deceased

The will of _____, deceased, having been:
    ❏ established by the oath of _____, a witness thereto, as being
       the Last Will and Testament of the decedent,
    ❏ self-proved as provided by by law
and presented to this Court, and no objection having been made to its probate, and the Court finding
that the decedent died on _____, it is

    ADJUDGED that the will dated _____ and attested by _____
_____ and _____as witnesses, is admitted to probate as
the Last Will and Testament of the decedent, and it is further

    ADJUDGED that _____ is appointed Personal
Representative of the estate, and that upon taking the Oath of Personal Representative, filing a
Designation of Resident Agent and Acceptance, and entering into a bond in the amount of
$_____, Letters of Administration shall be issued.

    ORDERED this _____

_____
Circuit Court Judge

Copy to:

IN THE CIRCUIT COURT FOR

_____

COUNTY, FLORIDA

PROBATE DIVISION

FILE NO.: _____

IN RE: ESTATE OF

**ORDER APPOINTING
PERSONAL REPRESENTATIVE
(WITHOUT WILL)**

Deceased

This Court having reviewed the Petition for Administration of the Estate of _____, deceased, and the Court finding that decedent died on _____, and that _____ is entitled to appointment as Personal Representative for the following reason(s): _____ _____it is

ADJUDGED that _____ is appointed Personal Representative of the estate, and that upon taking the Oath of Personal Representative, filing a Designation of Resident Agent and Acceptance, and entering into a bond in the amount of $_____, Letters of Administration shall be issued.

ORDERED this _____

_____
Circuit Court Judge

Copy to:

IN THE CIRCUIT COURT FOR

_____

COUNTY, FLORIDA

PROBATE DIVISION

FILE NO.: _____

IN RE: ESTATE OF

LETTERS OF ADMINISTRATION

Deceased

WHEREAS _____ has been appointed personal repre-sentative of the estate of the above-named decedent and has performed all acts required by law for issuance of letters of administration

NOW, THEREFORE, the undersigned circuit court judge hereby declares _____ _____ to be qualified under the laws of the state of Florida to serve as personal representative of the above-named estate with full power and authority to administer the estate accord-ing to law; to collect the property of the estate, to pay the debts and claims against the estate and to dis-tribute the assets of the estate according to law.

WITNESS my hand and the seal of this court this _____

_____
Circuit Court Judge

IN THE CIRCUIT COURT FOR

_____

COUNTY, FLORIDA

PROBATE DIVISION

FILE NO.: _____

IN RE: ESTATE OF

OATH OF WITNESS TO WILL

Deceased

STATE OF _____
COUNTY OF _____

_____, who, being first duly sworn, states that the original or copy of the will of _____, decedent, attached hereto, is the same will executed by the decedent and witnessed by the undersigned and _____
_____ as attesting witnesses on _____, _____ and that the decedent and witnesses signed the will at the end in the presence of each other and that the undersigned believes decedent was of sound mind and over eighteen years of age at the time of signing.

_____
Witness

Subscribed and sworn to before me
this _____ day of _____, _____

_____
Circuit Judge, Clerk or Commissioner

CERTIFICATE OF COMMISSIONER

I, _____, duly appointed Commissioner appointed as set forth in the attached Commission, hereby certify that _____ appeared before me this _____ day of _____, _____ , and after being duly sworn by me, executed the foregoing Oath of Witness to Will in my presence, and it was duly attested by me, and I hereby certify it to the Circuit Court Judge of _____ County, Florida.

IN WITNESS WHEREOF, I have hereunto set my hand and affixed my official seal this _____ day of _____, _____.

_____
Commissioner

IN THE CIRCUIT COURT FOR

_____

COUNTY, FLORIDA

PROBATE DIVISION

FILE NO.: _____

IN RE: ESTATE OF

**PETITION FOR APPOINTMENT
OF COMMISSIONER**

Deceased

Petitioner _____ hereby states that a Petition has been filed in this Court for the probate of the will of _____, deceased, that the will was executed on _____ at _____
_____.

The names of the witnesses to the will are as follows:_____
_____
and the witnesses are unable to appear before this court without great inconvenience.

Petitioner hereby requests that the Court appoint as a Commissioner: _____
_____ who is a _____, whose address is _____ to take the oath of _____, a witness to the execution of said will, whose address is _____.

Under penalties of perjury, I declare that I have read the foregoing Petition for Appointment of Commissioner, and that the facts alleged are true to the best of my knowledge and belief.

Dated: _____

_____
Petitioner

IN THE CIRCUIT COURT FOR

_____

COUNTY, FLORIDA

PROBATE DIVISION

FILE NO.: _____

IN RE: ESTATE OF

COMMISSION

Deceased

TO: _____ who is authorized by the laws of
_____ to administer oaths, GREETINGS:

      WHEREAS, a document purported to be the Last Will and Testament of _____
_____, deceased, has been offered to this Court for probate; and the witnesses to said will are unable to appear before this court without great inconvenience; and the oath of one of the witnesses is required by law before admitting the said will to probate;

      NOW, THEREFORE, the undersigned Circuit Court Judge in the above county and state, hereby appoints you, _____, as Commissioner of this Court to take the oath of the witness, _____ to prove the will;

      And you are hereby directed to certify the oath and file the executed commission, copy of the will, oath of the witness, and certificate of commissioner to this Court without delay.

      ORDERED THIS _____ day of _____, _____.

_____
Circuit Court Judge

IN THE CIRCUIT COURT FOR

_____

COUNTY, FLORIDA

PROBATE DIVISION

FILE NO.: _____

IN RE: ESTATE OF

NOTICE OF
PETITION FOR ADMINISTRATION
WITHOUT WILL

Deceased

TO:

YOU ARE HEREBY NOTIFIED that a Petition for Administration has been filed for the above estate, a copy of which is attached to this Notice. Any objections or defenses to the qualifications of the personal representative, the jurisdiction or the venue of the court, must be made in writing and served on the undersigned within 20 days after the date you are served with this Notice. The original must be filed with the Clerk of the above Court either before or immediately after service upon the undersigned.

If you fail to file and serve written defenses within the required time period, an order may be entered by the Court as requested in the petition. Any objections or defenses not so served and filed will be forever barred.

Date:_____

_____

Petitioner
Typed name:
Address:

Phone:

IN THE CIRCUIT COURT FOR

_____

COUNTY, FLORIDA

PROBATE DIVISION

FILE NO.: _____

IN RE: ESTATE OF

**NOTICE OF
PETITION FOR ADMINISTRATION
WITH WILL**

Deceased

TO:

    YOU ARE HEREBY NOTIFIED that a Petition for Administration has been filed for the above estate, a copy of which is attached to this Notice along with a copy of the Will proposed to be admitted to probate. Any objections or defenses to the validity of the will, qualifications of the personal representative, the jurisdiction or the venue of the court, must be made in writing and served on the undersigned within 20 days after the date you are served with this Notice. The original must be filed with the Clerk of the above Court either before or immediately after service upon the undersigned.

    If you fail to file and serve written defenses within the required time period, an order may be entered by the Court as requested in the petition. Any objections or defenses not so served and filed will be forever barred.

Dated: _____

_____
Petitioner
Typed name:
Address:

Phone:

IN THE CIRCUIT COURT FOR

_____

COUNTY, FLORIDA

PROBATE DIVISION

FILE NO.: _____

IN RE: ESTATE OF

NOTICE OF ADMINISTRATION

_____ Deceased

    Administration of the estate of _____, deceased, file number _____ has been filed in the Circuit Court for _____ County, Florida located at _____ _____. The personal representative's name and address are:_____ _____. The name and address of the personal representative's attorney (if any) are:_____ _____.

All interested persons are required to file with the court.:

    All claims against the estate within the time periods set forth in §733.702, Florida Statutes, to wit: within the later of 3 months after the date of the first publication of the notice of administration or, as to any creditor required to be served with a copy of the notice of administration, 30 days after the date of service of such copy of the notice on the creditor; and

    All objections by interested persons on whom notice was served that challenge the validity of the will, the qualifications of the personal representative, venue, or jurisdiction of the court within the later of 3 months after the date of the first publication of the notice or 30 days after the date of service of a copy of the notice on the objecting person,

or be forever barred.

The date of the first publication of this Notice is_____.

_____
Personal Representative

IN THE CIRCUIT COURT FOR

_____

COUNTY, FLORIDA

PROBATE DIVISION

FILE NO.: _____

IN RE: ESTATE OF

**RECEIPTS FOR
NOTICE BY MAIL**

Deceased

(Attach green post office
receipt cards to this sheet.
Use additional sheets if necessary.)

Form 56
(Rev. August 1997)

Department of the Treasury
Internal Revenue Service

Notice Concerning Fiduciary Relationship

(Internal Revenue Code sections 6036 and 6903)

OMB No. 1545-0013

Part I   Identification

Name of person for whom you are acting (as shown on the tax return)	Identifying number	Decedent's social security no.

Address of person for whom you are acting (number, street, and room or suite no.)

City or town, state, and ZIP code (If a foreign address, see instructions.)

Fiduciary's name

Address of fiduciary (number, street, and room or suite no.)

City or town, state, and ZIP code	Telephone number (optional) ( )

Part II   Authority

1   Authority for fiduciary relationship. Check applicable box:

a(1) ☐ Will and codicils or court order appointing fiduciary. Attach certified copy . .   (2) Date of death ....

b(1) ☐ Court order appointing fiduciary. Attach certified copy . . . .   (2) Date (see instructions) ....

c ☐ Valid trust instrument and amendments. Attach copy

d ☐ Other. Describe ▶ ....

Part III   Tax Notices

Send to the fiduciary listed in Part I all notices and other written communications involving the following tax matters:

2   Type of tax (estate, gift, generation-skipping transfer, income, excise, etc.) ▶ ---------------------------------

3   Federal tax form number (706, 1040, 1041, 1120, etc.) ▶ --

4   Year(s) or period(s) (if estate tax, date of death) ▶

Part IV   Revocation or Termination of Notice

Section A—Total Revocation or Termination

5   Check this box if you are revoking or terminating all prior notices concerning fiduciary relationships on file with the Internal Revenue Service for the same tax matters and years or periods covered by this notice concerning fiduciary relationship . ▶ ☐

Reason for termination of fiduciary relationship. Check applicable box:

a ☐ Court order revoking fiduciary authority. Attach certified copy.

b ☐ Certificate of dissolution or termination of a business entity. Attach copy.

c ☐ Other. Describe ▶

Section B—Partial Revocation

6a   Check this box if you are revoking earlier notices concerning fiduciary relationships on file with the Internal Revenue Service for the same tax matters and years or periods covered by this notice concerning fiduciary relationship . . . . ▶ ☐

b   Specify to whom granted, date, and address, including ZIP code, or refer to attached copies of earlier notices and authorizations
▶ ---

Section C—Substitute Fiduciary

7   Check this box if a new fiduciary or fiduciaries have been or will be substituted for the revoking or terminating fiduciary(ies) and specify the name(s) and address(es), including ZIP code(s), of the new fiduciary(ies) . . . . ▶ ☐

Part V   Court and Administrative Proceedings

Name of court (if other than a court proceeding, identify the type of proceeding and name of agency)	Date proceeding initiated
Address of court	Docket number of proceeding

City or town, state, and ZIP code	Date	Time	a.m. p.m.	Place of other proceedings

I certify that I have the authority to execute this notice concerning fiduciary relationship on behalf of the taxpayer.

Please Sign Here

▶ _____   _____   _____
   Fiduciary's signature   Title, if applicable   Date

▶ _____   _____   _____
   Fiduciary's signature   Title, if applicable   Date

For Paperwork Reduction Act and Privacy Act Notice, see back page.   Cat. No. 16375I   Form **56** (Rev. 8-97)

General Instructions

Section references are to the Internal Revenue Code unless otherwise noted.

Purpose of Form

You may use Form 56 to notify the IRS of the creation or termination of a fiduciary relationship under section 6903 and to give notice of qualification under section 6036.

Who Should File

The fiduciary (see **Definitions** below) uses Form 56 to notify the IRS of the creation, or termination, of a fiduciary relationship under section 6903. For example, if you are acting as fiduciary for an individual, a decedent's estate, or a trust, you may file Form 56. If notification is not given to the IRS, notices sent to the last known address of the taxable entity, transferee, or other person subject to tax liability are sufficient to satisfy the requirements of the Internal Revenue Code.

Receivers and assignees for the benefit of creditors also file Form 56 to give notice of qualification under section 6036. However, a bankruptcy trustee, debtor in possession, or other like fiduciary in a bankruptcy proceeding is not required to give notice of qualification under section 6036. Trustees, etc., in bankruptcy proceedings are subject to the notice requirements under title 11 of the United States Code (Bankruptcy Rules).

Definitions

Fiduciary. A fiduciary is any person acting in a fiduciary capacity for any other person (or terminating entity), such as an administrator, conservator, designee, executor, guardian, receiver, trustee of a trust, trustee in bankruptcy, personal representative, person in possession of property of a decedent's estate, or debtor in possession of assets in any bankruptcy proceeding by order of the court.

Person. A person is any individual, trust, estate, partnership, association, company or corporation.

Decedent's estate. A decedent's estate is a taxable entity separate from the decedent that comes into existence at the time of the decedent's death. It generally continues to exist until the final distribution of the assets of the estate is made to the heirs and other beneficiaries.

Terminating entities. A terminating entity, such as a corporation, partnership, trust, etc., only has the legal capacity to establish a fiduciary relationship while it is in existence. Establishing a fiduciary relationship prior to termination of the entity allows the fiduciary to represent the entity on all tax matters after it is terminated.

When and Where To File

Notice of fiduciary relationship. Generally, you should file Form 56 when you create (or terminate) a fiduciary relationship. To receive tax notices upon creation of a fiduciary relationship, file Form 56 with the Internal Revenue Service Center where the person for whom you are acting is required to file tax returns. However, when a fiduciary relationship is first created, a fiduciary who is required to file a return can file Form 56 with the first tax return filed.

Proceedings (other than bankruptcy) and assignments for the benefit of creditors. A fiduciary who is appointed or authorized to act as:

- A receiver in a receivership proceeding or similar fiduciary (including a fiduciary in aid of foreclosure), or
- An assignee for the benefit of creditors, must file Form 56 on, or within 10 days of, the date of appointment with the Chief, Special Procedures Staff, of the district office of the IRS having jurisdiction over the person for whom you are acting.

The receiver or assignee may also file a separate Form 56 with the service center where the person for whom the fiduciary is acting is required to file tax returns to provide the notice required by section 6903.

Specific Instructions

Part I—Identification

Provide all the information called for in this part.

Identifying number. If you are acting for an individual, an individual debtor, or other person whose assets are controlled, the identifying number is the social security number (SSN). If you are acting for a person other than an individual, including an estate or trust, the identifying number is the employer identification number (EIN).

Decedent's SSN. If you are acting on behalf of a decedent, enter the decedent's SSN shown on his or her final Form 1040 in the space provided.

Address. Include the suite, room, or other unit number after the street address.

If the postal service does not deliver mail to the street address and the fiduciary (or person) has a P.O. box, show the box number instead of the street address.

For a foreign address, enter the information in the following order: city, province or state, and country. Follow the country's practice for entering the postal code. Please **do not** abbreviate the country name.

Part II—Authority

Line 1a. Check the box on line 1a if the decedent died **testate** (i.e., having left a valid will) and enter the decedent's date of death.

Line 1b. Check the box on line 1b if the decedent died **intestate** (i.e., without leaving a valid will). Also, enter the decedent's date of death and write "Date of Death" next to the date.

Assignment for the benefit of creditors. Enter the date the assets were assigned to you and write "Assignment Date" after the date.

Proceedings other than bankruptcy. Enter the date you were appointed or took possession of the assets of the debtor or other person whose assets are controlled.

Part III—Tax Notices

Complete this part if you want the IRS to send you tax notices regarding the person for whom you are acting.

Line 2. Specify the type of tax involved. This line should also identify a transferee tax liability under section 6901 or fiduciary tax liability under 31 U.S.C. 3713(b) when either exists.

Part IV—Revocation or Termination of Notice

Complete this part only if you are revoking or terminating a prior notice concerning a fiduciary relationship. Completing this part will relieve you of any further duty or liability as a fiduciary if used as a notice of termination.

Part V—Court and Administrative Proceedings

Complete this part only if you have been appointed a receiver, trustee, or fiduciary by a court or other governmental unit in a proceeding other than a bankruptcy proceeding.

If proceedings are scheduled for more than one date, time, or place, attach a separate schedule of the proceedings.

Assignment for the benefit of creditors.— You must attach the following information:

1. A brief description of the assets that were assigned, and

2. An explanation of the action to be taken regarding such assets, including any hearings, meetings of creditors, sale, or other scheduled action.

Signature

Sign Form 56 and enter a title describing your role as a fiduciary (e.g., assignee, executor, guardian, trustee, personal representative, receiver, or conservator).

Paperwork Reduction Act and Privacy Act Notice. We ask for the information on this form to carry out the Internal Revenue laws of the United States. Form 56 is provided for your convenience and its use is voluntary. Under section 6109 you must disclose the social security number or employer identification number of the individual or entity for which you are acting. The principal purpose of this disclosure is to secure proper identification of the taxpayer. We also need this information to gain access to the tax information in our files and properly respond to your request. If you do not disclose this information, we may suspend processing the notice of fiduciary relationship and not consider this as proper notification until you provide the information.

You are not required to provide the information requested on a form that is subject to the Paperwork Reduction Act unless the form displays a valid OMB control number. Books or records relating to a form or its instructions must be retained as long as their contents may become material in the administration of any Internal Revenue law. Generally, tax returns and return information are confidential as required by section 6103.

The time needed to complete and file this form will vary depending on individual circumstances. The estimated average time is:

Recordkeeping	8 min.
Learning about the law or the form	32 min.
Preparing the form	46 min.
Copying, assembling, and sending the form to the IRS . .	15 min.

If you have comments concerning the accuracy of these time estimates or suggestions for making this form simpler, we would be happy to hear from you. You can write to the Tax Forms Committee, Western Area Distribution Center, Rancho Cordova, CA 95743-0001. **DO NOT** send Form 56 to this address. Instead, see **When and Where To File** on this page.

Form **SS-4**

(Rev. April 2000)
Department of the Treasury
Internal Revenue Service

Application for Employer Identification Number

(For use by employers, corporations, partnerships, trusts, estates, churches, government agencies, certain individuals, and others. See instructions.)

▶ Keep a copy for your records.

EIN

OMB No. 1545-0003

1 Name of applicant (legal name) (see instructions)	

Please type or print clearly.

2 Trade name of business (if different from name on line 1)	**3** Executor, trustee, "care of" name
4a Mailing address (street address) (room, apt., or suite no.)	**5a** Business address (if different from address on lines 4a and 4b)
4b City, state, and ZIP code	**5b** City, state, and ZIP code

6 County and state where principal business is located

7 Name of principal officer, general partner, grantor, owner, or trustor—SSN or ITIN may be required (see instructions) ▶ _____

8a Type of entity (Check only one box.) (see instructions)

Caution: *If applicant is a limited liability company, see the instructions for line 8a.*

☐ Sole proprietor (SSN) _____ _____
☐ Partnership   ☐ Personal service corp.
☐ REMIC   ☐ National Guard
☐ State/local government   ☐ Farmers' cooperative
☐ Church or church-controlled organization
☐ Other nonprofit organization (specify) ▶ _____
☐ Other (specify) ▶ _____

☐ Estate (SSN of decedent) _____ _____
☐ Plan administrator (SSN) _____ _____
☐ Other corporation (specify) ▶ _____
☐ Trust
☐ Federal government/military
(enter GEN if applicable) _____

8b If a corporation, name the state or foreign country (if applicable) where incorporated

State	Foreign country

9 Reason for applying (Check only one box.) (see instructions)

☐ Started new business (specify type) ▶ _____

☐ Hired employees (Check the box and see line 12.)
☐ Created a pension plan (specify type) ▶ _____

☐ Banking purpose (specify purpose) ▶ _____
☐ Changed type of organization (specify new type) ▶ _____
☐ Purchased going business
☐ Created a trust (specify type) ▶ _____
☐ Other (specify) ▶ _____

10 Date business started or acquired (month, day, year) (see instructions)	**11** Closing month of accounting year (see instructions)

12 First date wages or annuities were paid or will be paid (month, day, year). **Note:** *If applicant is a withholding agent, enter date income will first be paid to nonresident alien. (month, day, year)* . . . . ▶

13 Highest number of employees expected in the next 12 months. **Note:** *If the applicant does not expect to have any employees during the period, enter -0-. (see instructions)* . . . . ▶	Nonagricultural	Agricultural	Household

14 Principal activity (see instructions) ▶

15 Is the principal business activity manufacturing? . . . . If "Yes," principal product and raw material used ▶	☐ Yes	☐ No

16 To whom are most of the products or services sold? Please check one box.
☐ Public (retail)   ☐ Other (specify) ▶
☐ Business (wholesale)   ☐ N/A

17a Has the applicant ever applied for an employer identification number for this or any other business? . . . . ☐ Yes ☐ No
Note: *If "Yes," please complete lines 17b and 17c.*

17b If you checked "Yes" on line 17a, give applicant's legal name and trade name shown on prior application, if different from line 1 or 2 above.
Legal name ▶   Trade name ▶

17c Approximate date when and city and state where the application was filed. Enter previous employer identification number if known.

Approximate date when filed (mo., day, year)	City and state where filed	Previous EIN

Under penalties of perjury, I declare that I have examined this application, and to the best of my knowledge and belief, it is true, correct, and complete.	Business telephone number (include area code) ( )
	Fax telephone number (include area code) ( )
Name and title (Please type or print clearly.) ▶	

Signature ▶   Date ▶

Note: *Do not write below this line. For official use only.*

Please leave blank ▶	Geo.	Ind.	Class	Size	Reason for applying

For Privacy Act and Paperwork Reduction Act Notice, see page 4.   Cat. No. 16055N   Form **SS-4** (Rev. 4-2000)

General Instructions

Section references are to the Internal Revenue Code unless otherwise noted.

Purpose of Form

Use Form SS-4 to apply for an employer identification number (EIN). An EIN is a nine-digit number (for example, 12-3456789) assigned to sole proprietors, corporations, partnerships, estates, trusts, and other entities for tax filing and reporting purposes. The information you provide on this form will establish your business tax account.

Caution: *An EIN is for use in connection with your business activities only. Do **not** use your EIN in place of your social security number (SSN).*

Who Must File

You must file this form if you have not been assigned an EIN before and:

- You pay wages to one or more employees including household employees.

- You are required to have an EIN to use on any return, statement, or other document, even if you are not an employer.

- You are a withholding agent required to withhold taxes on income, other than wages, paid to a nonresident alien (individual, corporation, partnership, etc.). A withholding agent may be an agent, broker, fiduciary, manager, tenant, or spouse, and is required to file **Form 1042,** Annual Withholding Tax Return for U.S. Source Income of Foreign Persons.

- You file **Schedule C,** Profit or Loss From Business, **Schedule C-EZ,** Net Profit From Business, or **Schedule F,** Profit or Loss From Farming, of **Form 1040,** U.S. Individual Income Tax Return, **and** have a Keogh plan or are required to file excise, employment, or alcohol, tobacco, or firearms returns.

The following must use EINs even if they do not have any employees:

- State and local agencies who serve as tax reporting agents for public assistance recipients, under Rev. Proc. 80-4, 1980-1 C.B. 581, should obtain a separate EIN for this reporting. See **Household employer** on page 3.

- Trusts, except the following:

  1. Certain grantor-owned trusts. (See the **Instructions for Form 1041,** U.S. Income Tax Return for Estates and Trusts.)

  2. Individual retirement arrangement (IRA) trusts, unless the trust has to file **Form 990-T,** Exempt Organization Business Income Tax Return. (See the **Instructions for Form 990-T.)**

- Estates

- Partnerships

- REMICs (real estate mortgage investment conduits) (See the **Instructions for Form 1066,** U.S. Real Estate Mortgage Investment Conduit (REMIC) Income Tax Return.)

- Corporations

- Nonprofit organizations (churches, clubs, etc.)

- Farmers' cooperatives

- Plan administrators (A plan administrator is the person or group of persons specified as the administrator by the instrument under which the plan is operated.)

When To Apply for a New EIN

New Business. If you become the new owner of an existing business, **do not** use the EIN of the former owner. **If you already have an EIN, use that number.** If you do not have an EIN, apply for one on this form. If you become the "owner" of a corporation by acquiring its stock, use the corporation's EIN.

Changes in Organization or Ownership. If you already have an EIN, you may need to get a new one if either the organization or ownership of your business changes. If you incorporate a sole proprietorship or form a partnership, you must get a new EIN. However, **do not** apply for a new EIN if:

- You change only the name of your business,

- You elected on **Form 8832,** Entity Classification Election, to change the way the entity is taxed, or

- A partnership terminates because at least 50% of the total interests in partnership capital and profits were sold or exchanged within a 12-month period. (See Regulations section 301.6109-1(d)(2)(iii).) The EIN for the terminated partnership should continue to be used.

Note: *If you are electing to be an "S corporation," be sure you file **Form 2553,** Election by a Small Business Corporation.*

File Only One Form SS-4. File only one Form SS-4, regardless of the number of businesses operated or trade names under which a business operates. However, each corporation in an affiliated group must file a separate application.

EIN Applied for, But Not Received. If you do not have an EIN by the time a return is due, write "Applied for" and the date you applied in the space shown for the number. **Do not** show your social security number (SSN) as an EIN on returns.

If you do not have an EIN by the time a tax deposit is due, send your payment to the Internal Revenue Service Center for your filing area. (See **Where To Apply** below.) Make your check or money order payable to "United States Treasury" and show your name (as shown on Form SS-4), address, type of tax, period covered, and date you applied for an EIN. Send an explanation with the deposit.

For more information about EINs, see **Pub. 583,** Starting a Business and Keeping Records, and **Pub. 1635,** Understanding Your EIN.

How To Apply

You can apply for an EIN either by mail or by telephone. You can get an EIN immediately by calling the Tele-TIN number for the service center for your state, or you can send the completed Form SS-4 directly to the service center to receive your EIN by mail.

Application by Tele-TIN. Under the Tele-TIN program, you can receive your EIN by telephone and use it immediately to file a return or make a payment. To receive an EIN by telephone, complete Form SS-4, then call the Tele-TIN number listed for your state under **Where To Apply.** The person making the call must be authorized to sign the form. (See **Signature** on page 4.)

An IRS representative will use the information from the Form SS-4 to establish your account and assign you an EIN. Write the number you are given on the upper right corner of the form and sign and date it.

Mail or fax (facsimile) the signed Form SS-4 **within 24 hours** to the Tele-TIN Unit at the service center address for your state. The IRS representative will give you the fax number. The fax numbers are also listed in Pub. 1635.

Taxpayer representatives can receive their client's EIN by telephone if they first send a fax of a completed **Form 2848,** Power of Attorney and Declaration of Representative, or **Form 8821,** Tax Information Authorization, to the Tele-TIN unit. The Form 2848 or Form 8821 will be used solely to release the EIN to the representative authorized on the form.

Application by Mail. Complete Form SS-4 at least 4 to 5 weeks before you will need an EIN. Sign and date the application and mail it to the service center address for your state. You will receive your EIN in the mail in approximately 4 weeks.

Where To Apply

The Tele-TIN numbers listed below will involve a long-distance charge to callers outside of the local calling area and can be used only to apply for an EIN. **The numbers may change without notice.** Call 1-800-829-1040 to verify a number or to ask about the status of an application by mail.

If your principal business, office or agency, or legal residence in the case of an individual, is located in: ▼	Call the Tele-TIN number shown or file with the Internal Revenue Service Center at: ▼
Florida, Georgia, South Carolina	Attn: Entity Control Atlanta, GA 39901 770-455-2360
New Jersey, New York (New York City and counties of Nassau, Rockland, Suffolk, and Westchester)	Attn: Entity Control Holtsville, NY 00501 516-447-4955
New York (all other counties), Connecticut, Maine, Massachusetts, New Hampshire, Rhode Island, Vermont	Attn: Entity Control Andover, MA 05501 978-474-9717
Illinois, Iowa, Minnesota, Missouri, Wisconsin	Attn: Entity Control Stop 6800 2306 E. Bannister Rd. Kansas City, MO 64999 816-926-5999
Delaware, District of Columbia, Maryland, Pennsylvania, Virginia	Attn: Entity Control Philadelphia, PA 19255 215-516-6999
Indiana, Kentucky, Michigan, Ohio, West Virginia	Attn: Entity Control Cincinnati, OH 45999 859-292-5467

Kansas, New Mexico, Oklahoma, Texas	Attn: Entity Control Austin, TX 73301 512-460-7843
Alaska, Arizona, California (counties of Alpine, Amador, Butte, Calaveras, Colusa, Contra Costa, Del Norte, El Dorado, Glenn, Humboldt, Lake, Lassen, Marin, Mendocino, Modoc, Napa, Nevada, Placer, Plumas, Sacramento, San Joaquin, Shasta, Sierra, Siskiyou, Solano, Sonoma, Sutter, Tehama, Trinity, Yolo, and Yuba), Colorado, Idaho, Montana, Nebraska, Nevada, North Dakota, Oregon, South Dakota, Utah, Washington, Wyoming	Attn: Entity Control Mail Stop 6271 P.O. Box 9941 Ogden, UT 84201 801-620-7645
California (all other counties), Hawaii	Attn: Entity Control Fresno, CA 93888 559-452-4010
Alabama, Arkansas, Louisiana, Mississippi, North Carolina, Tennessee	Attn: Entity Control Memphis, TN 37501 901-546-3920
If you have no legal residence, principal place of business, or principal office or agency in any state	Attn: Entity Control Philadelphia, PA 19255 215-516-6999

Specific Instructions

The instructions that follow are for those items that are not self-explanatory. Enter N/A (nonapplicable) on the lines that do not apply.

Line 1. Enter the legal name of the entity applying for the EIN exactly as it appears on the social security card, charter, or other applicable legal document.

Individuals. Enter your first name, middle initial, and last name. If you are a sole proprietor, enter your individual name, not your business name. Enter your business name on line 2. Do not use abbreviations or nicknames on line 1.

Trusts. Enter the name of the trust.

Estate of a decedent. Enter the name of the estate.

Partnerships. Enter the legal name of the partnership as it appears in the partnership agreement. **Do not** list the names of the partners on line 1. See the specific instructions for line 7.

Corporations. Enter the corporate name as it appears in the corporation charter or other legal document creating it.

Plan administrators. Enter the name of the plan administrator. A plan administrator who already has an EIN should use that number.

Line 2. Enter the trade name of the business if different from the legal name. The trade name is the "doing business as" name.

Note: *Use the full legal name on line 1 on all tax returns filed for the entity. However, if you enter a trade name on line 2 and choose to use the trade name instead of the legal name, enter the trade name on all returns you file. To prevent processing delays and errors, always use either the legal name only or the trade name only on all tax returns.*

Line 3. Trusts enter the name of the trustee. Estates enter the name of the executor, administrator, or other fiduciary. If the entity applying has a designated person to receive tax information, enter that person's name as the "care of" person. Print or type the first name, middle initial, and last name.

Line 7. Enter the first name, middle initial, last name, and SSN of a principal officer if the business is a corporation; of a general partner if a partnership; of the owner of a single member entity that is disregarded as an entity separate from its owner; or of a grantor, owner, or trustor if a trust. If the person in question is an alien individual with a previously assigned individual taxpayer identification number (ITIN), enter the ITIN in the space provided, instead of an SSN. You are not required to enter an SSN or ITIN if the reason you are applying for an EIN is to make an entity classification election (see Regulations section 301.7701-1 through 301.7701-3), and you are a nonresident alien with no effectively connected income from sources within the United States.

Line 8a. Check the box that best describes the type of entity applying for the EIN. If you are an alien individual with an ITIN previously assigned to you, enter the ITIN in place of a requested SSN.

Caution: *This is not an election for a tax classification of an entity. See "Limited liability company (LLC)" below.*

If not specifically mentioned, check the "Other" box, enter the type of entity and the type of return that will be filed (for example, common trust fund, Form 1065). Do not enter N/A. If you are an alien individual applying for an EIN, see the **Line 7** instructions above.

Sole proprietor. Check this box if you file Schedule C, C-EZ, or F (Form 1040) and have a qualified plan, or are required to file excise, employment, or alcohol, tobacco, or firearms returns, or are a payer of gambling winnings. Enter your SSN (or ITIN) in the space provided. If you are a nonresident alien with are a nonresident alien with no effectively

connected income from sources within the United States, you do not need to enter an SSN or ITIN.

REMIC. Check this box if the entity has elected to be treated as a real estate mortgage investment conduit (REMIC). See the Instructions for Form 1066 for more information.

Other nonprofit organization. Check this box if the nonprofit organization is other than a church or church-controlled organization and specify the type of nonprofit organization (for example, an educational organization).

If the organization also seeks tax-exempt status, you must file either **Package 1023,** Application for Recognition of Exemption, or **Package 1024,** Application for Recognition of Exemption Under Section 501(a). Get **Pub. 557,** Tax Exempt Status for Your Organization, for more information.

Group exemption number (GEN). If the organization is covered by a group exemption letter, enter the four-digit GEN. (Do not confuse the GEN with the nine-digit EIN.) If you do not know the GEN, contact the parent organization. Get Pub. 557 for more information about group exemption numbers.

Withholding agent. If you are a withholding agent required to file Form 1042, check the "Other" box and enter "Withholding agent."

Personal service corporation. Check this box if the entity is a personal service corporation. An entity is a personal service corporation for a tax year only if:

● The principal activity of the entity during the testing period (prior tax year) for the tax year is the performance of personal services substantially by employee-owners, and

● The employee-owners own at least 10% of the fair market value of the outstanding stock in the entity on the last day of the testing period.

Personal services include performance of services in such fields as health, law, accounting, or consulting. For more information about personal service corporations, see the **Instructions for Forms 1120 and 1120-A,** and **Pub. 542,** Corporations.

Limited liability company (LLC). See the definition of limited liability company in the **Instructions for Form 1065,** U.S. Partnership Return of Income. An LLC with two or more members can be a partnership or an association taxable as a corporation. An LLC with a single owner can be an association taxable as a corporation or an entity disregarded as an entity separate from its owner. See Form 8832 for more details.

Note: *A domestic LLC with at least two members that does not file Form 8832 is classified as a partnership for Federal income tax purposes.*

● If the entity is classified as a partnership for Federal income tax purposes, check the "partnership" box.

● If the entity is classified as a corporation for Federal income tax purposes, check the "Other corporation" box and write "limited liability co." in the space provided.

● If the entity is disregarded as an entity separate from its owner, check the "Other" box and write in "disregarded entity" in the space provided.

Plan administrator. If the plan administrator is an individual, enter the plan administrator's SSN in the space provided.

Other corporation. This box is for any corporation other than a personal service corporation. If you check this box, enter the type of corporation (such as insurance company) in the space provided.

Household employer. If you are an individual, check the "Other" box and enter "Household employer" and your SSN. If you are a state or local agency serving as a tax reporting agent for public assistance recipients who become household employers, check the "Other" box and enter "Household employer agent." If you are a trust that qualifies as a household employer, you do not need a separate EIN for reporting tax information relating to household employees; use the EIN of the trust.

QSub. For a qualified subchapter S subsidiary (QSub) check the "Other" box and specify "QSub."

Line 9. Check only **one** box. Do not enter N/A.

Started new business. Check this box if you are starting a new business that requires an EIN. If you check this box, enter the type of business being started. **Do not** apply if you already have an EIN and are only adding another place of business.

Hired employees. Check this box if the existing business is requesting an EIN because it has hired or is hiring employees and is therefore required to file employment tax returns. **Do not** apply if you already have an EIN and are only hiring employees. For information on the applicable employment taxes for family members, see **Circular E,** Employer's Tax Guide (Publication 15).

Created a pension plan. Check this box if you have created a pension plan and need an EIN for reporting purposes. Also, enter the type of plan.

Note: *Check this box if you are applying for a trust EIN when a new pension plan is established.*

Banking purpose. Check this box if you are requesting an EIN for banking purposes only, and enter the banking purpose (for example, a bowling league for depositing dues or an investment club for dividend and interest reporting).

Changed type of organization. Check this box if the business is changing its type of organization, for example, if the business was a sole proprietorship and has been incorporated or has become a partnership. If you check this box, specify in the space provided the type of change made, for example, "from sole proprietorship to partnership."

Purchased going business. Check this box if you purchased an existing business. **Do not** use the former owner's EIN. **Do not** apply for a new EIN if you already have one. Use your own EIN.

Created a trust. Check this box if you created a trust, and enter the type of trust created. For example, indicate if the trust is a nonexempt charitable trust or a split-interest trust.

Note: *Do not check this box if you are applying for a trust EIN when a new pension plan is established. Check "Created a pension plan."*

Exception. Do **not** file this form for certain grantor-type trusts. The trustee does not need an EIN for the trust if the trustee furnishes the name and TIN of the grantor/owner and the address of the trust to all payors. See the Instructions for Form 1041 for more information.

Other (specify). Check this box if you are requesting an EIN for any other reason, and enter the reason.

Line 10. If you are starting a new business, enter the starting date of the business. If the business you acquired is already operating, enter the date you acquired the business. Trusts should enter the date the trust was legally created. Estates should enter the date of death of the decedent whose name appears on line 1 or the date when the estate was legally funded.

Line 11. Enter the last month of your accounting year or tax year. An accounting or tax year is usually 12 consecutive months, either a calendar year or a fiscal year (including a period of 52 or 53 weeks). A calendar year is 12 consecutive months ending on December 31. A fiscal year is either 12 consecutive months ending on the last day of any month other than December or a 52-53 week year. For more information on accounting periods, see **Pub. 538**, Accounting Periods and Methods.

Individuals. Your tax year generally will be a calendar year.

Partnerships. Partnerships generally must adopt one of the following tax years:

- The tax year of the majority of its partners,
- The tax year common to all of its principal partners,
- The tax year that results in the least aggregate deferral of income, or
- In certain cases, some other tax year.

See the Instructions for Form 1065 for more information.

REMIC. REMICs must have a calendar year as their tax year.

Personal service corporations. A personal service corporation generally must adopt a calendar year unless:

- It can establish a business purpose for having a different tax year, or
- It elects under section 444 to have a tax year other than a calendar year.

Trusts. Generally, a trust must adopt a calendar year except for the following:

- Tax-exempt trusts,
- Charitable trusts, and
- Grantor-owned trusts.

Line 12. If the business has or will have employees, enter the date on which the business began or will begin to pay wages. If the business does not plan to have employees, enter N/A.

Withholding agent. Enter the date you began or will begin to pay income to a nonresident alien. This also applies to individuals who are required to file Form 1042 to report alimony paid to a nonresident alien.

Line 13. For a definition of agricultural labor (farmwork), see **Circular A,** Agricultural Employer's Tax Guide (Publication 51).

Line 14. Generally, enter the exact type of business being operated (for example, advertising agency, farm, food or beverage establishment, labor union, real estate agency, steam laundry, rental of coin-operated vending machine, or investment club). Also state if the business will involve the sale or distribution of alcoholic beverages.

Governmental. Enter the type of organization (state, county, school district, municipality, etc.).

Nonprofit organization (other than governmental). Enter whether organized for religious, educational, or humane purposes, and the principal activity (for example, religious organization—hospital, charitable).

Mining and quarrying. Specify the process and the principal product (for example, mining bituminous coal, contract drilling for oil, or quarrying dimension stone).

Contract construction. Specify whether general contracting or special trade contracting. Also, show the type of work normally performed (for example, general contractor for residential buildings or electrical subcontractor).

Food or beverage establishments. Specify the type of establishment and state whether you employ workers who receive tips (for example, lounge—yes).

Trade. Specify the type of sales and the principal line of goods sold (for example, wholesale dairy products, manufacturer's representative for mining machinery, or retail hardware).

Manufacturing. Specify the type of establishment operated (for example, sawmill or vegetable cannery).

Signature. The application must be signed by (a) the individual, if the applicant is an individual, (b) the president, vice president, or other principal officer, if the applicant is a corporation, (c) a responsible and duly authorized member or officer having knowledge of its affairs, if the applicant is a partnership or other unincorporated organization, or (d) the fiduciary, if the applicant is a trust or an estate.

How To Get Forms and Publications

Phone. You can order forms, instructions, and publications by phone 24 hours a day, 7 days a week. Just call 1-800-TAX-FORM (1-800-829-3676). You should receive your order or notification of its status within 10 workdays.

Personal computer. With your personal computer and modem, you can get the forms and information you need using IRS's Internet Web Site at www.irs.gov or File Transfer Protocol at ftp.irs.gov.

CD-ROM. For small businesses, return preparers, or others who may frequently need tax forms or publications, a CD-ROM containing over 2,000 tax products (including many prior year forms) can be purchased from the National Technical Information Service (NTIS).

To order **Pub. 1796,** Federal Tax Products on CD-ROM, call **1-877-CDFORMS** (1-877-233-6767) toll free or connect to www.irs.gov/cdorders

The time needed to complete and file this form will vary depending on individual circumstances. The estimated average time is:

Recordkeeping	7 min.
Learning about the law or the form	22 min.
Preparing the form	46 min.
Copying, assembling, and sending the form to the IRS . .	20 min.

If you have comments concerning the accuracy of these time estimates or suggestions for making this form simpler, we would be happy to hear from you. You can write to the Tax Forms Committee, Western Area Distribution Center, Rancho Cordova, CA 95743-0001. **Do not** send the form to this address. Instead, see **Where To Apply** on page 2.

FLORIDA

DEPARTMENT OF REVENUE

Affidavit of No Florida Estate Tax Due	DR-312 N. 01/00

(for decedents dying on or after January 1, 2000)

_____

(this space available for case style of estate probate proceeding)   (for official use only)

STATE OF _____

COUNTY OF _____

I, the undersigned, _____ , do hereby state:

(print name of personal representative)

1. I am the Personal Representative as defined in s. 198.01 or s. 731.201, Florida Statutes (F.S.), as the case may be,

   of the Estate of _____ .

   (print name of decedent)

2. The decedent referenced above, whose Social Security Number is _____, died

   on _____/_____/_____, and was domiciled, as defined in s. 198.015, F.S., at the time of death in the state

   (date of death)

   of _____ .

   On date of death, the decedent was (check one): ❑ a U.S. citizen ❑ <u>not</u> a U.S. citizen

3. A federal estate tax return (federal Form 706 or 706-NA) is not required to be filed for the Estate.

4. The Estate does not owe Florida estate tax pursuant to Chapter 198, F.S.

5. I acknowledge personal liability for distribution in whole or in part of any of the Estate by having obtained release of such property from the lien of the Florida estate tax.

Under penalties of perjury, I declare that I have read this Affidavit and that the facts stated are true.

Executed this _____ day of _____, 20 _____ .

Signature: _____

Print Name: _____

Mailing Address: _____

_____ Telephone: _____

STATE OF _____

COUNTY OF _____

Sworn to (or affirmed) and subscribed before me by _____

on this _____ day of _____, 20_____ .

Personally known _____
Or Produced Identification _____
Type of Identification Produced_____

Signature of Notary: _____

_____
(Print, Type, or Stamp Name of Notary)

- **Use this form ONLY for decedents dying on or after January 1, 2000.**
- **File this form with the clerk of the court. Do not mail it to the Florida Department of Revenue.**

General Information

Effective January 1, 2000 (for decedents dying on or after January 1, 2000 ONLY), estates are no longer required to file a *Preliminary Notice and Report* (DR-301) with the Florida Department of Revenue. If Florida estate tax is not due; and a federal estate tax return (federal Form 706 or 706-NA) is not required to be filed, the personal representatives of such estates are to complete Florida Form DR-312, *Affidavit of No Florida Estate Tax Due*. Note that the definition of "personal representative" in Chapter 198 includes any person who is in actual or constructive possession. Therefore, this affidavit may be used by "persons in possession" of any property included in the decedent's gross estate. **Form DR-312 must be recorded directly with the clerk of the circuit court in the county or counties where the decedent owned property. DO NOT send this form to the Florida Department of Revenue.**

Form DR-312 is admissible as evidence of nonliability for Florida estate tax and will remove the Department's estate tax lien. The Florida Department of Revenue will no longer issue *Nontaxable Certificates* for estates of persons dying on or after January 1, 2000 for which the DR-312 has been duly filed and no federal Form 706 or 706-NA is due.

The 3-inch by 3-inch space in the upper right corner is for the exclusive use of the clerk of the court. Do not write, mark or stamp in that space.

Where to File Form DR-312

File this form with the clerk of the court in the appropriate county. **Do not send this form to the Florida Department of Revenue.**

When to Use Form DR-312

Form DR-312 should be used when an estate is not subject to Florida estate tax under Chapter 198, Florida Statutes (F.S.), and a federal estate tax return (federal Form 706 or 706-NA) is not required to be filed.

Federal thresholds for filing federal Form 706 only: (For informational purposes only. Please confirm with Form 706 instructions.)

Date of Death (year)	Dollar Threshold for Filing Form 706 (value of gross estate)
2000 and 2001	$675,000
2002 and 2003	$700,000
2004	$850,000
2005	$950,000
2006 and thereafter	$1,000,000

For thresholds for filing federal Form 706-NA (nonresident alien decedent), contact your local IRS office.

If an administration proceeding is pending for an estate, Form DR-312 may be filed in that proceeding. The case style of the proceeding should be added in the large blank space in the upper left portion of the DR-312. Form DR-312 should be filed with the clerk of court and duly recorded in the public records of the county or counties where the decedent owned property.

Need Assistance?

For **forms and general information,** call Taxpayer Services, Monday-Friday, 8 a.m. to 5 p.m., ET, at 1-800-352-3671 (in Florida only) or 850-488-6800. From the option menu, select *Information on Taxes or Forms.*

Hearing or speech impaired persons may call the TDD line at 1-800-367-8331 or 850-922-1115.

Visit our web site at:
Form DR-312 can be downloaded from our Internet website at:
http://sun6.dms.state.fl.us/dor

For a **detailed written response** to your questions, write: Florida Department of Revenue, Estate Tax Unit, 5050 W. Tennessee St., Tallahassee, Florida 32399-0155.

Get the forms you need fast by **FAX on Demand!** Call seven days a week, 24 hours a day, at 850-922-3676 from your FAX machine telephone and follow the instructions.

Reference Material
Chapter 12C-3, Florida Administrative Code and Chapter 198, Florida Statutes. Tax statutes and rules are available online at:
http://taxlaw.state.fl.us

IN THE CIRCUIT COURT FOR

_____

COUNTY, FLORIDA

PROBATE DIVISION

FILE NO.: _____

IN RE: ESTATE OF

INVENTORY

Deceased

The following inventory is a complete listing of all property of the estate of _____ _____, deceased, of which the undersigned personal representative has knowledge:

Florida real estate, homestead:

Value: $

Florida real estate, non-homestead:

Value: $

Personal property of any kind or location:

Value: $ _____

Total value of all property of the estate except homestead: $

     Copies of this inventory have been served on the Florida Department of Revenue, Tallahassee, Florida 32301, and on the following:

     Under penalties of perjury, I declare that I have read the foregoing, and the facts alleged are true, to the best of my knowledge and belief.

Dated:_____

_____
Personal Representative

IN THE CIRCUIT COURT FOR

_____

COUNTY, FLORIDA

PROBATE DIVISION

FILE NO.: _____

IN RE: ESTATE OF

Deceased

**WAIVER OF ACCOUNTING AND OF
SERVICE OF PETITION FOR DISCHARGE,
RECEIPT OF BENEFICIARY AND
CONSENT TO DISCHARGE**

The undersigned beneficiary, whose social security or tax identification number is _____ hereby waives the filing and service of any accounting by the personal representative, waives service and notice of the Petition for Discharge of the personal representative and acknowledges receipt from the personal representative of the above estate the following as complete distribution of the undersigned's share:

The undersigned releases the personal representative from further liability regarding the estate and consents to discharge of the personal representative without notice or delay.

Dated _____

_____
Beneficiary
Name typed:_____
Address:

IN RE: ESTATE OF _____

PROBATE DIVISION
File Number_____

_____ Deceased.

Division_____

_____ACCOUNTING OF PERSONAL REPRESENTATIVE

From:_____,20___, through:_____,20___.

(If this is a FINAL accounting, the amount and manner of determining compensation for attorneys for the personal representative(s) are disclosed on Schedule F, unless the disclosure is waived pursuant to Section 733.6171 (9) of the Florida Statutes by the parties bearing the impact of the compensation.

It is important that this accounting be carefully examined. Requests for additional information and any questions should be addressed to the personal representative(s) or the attorneys for the personal representative(s), the names and addresses of whom are set forth below.)

SUMMARY

I. <u>Starting Balance</u>
    Assets per Inventory or on
    hand at close of last accounting
    period. $_____

II. <u>Receipts</u>

Schedule A—Income	$_____	
Principal	$_____	
Total Receipts		$_____
Subtotal		$_____

III. <u>Disbursements</u>

Schedule B—Income	$_____	
Principal	$_____	
Total Disbursements		$_____
Subtotal		$_____

IV. <u>Distributions</u>

Schedule C: Income	$_____	
Principal Distributions	$_____	
Total Distributions		$_____
Subtotal		$_____

V. <u>Capital Transactions and Adjustments</u>
    Schedule D—Net Gain or Loss $_____

VI. <u>Assets on Hand at Close of Accounting Period</u>
    Schedule E—Cash and Other Assets $_____

Under penalties of perjury, the undersigned personal representative(s) declare(s) that I (we) have read and examined this accounting and that the facts and figures set forth in the Summary and the attached Schedules are true, to the best of my (our knowledge and belief, and that it is a complete report of all cash and property transactions and of all receipts and disbursements by me (us) as personal representative(s) of the estate of _____

_____deceased, from_____,
20____through_____,20___.

Signed on _____,20____.
Attorney for Personal Representative:

Personal Representative:

_____

_____

Attorney

_____

    NAME

Florida Bar No._____

_____

_____

_____

_____

_____

_____
          (address)
          (address)

Telephone:_____
[Print or type names under all]
[signature lines]

IN THE CIRCUIT COURT FOR

_____

COUNTY, FLORIDA

IN RE: ESTATE OF

PROBATE DIVISION

File Number_____

Deceased.

Division_____

_____ACCOUNTING OF PERSONAL REPRESENTATIVE.
ESTATE OF_____
From:_____,20____, Through:_____,20____.

_____

<u>Schedule A</u>   Receipts During Period
(Does not include receipts from sale of other dispositions of principal assets. Such transactions are shown on Schedule D.)

Date	Brief Description of Items	Income	Principal

(Schedule A should reflect only those items received during administration that are not shown on the inventory. Classification of items as income or principal is to be in accordance with the provisions of the Florida Principal and Income Act, Chapter 738, Florida Statutes.)

IN THE CIRCUIT COURT FOR

_____

COUNTY, FLORIDA

IN RE: ESTATE OF

PROBATE DIVISION

File Number_____

Deceased.

Division_____

_____ACCOUNTING OF PERSONAL REPRESENTATIVE.

ESTATE OF_____

From:_____,20_____, Through:_____,20_____.

SCHEDULE B
DISBURSEMENTS

Deceased

FOR THE PERIOD COMMENCING: _____

THROUGH: _____

SCHEDULE—B   Disbursements and Distributions

(Does not include purchases of principal assets. Such transactions are shown on Schedule C.)

Date	Brief Description of Items	Income	Principal

IN THE CIRCUIT COURT FOR

_____

COUNTY, FLORIDA

IN RE: ESTATE OF

PROBATE DIVISION

File Number_____

Deceased.

Division_____

_____ACCOUNTING OF PERSONAL REPRESENTATIVE.

ESTATE OF_____

From:_____,20____, Through:_____,20____.

SCHEDULE C
CAPITAL TRANSACTIONS

Deceased

FOR THE PERIOD COMMENCING: _____

THROUGH: _____

SCHEDULE—C   Capital Transactions and Adjustments

(Do not show distributions. Distributions are shown on Schedule B.)

Date	Brief Description of Items	Income	Principal

IN THE CIRCUIT COURT FOR

_____

COUNTY, FLORIDA

IN RE: ESTATE OF

PROBATE DIVISION

File Number_____

Deceased.

Division_____

_____ACCOUNTING OF PERSONAL REPRESENTATIVE.

ESTATE OF_____

From:_____,20____, Through:_____,20____.

SCHEDULE D
CAPITAL TRANSACTIONS

Deceased

FOR THE PERIOD COMMENCING: _____

THROUGH: _____

SCHEDULE—D   Assets on Hand at Close of Accounting Period
(Indicate where held and legal description, certificate
numbers, or other identification.)

	Estimated Current Value	Carrying Value
OTHER ASSETS TOTAL		

CASH:

CASH TOTAL

TOTAL ASSETS (entered as Item V on Summary) $_____

IN THE CIRCUIT COURT FOR

_____

COUNTY, FLORIDA

PROBATE DIVISION

FILE NO.: _____

IN RE: ESTATE OF

PETITION FOR DISCHARGE

Deceased

Petitioner, alleges:

1. Petitioner is personal representative of the estate of _____,
deceased.

2. Petitioner has fully administered the estate by making payment, settlement, or other disposition of all claims and debts that were presented and all taxes and expenses of administration.

3. Accompanying this Petition is a complete report (Final Accounting) of all receipts and disbursements since the date of the last annual accounting or, if none, from the commencement of administration.

4. The compensation paid to the personal representative, attorneys, accountants, appraisers, or other agents employed by the personal representative is as follows:

5. The personal representative proposes to distribute the remaining assets of the estate as follows:

A. Prior distributions:

B. Property remaining in the hands of the personal representative:

C. Proposed distribution of the remaining assets:

6. Any objections to the accounting, the compensation paid or proposed to be paid, or the proposed distribution of assets must be filed within 30 days from the date of service of the last of the petition for discharge or final accounting; and within 90 days of filing an objection a notice of hearing thereon must be served or the objection is abandoned.

7. Objections, if any, shall be in writing and shall state with particularity the item or items to which the objection is directed and the grounds on which the objection is based.

8. This petition and the Final Accounting are being served upon the following interested persons:

Wherefore the undersigned petitioner requests that this Court enter its order discharging petitioner as personal representative and releasing the surety on any bond which may have been posted in this estate.

Under penalties of perjury, I declare that I have read the foregoing, and the facts alleged are true, to the best of my knowledge and belief.

Date_____

_____
Personal Representative

IN THE CIRCUIT COURT FOR

_____

COUNTY, FLORIDA

PROBATE DIVISION

FILE NO.: _____

IN RE: ESTATE OF

ORDER OF DISCHARGE

Deceased

This cause came before the Court on the Petition for Discharge of _____ _____ as personal representative of the above estate and the Court finding that the estate has been properly distributed and that claims of creditors have been paid or otherwise disposed of, it is

ORDERED, ADJUDGED AND DECREED that the personal representative is discharged and the surety on the bond, if any, is released from further liability.

Dated:_____

_____
Circuit Court Judge

IN THE CIRCUIT COURT FOR

_____

COUNTY, FLORIDA

PROBATE DIVISION

FILE NO.: _____

IN RE: ESTATE OF

                                                                    PETITION FOR
                                                                    FAMILY ADMINISTRATION
                    Deceased   **WITH WILL**

Petitioner alleges:

1. The interest of the Petitioners in this estate is as beneficiaries under the will. The name and office address of petitioner's attorney (if any) is as follows: _____ _____.

2. The name, last known address and social security number of decedent are: _____ _____. The date and place of death are _____. Decedent was domiciled in _____ County, State of _____.

3. The names and addresses of the beneficiaries and decedent's spouse (if any) , their relationship and the date of birth of any minors are as follows:

| | | Birth date |
| Name and Address: | Relationship: | if under 18: |

4. Venue for this proceeding is in this county because _____ _____.

5. The assets in the gross estate for estate tax purposes are as follows:

and the estate will not be required to file an estate tax return with the Internal Revenue Service.

6. The unrevoked will of decedent is dated _____ and the unrevoked codicils of decedent are dated _____.

7. Petitioner(s) is/are not aware of any other unrevoked wills or codicils.

8. The original of decedent's last will is in the possession of the court or accompanies this petition.

9. Petitioners are entitled to family administration because the beneficiaries under the will are all either a surviving spouse, lineal descendant or lineal ascendant and any devise to others constitutes only a minor part of the estate; the decedent's will does not direct administration under chapter 733; the gross estate, as of the date of death, for federal estate tax purposes is less than $60,000; and the entire estate consists of personal property.

10. Regarding debts of the estate:
    ☐ A. The estate is not indebted
    ☐ B. All creditors' claims are barred

11. The petitioners propose to distribute the estate as follows:
Beneficiary: Share:

Under penalties of perjury, I declare that I have read the foregoing, and the facts alleged therein are true, to the best of my knowledge and belief.

Executed this date _____.

Petitioners:

_____

_____

_____

_____

IN THE CIRCUIT COURT FOR

_____

COUNTY, FLORIDA

PROBATE DIVISION

FILE NO.: _____

IN RE: ESTATE OF

ORDER OF
FAMILY ADMINISTRATION
WITH WILL

Deceased

This cause came before the Court upon the Petition for Family Administration of the estate of _____, deceased, and the court finding that decedent died on _____ at _____ that the material allegations of the petition are true; that decedent's Last Will and Testament, executed on _____ has been admitted to probate; that this estate qualifies for family administration, it is

ADJUDGED that there be immediate distribution of the assets of the decedent, subject to this Family Administration, as follows:

ADJUDGED FURTHER, that the above-listed beneficiaries shall be entitled to receive and collect the shares of the estate distributed to them and to maintain actions to enforce their rights to the property; and that those holding the property of the decedent, including those in whose name decedent's securities (if any) are registered, are hereby authorized and directed to transfer and turn over such property to the beneficiaries without accountability to anyone else for the property.

ORDERED this _____ day of _____, _____

_____

_____
Circuit Court Judge

IN THE CIRCUIT COURT FOR

_____

COUNTY, FLORIDA

PROBATE DIVISION

FILE NO.: _____

IN RE: ESTATE OF

**PETITION FOR
FAMILY ADMINISTRATION
WITHOUT WILL**

Deceased

Petitioner alleges:

1. The interest of the Petitioners in this estate is as heirs at law of the decedent. The name and office address of petitioners' attorney (if any) is as follows: _____
_____.

2. The name, last known address and social security number of decedent are: _____
__ _____. The date and place of death are _____. Decedent was domiciled in _____ County, State of _____.

3. The names and addresses of the beneficiaries and decedent's spouse (if any) , their relationship and the date of birth of any minors are as follows:

Name and Address:

Relationship:

Birth date
if under 18:

4. Venue for this proceeding is in this county because _____
_____.

5. The assets in the gross estate for estate tax purposes are as follows:

and the estate will not be required to file an estate tax return with the Internal Revenue Service.

6. Petitioner(s) is/are not aware of any other unrevoked wills or codicils.

7. Petitioners are entitled to family administration because the beneficiaries are all either a surviving spouse, lineal descendant or lineal ascendant without will; the gross estate, as of the date of death, for federal estate tax purposes is less than $60,000; and the entire estate consists of personal property.

8. Regarding debts of the estate:
   ☐ A. The estate is not indebted
   ☐ B. All creditors' claims are barred

9. The petitioners propose to distribute the estate as follows:

Beneficiary: Share:

Under penalties of perjury, I declare that I have read the foregoing, and the facts alleged therein are true, to the best of my knowledge and belief.

Executed this date _____.

Petitioners:

_____

_____

_____

_____

IN THE CIRCUIT COURT FOR

_____

COUNTY, FLORIDA

PROBATE DIVISION

FILE NO.: _____

IN RE: ESTATE OF

**ORDER OF
FAMILY ADMINISTRATION
WITHOUT WILL**

Deceased

This cause came before the Court upon the Petition for Family Administration of the estate of _____, deceased, and the court finding that decedent died on _____ at _____ that the material allegations of the petition are true and that this estate qualifies for Family Administration, it is

ADJUDGED that there be immediate distribution of the assets of the decedent, subject to this Family Administration, as follows:

ADJUDGED FURTHER, that the above-listed beneficiaries shall be entitled to receive and collect the shares of the estate distributed to them and to maintain actions to enforce their rights to the property; and that those holding the property of the decedent, including those in whose name decedent's securities (if any) are registered, are hereby authorized and directed to transfer and turn over such property to the beneficiaries without accountability to anyone else for the property.

ORDERED this _____ day of _____, _____

_____
Circuit Court Judge

IN THE CIRCUIT COURT FOR

_____

COUNTY, FLORIDA

PROBATE DIVISION

FILE NO.: _____

IN RE: ESTATE OF

**PETITION FOR
SUMMARY ADMINISTRATION
WITH WILL**

Deceased

Petitioner alleges:

1. The interest of the Petitioners in this estate is as beneficiaries under the will. The name and office address of petitioner's attorney (if any) is as follows: _____

_____.

2. The name, last known address and social security number of decedent are: _____

_____. The date and place of death are _____. Decedent was domiciled in _____ County, State of _____.

3. So far as is known, the names and addresses of the beneficiaries and decedent's spouse (if any), their relationship and the date of birth of any minors are as follows:

Name and Address:	Relationship:	Birth date if under 18:

4. Venue for this proceeding is in this county because _____

_____.

5. Regarding debts of the estate:

    A. The estate is not indebted

    B. All creditors' claims are barred

    C. Provision for payment of debts has been made

6. The nature and approximate value of the assets in this estate subject to probate in the State of Florida is:

Total value is approximately $_____.

7. The unrevoked will of decedent is dated _____ and the unrevoked codicils of decedent are dated _____.

8. Petitioner(s) is/are not aware of any other unrevoked wills or codicils.

9. The original of decedent's last will is in the possession of the court or accompanies this petition.

10. Petitioners are entitled to summary administration because the decedent's will does not direct administration as required by chapter 733 and
   ❑ A. The value of the estate subject to administration in this state, less the value of property exempt from claims of creditors, is less than $25,000
   ❑ B. The decedent has been dead for more than 2 years.

11. The petitioners propose to distribute the estate as follows:

Beneficiary: Share:

Under penalties of perjury, I declare that I have read the foregoing, and the facts alleged therein are true, to the best of my knowledge and belief.

Date _____.

Petitioners:

_____

_____

_____

_____

IN THE CIRCUIT COURT FOR

_____

COUNTY, FLORIDA

PROBATE DIVISION

FILE NO.: _____

IN RE: ESTATE OF

ORDER OF
SUMMARY ADMINISTRATION
WITH WILL

Deceased

  This cause came before the Court upon the Petition for Summary Administration of the estate of _____, deceased ,and the court finding that decedent died on _____ at _____ that the material allegations of the petition are true; that decedent's Last Will and Testament, executed on _____ has been admitted to probate; that this estate qualifies for summary administration, it is

  ADJUDGED that there be immediate distribution of the assets of the decedent, subject to this Summary Administration, as follows:

  ADJUDGED FURTHER, that the above-listed beneficiaries shall be entitled to receive and collect the shares of the estate distributed to them and to maintain actions to enforce their rights to the property; and that those holding the property of the decedent, including those in whose name decedent's securities (if any) are registered, are hereby authorized and directed to transfer and turn over such property to the beneficiaries without accountability to anyone else for the property.

  ORDERED this _____ day of _____, _____

_____
Circuit Court Judge

IN THE CIRCUIT COURT FOR

_____

COUNTY, FLORIDA

PROBATE DIVISION

FILE NO.: _____

IN RE: ESTATE OF

**PETITION FOR
SUMMARY ADMINISTRATION
WITHOUT WILL**

Deceased

Petitioner alleges:

1. The interest of the Petitioners in this estate is as heirs at law of the decedent. The name and office address of petitioners' attorney (if any) is as follows: _____ _____.

2. The name, last known address and social security number of decedent are: _____ — _____. The date and place of death are _____. Decedent was domiciled in _____ County, State of _____.

3. So far as is known, the names and addresses of the beneficiaries and decedent's spouse (if any), their relationship and the date of birth of any minors are as follows:

Name and Address:	Relationship:	Birth date if under 18:

4. Venue for this proceeding is in this county because _____ _____ .

5. Regarding debts of the estate:
   - ❏ A. The estate is not indebted
   - ❏ B. All creditors' claims are barred
   - ❏ C. Provision for payment of debts has been made

6. The nature and approximate value of the assets in this estate subject to probate in the State of Florida is:

Total value is approximately $_____.

7. Petitioner(s) is/are not aware of any unrevoked wills or codicils.

9. Petitioners are entitled to summary administration because the decedents did not leave a will and

        ❏ A. The value of the estate subject to administration in this state, less the value of property exempt from claims of creditors, is less than $25,000

        ❏ B. The decedent has been dead for more than 2 years.

10. The petitioners propose to distribute the estate as follows:

<u>Beneficiary:</u>   <u>Share:</u>

Under penalties of perjury, I declare that I have read the foregoing, and the facts alleged therein are true, to the best of my knowledge and belief.

Date _____.

Petitioners:

_____

_____

_____

_____

IN THE CIRCUIT COURT FOR

_____

COUNTY, FLORIDA

PROBATE DIVISION

FILE NO.: _____

IN RE: ESTATE OF

ORDER OF
SUMMARY ADMINISTRATION
WITHOUT WILL

Deceased

This cause came before the Court upon the Petition for Summary Administration of the estate of _____, deceased, and the court finding that decedent died on _____ at _____ that the material allegations of the petition are true and that this estate qualifies for Summary Administration, it is

ADJUDGED that there be immediate distribution of the assets of the decedent, subject to this Summary Administration, as follows:

ADJUDGED FURTHER, that the above-listed beneficiaries shall be entitled to receive and collect the shares of the estate distributed to them and to maintain actions to enforce their rights to the property; and that those holding the property of the decedent, including those in whose name decedent's securities (if any) are registered, are hereby authorized and directed to transfer and turn over such property to the beneficiaries without accountability to anyone else for the property.

ORDERED this _____ day of _____, _____

_____
Circuit Court Judge

IN THE CIRCUIT COURT FOR
_____

COUNTY, FLORIDA

PROBATE DIVISION

FILE NO.: _____

IN RE: ESTATE OF

**PETITION FOR
DISPOSITION OF
PERSONAL PROPERTY
WITHOUT ADMINISTRATION**

Deceased

1. The undersigned petitioner(s) are _____ of
_____ who died on _____ at
_____ and was a resident of _____, residing at
_____.

2. After diligent search the undersigned believe the decedent

    A. Left no unrevoked will.

    B. Left a will which accompanies this petition or has previously been deposited with this court.

3. The names and addresses of the beneficiaries and decedent's spouse (if any), their relationship and the date of birth of any minors are as follows:

Name and Address:	Relationship:	Birth date if under 18:

4. The decedent has left only personal property exempt under the provisions of s. 732.402, personal property exempt from the claims of creditors under the Constitution of Florida, and nonexempt personal property the value of which does not exceed the sum of the amount of preferred funeral expenses and reasonable and necessary medical and hospital expenses of the last 60 days of the last illness as follows:

A. Exempt property consisting of household furniture, furnishings and appliances in decedent's usual place of abode up to a net value of $10,000 as of the date of death:

B. Exempt property under Article X, section 4 of the Florida Constitution:

C. Nonexempt property:

5. The amount of preferred funeral expenses and reasonable and necessary medical and hospital expenses of the last 60 days of the last illness was as follows: (include statements or receipts)

6. The petitioners propose to distribute the estate as follows:

<u>Name:</u>   <u>Share:</u>

Under penalties of perjury, I declare that I have read the foregoing, and the facts alleged therein are true, to the best of my knowledge and belief.

Dated: _____.

Petitioners:

_____

_____

_____

_____

IN THE CIRCUIT COURT FOR

_____

COUNTY, FLORIDA

PROBATE DIVISION

FILE NO.: _____

IN RE: ESTATE OF

**ORDER OF DISTRIBUTION
OF PERSONAL PROPERTY
WITHOUT ADMINISTRATION**

Deceased

This cause came before the Court upon the Petition for Distribution of Personal Property Without Administration of _____, deceased, and the court finding that decedent died on _____ at _____ that the petitioners are entitled to disposition without administration, it is

ADJUDGED that there be immediate distribution of the assets of the decedent, subject to this Family Administration, as follows:

Person: Property:

ADJUDGED FURTHER, that the above-listed persons shall be entitled to receive and collect the shares of the estate distributed to them and to maintain actions to enforce their rights to the property; and that those holding the property of the decedent, including those in whose name decedent's securities (if any) are registered, are hereby authorized and directed to transfer and turn over such property to the beneficiaries without accountability to anyone else for the property.

ORDERED this _____ day of _____, _____

_____
Circuit Court Judge

form 35

TO: United States Department of the Treasury
     Internal Revenue Service
     Atlanta, Georgia 39901

APPLICATION FOR INCOME TAX REFUND
UNDER FLORIDA STATUTES §735.302

The undersigned who is/are the _____
of_____decedent, who died
at _____ on _____, a copy of
his/her death certificate being attached to this Application, hereby
state as follows:

1. That the decedent's social security number is
_____.

2. That the decedent filed an income tax return for the year
ending_____.

3. That the decedent is entitled to an income tax refund in the
amount of $_____.

4. That

   ❏ a.) the decedent was not indebted;

   ❏ b.) provision has been made for the payment of decedent's
          debts as follows:

   ❏ c.) the entire estate is exempt from the claims of
          creditors under the Constitution and the statutes
          of Florida.

5. That no administration of the estate has been initiated, and,
to the best of applicant's knowledge, none is intended.

6. The refund should be paid to _____

Under penalties of perjury, I declare that I have read the foregoing, and the facts alleged therein are true, to the best of my
knowledge and belief.

Date:_____

_____
Name:
Address:

170

IN THE CIRCUIT COURT FOR

_____

COUNTY, FLORIDA

PROBATE DIVISION

FILE NO.: _____

IN RE: ESTATE OF

NOTICE TO CREDITORS
SUMMARY ADMINISTRATION

Deceased

    Administration of the estate of _____, deceased, file number _____ has been filed in the Circuit Court for _____ County, Florida, located at _____ _____. The name and address of the person publishing this notice are: _____. The name and address of the personal representative's attorney (if any) are: _____ _____.

All persons having claims or demands against the estate are notified that an order of summary administration has been entered by the court. The total cash value of the estate is $_____ and the persons to whom it was assigned are:

Name: Address:

All claims against the estate must be filed within the time periods set forth in §733.702, Florida Statutes, to wit: within the later of 3 months after the date of the first publication of the notice of administration or, as to any creditor required to be served with a copy of this notice, 30 days after the date of service of such copy of the notice on the creditor or be forever barred.

The date of the first publication of this Notice is_____.

_____

IN THE CIRCUIT COURT FOR

_____

COUNTY, FLORIDA

PROBATE DIVISION

FILE NO.: _____

IN RE: ESTATE OF

**PETITION TO DETERMINE
EXEMPT PROPERTY**

Deceased

1. The petitioner who is the _____ of the decedent in this action hereby requests this court determine that the following property is exempt:

Property: Basis for exemption: Value:

2. The name and address of the decedent's spouse, if any, are:

_____

3. If decedent was not married at the time of death the names and addresses (and birthdates if minors) of decedent's children entitled by law to the exempt property are:

_____

_____

_____

_____

4. None of the property claimed to be exempt has been specifically or demonstrably devised to anyone other than petitioner.

5. Other than petitioner the only person(s) having an interest in this proceeding are:
Name: Address:

Petitioner requests that an order be entered determining that _____
_____ is entitled to the above-described property as exempt property under Florida law and authorizing and directing the personal representative of this estate to deliver this property to petitioner.

Under penalties of perjury, I declare that I have read the foregoing, and the facts are true, to the best of my knowledge and belief.

I HEREBY CERTIFY that a true and correct copy of the foregoing was mailed this _____ day of _____, 20____ to the following:

Date:_____

_____
PETITIONER

IN THE CIRCUIT COURT FOR

_____

COUNTY, FLORIDA

PROBATE DIVISION

FILE NO.: _____

IN RE: ESTATE OF

                                 Deceased

**ORDER DETERMINING
EXEMPT PROPERTY**

     On the Petition to Determine Exempt Property filed by _____
the court finds that proper notice has been given and that the property is exempt under Florida law and
it is therefore:

     ADJUDGED that _____ is entitled to the following
property as exempt under Florida law:

Description: Value:

and it is further

     ADJUDGED that the personal representative of the estate shall turn over the exempt property
to _____.

ORDERED this _____

                           _____
                           Circuit Court Judge

IN THE CIRCUIT COURT FOR

_____

COUNTY, FLORIDA

PROBATE DIVISION

FILE NO.: _____

IN RE: ESTATE OF

BOND OF
PERSONAL REPRESENTATIVE

Deceased

We, _____ as principal and

_____ as surety, are held and firmly

bound unto the Honorable _____ , as governor of the state of

Florida, and to his or her successors in office, in the sum of _____

_____dollars ($_____) for the payment whereof we bind ourselves, our

heirs, executors, and administrators, jointly and severally.

The condition of this bond is that, if _____ , the Personal

Representative of the above-named estate performs faithfully all his/her duties as such Personal

Representative, then this bond is to be void; otherwise to remain in full force and effect.

In witness whereof we have subscribed our names on _____ , 20_____

_____

Principal

_____

Surety

Approved on _____ , 20_____.

_____

AFFIDAVIT OF CONTINUOUS MARRIAGE

STATE OF FLORIDA   )

COUNTY OF_____)

      BEFORE ME, the undersigned authority personally appeared _____ _____, who upon being duly sworn, deposes and says as follows:

      1. That affiant and _____ were lawfully married on the ___ day of _____, 20_____ in_____, and were continuously married since that date until the date of death of_____ _____ on _____

      2. That the undersigned affiant and _____ took title on or about _____, as husband and wife in an Estate by the Entireties to the following property located in _____ County, Florida:

      3. That affiant and _____ owned the above-described property as tenants by entireties continuously until the death of _____.

      4. That a certified copy of the death certificate of _____ is attached hereto.

      FURTHER Affiant sayeth not.

                                                  _____

                                                  (Printed or Typed)

      Acknowledged before me this _____ day of _____, _____, by _____, who is personally known to me or who produced _____as identification and who did take an oath.

                                                _____

                                             NOTARY PUBLIC

                                             Commission No.:

                                             My Commission expires:

IN THE CIRCUIT COURT FOR

_____

COUNTY, FLORIDA

PROBATE DIVISION

FILE NO.: _____

IN RE: ESTATE OF

STATEMENT REGARDING CREDITORS

Deceased

The undersigned, being the personal representative of the above-captioned estate hereby states that he/she has made a diligent search for creditors of the estate as follows:

After such search he/she has found the following creditors:

		Served with Notice or Actual Notice
Name	Address	

Under penalties of perjury, I declare that I have read the foregoing, and the facts alleged therein are true, to the best of my knowledge and belief.

Dated:_____

_____
Personal Representative

IN THE CIRCUIT COURT OF THE _____ SIXTH JUDICIAL CIRCUIT,
IN AND FOR _____ COUNTY, FLORIDA
PROBATE DIVISION

IN RE: ESTATE OF

_____,

Deceased.

CASE NO. _____

**PETITION TO DETERMINE
HOMESTEAD REAL PROPERTY**

Petitioner_____, as personal representative of
this estate, alleges::

    1. The decedent, _____, died on
_____, domiciled in _____ County, Florida.

    2. At the time of the decedent's death, the decedent owned the following real property
as his/her residence:

    3. The names and addresses of the decedent's surviving spouse, if any, and surviving lineal descendants, if any, and their respective relationships to the decedent, and their dates of birth, are:

Name & Address   Relationship   Date of Birth

    4. The property described in paragraph 2 above constituted the homestead of the decedent within the meaning of Article X, Section 4 of the Constitution of the State of Florida, and upon the decedent's death descended to the following persons in the shares indicated:

5. In addition to the person(s) listed in paragraph 3 above, the following person(s) have an interest in this probate proceeding:

Name   Address

Petitioner requests that the court enter an order determining that the property described in paragraph 2 above constituted the homestead of the decedent, and that, upon the date of death, it descended as forth in paragraph 4 above.

Under penalties of perjury, I declare that I have read the foregoing, and the facts alleged are true, to the best of my knowledge and belief.

Dated: _____

_____
Signature of Personal Representative

CERTIFICATE OF SERVICE

I HEREBY CERTIFY that a copy of the forgoing has been furnished to: _____
_____,
by mail, this _____ day of _____, _____.

IN THE CIRCUIT COURT OF THE _____ JUDICIAL CIRCUIT,
IN AND FOR _____ COUNTY, FLORIDA
PROBATE DIVISION

IN RE: ESTATE OF

CASE NO. _____

_____,

ORDER DETERMINING
HOMESTEAD REAL PROPERTY

Deceased.

On the petition of _____, personal representative, for an order determining homestead of the above decedent, the court finding that all interested persons have been served proper notice of hearing, or have waived notice thereof; that the material allegations of the petition are true; that the decedent was domiciled in _____ County, Florida, at the time of death; that the decedent was survived by a spouse and by lineal descendants; and that at the time of the decedent's death he owned certain property as his residence; it is

ADJUDGED that the following described property:

constituted the homestead of the above decedent within the meaning of Article X, Section 4 of the Constitution of the State of Florida.

ADJUDGED FURTHER that the title to the above-described property descended to the following persons, as tenants in common, with each such person having the share indicated, as follows:

<u>Name</u>   <u>Share</u>

ADJUDGED FURTHER that the personal representative is authorized and directed to surrender to those persons all or any part of the above-described property which may be in the possession or control of the personal representative, and that the personal representative shall have no further responsibility with respect thereto.

ORDERED this_____ day of _____, _____.

_____
Circuit Judge

IN THE CIRCUIT COURT OF THE _____ JUDICIAL CIRCUIT,
IN AND FOR _____ COUNTY, FLORIDA
PROBATE DIVISION

IN RE: ESTATE OF

CASE NO. _____

_____,

**PETITION TO ALLOW
CONVERSION FROM FORMAL
TO SUMMARY ADMINISTRATION**

Petitioner states as follows:

1. Formal Administration in this proceeding was commenced in this court on _____.

2. The estate now falls within the requirements of Summary Administration for the following reasons, as the decedent's will does not direct formal administration, and (select one):

❏   The entire value of the estate subject to administration in this State, less the amount exempt from creditors, has been determined to be less that $25,000.

❏   The decedent has been dead for more than 2 years.

WHEREFORE, Petitioner requests that the Court convert the Formal Administration to Summary Administration.

_____
Petitioner

Copies furnished to:

form 45

FLORIDA

DEPARTMENT OF REVENUE

Mail To:
Florida Department of Revenue
5050 W Tennessee Street
Tallahassee FL 32399-0155
Include $5.00 fee.

Preliminary Notice and Report
Chapter 198, Florida Statutes, Notice of Death

DR-301
R. 07/99

Important Notice: Five dollar ($5.00) fee required for issuance of a nontaxable certificate. Failure to complete all blank spaces will result in delaying the issuance of the proper certificate. If none, show "none."

Decedent's First Name and Middle Initial	Decedent's Last Name	Decedent's Social Security Number

Residence (Domicile) at Time of Death (County, State)	Date of Domicile	Florida Counties in Which Decedent Owned Real Estate:	Date of Death

Name, Title, and Address of Personal Representative, or Person in Possession of Decedent's Property

Name, Address, and Telephone Number of Attorney for Estate

If Estate is Being Administered, Give Title and Location of Court and Date of Appointment as Representative:

Send the Nontaxable Certificate to the Following Address:	Spouse Name	Social Security Number

Will this estate be filing a Federal Estate Tax Return? ☐ Yes ☐ No | Federal Estate I.D. # (If acquired)

The decedent left an estate which consisted of: (   ) only Florida property; (   ) property situated both within and outside the State of Florida. The property is described below. Attach schedule if needed.

Real estate in Florida (attach legal description for each piece of real property in which decedent owned any interest):

_____ $ _____
_____ $ _____
Tangible personal property in Florida: _____ $ _____

All Other Property Wherever Situated:

Real estate not in Florida: _____ $ _____
Stocks: _____ $ _____
Bonds: _____ $ _____
Mortgages: _____ $ _____
Notes: _____ $ _____
Cash: _____ $ _____
Insurance on decedent's life and annuities: _____ $ _____

All other property including, but not limited to, jointly owned property (other than real estate) and Powers

of Appointment: _____ $ _____
Transfers during decedent's life: _____ $ _____

TOTAL $ _____

FOR OFFICE USE ONLY

I, _____ hereby acknowledge
     (Print name of personal representative or person authorized under s. 198.01(2), F.S.)

under oath that I have read the foregoing report and that the statements therein contained are true and that the same

correctly disclose all of the assets of the decedent named therein wherever located to the best of my knowledge and belief.

_____
     (Signature of personal representative or person authorized under s. 198.01(2), F.S.)

_____
     (Title)   (Date)

State of _____ County of _____

Sworn to and subscribed before me this _____ day of _____, _____
                                              Day   Month   Year

_____ or _____
Signature of Circuit Judge   Print, Type or Stamp Name of Notary

Personally known _____ or produced identification _____.

Type of identification produced _____

INSTRUCTIONS

THIS FORM IS TO BE FILED:

- For all resident estates for the purpose of determining estate tax liability.
- For all non-resident estates owning real estate and tangible personal property in Florida.
- By domiciliary personal representatives and verified by the Judge of the Circuit Court or acknowledged before a notary public.
- If the estate is required to file a return with the federal government, a copy of federal Form 706 should be filed with this office on or before nine months after date of death along with any estate tax due Florida.

1. Any person who fails to timely file a required return, willfully fails to pay the tax, keep such records, etc. (in addition to other penalties) is guilty of a misdemeanor of the first degree punishable under ss. 775.082 or 775.083, F.S. Any person who willfully aids or assists in preparing or filing a fraudulent return is guilty of a felony of the third degree punishable under ss. 775.082,775.083, or 775.084, F.S. (ss. 198.37,198.38, F.S.).

In addition to any unpaid tax plus interest from the due date until paid, additional penalties are:

Late Payment Penalty: 10% of the unpaid tax if the tax and penalty are paid within 30 days of the due date; thereafter the penalty rises to 20%.
Failure to Pay Penalty: 10% per month to a maximum of 50% of the tax due.
Fraud Penalty: 100% of the total deficiency if any part of the deficiency is made with intent to defraud.
[It is possible for the Department to impose all three penalties and interest on the same taxpayer for the same return (ss.198.15,198.18, F.S.).]

2. This notice should be made within two months after appointment of the personal representative of the estate of every resident and non-resident of Florida whose estate included real estate regardless of the value of the estate. If no personal representative is appointed the person in actual or constructive possession of the decedent's property should make this report within two months after the death of the decedent.

3. In case the estate of either a resident or non-resident within and outside the State of Florida is required to file a federal return, the personal representative is required to make and file (in addition to this notice) a complete return which will describe the property of the decedent item-by-item and show various deductions for debts, etc.

4. In every case where this notice is required to be made, a receipt for the amount of the tax paid (if tax is found due the State of Florida) or a nontaxable certificate (if it is found no tax is due the State of Florida) is required to be filed with the Circuit Judge of the County in the State of Florida in which domiciliary or ancillary administration or probate proceedings is pending before the judge is authorized to grant a discharge in the estate, and may be filed for record in the office of the Clerk of the Circuit Court of any other county in Florida in which property of the estate is located.

5. Date of Domicile: Attach copies of: Declaration of Domicile Recorded with Clerk of Court, Ad Valorem Tax Bill, oldest Homestead Exemption obtained, Florida Driver License, Voter's Registration card, etc.

6. In case decedent was a resident of Florida and left an estate not subject to federal return and it is found necessary or desirable to show the estate not liable to Florida for estate tax, the personal representative may obtain a nontaxable certificate by filing this notice and paying the fee of $5.00.

7. Every estate not required to file federal Form 706 should secure a non-taxable certificate where there is real estate, to clear title.

    Note: The nontaxable certificate cannot be mailed to anyone other than the personal representative, spouse, or attorney of record without written authorization .

8. In the case of a resident of the State of Florida, the amount of the tax to be paid, if any, is the amount of credit allowed by the Federal Government on account of taxes paid to a state, or the balance of such credit amount which is not used in payment of constitutionally valid estate, inheritance, legacy and succession taxes of another state on account of property of the decedent located there.

9. In case of a non-resident of Florida, the amount of tax to be paid, if any, is the proportion of the allowable credit from federal tax that the gross value of the Florida property bears to the entire gross estate wherever situated.

Gross estate - The gross estate of decedents dying on or after July 1, 1964, as defined in section 2031 (a) of the Internal Revenue Code, comprises property of the decedent wherever situated. The gross estate includes:

a. Property in which the decedent at the time of his death had any beneficial interest.
b. Interest of surviving spouse, as dower, courtesy, or estate in lieu thereof.
c. Property transferred by the decedent during his life by trust or otherwise (other than by bona fide sale for an adequate and full consideration in money or money's worth) as follows: (1) Transfers made in contemplation of death if made within 3 years prior to death; (2) transfers intended to take effect in possession or enjoyment at or after the decedent's death; (3) transfers under which the decedent reserved or retained (in whole or in part) the use, possession, rents, or other income, or enjoyment of the transferred property, for his life, or for a period not ascertainable without reference to his death, or for a period of such duration as to evidence an intention that it should extend to his death, including also the reservation or retention of the use, possession, rents, or other income, the actual enjoyment of which was to await the termination of a transferred precedent interest or estate, (4) transfers under which the decedent retained the right either alone or in conjunction with another person or persons, to designate who should possess or enjoy the property or the income therefrom; and (5) transfers under which the enjoyment of the transferred property was subject at decedent's death to a change through the exercise, either by the decedent alone or in conjunction with another person or persons, of a power to alter, amend, revoke, or terminate, or where such a power was relinquished in contemplation of decedent's death.
d. Annuities received by any beneficiary by reason of surviving the decedent.
e. Property owned jointly or in tenancy by the entirety, with right of survivorship.
f. Property subject to a general power of appointment, including property with respect to which the decedent exercised or released the power during his lifetime.
g. Insurance upon the life of the decedent, including insurance receivable by beneficiaries other than the estate.

NON-RESIDENT ALIENS include only property having a tax situs in the United States.

Section 198.01 (2) -"Personal Representative" - means the executor, administrator or curator of the decedent or if there is no executor, administrator or curator appointed, qualified and acting, then any person who is in the actual or constructive possession of any property included in the gross estate of the decedent or any other person who is required to file a return or pay the taxes due under any provision of this chapter.

form 46

FLORIDA

DEPARTMENT OF REVENUE

Application for Waiver and Release of Florida Estate Tax Lien

DR-308
R. 10/99

In accordance with the provisions of Chapter 198, Florida Statutes, application is hereby made for issuance of a certificate releasing the lien for estate tax on the property belonging to, or forming part of, the gross estate of the decedent identified below.

Name of Decedent: _____ Date of Death: _____

County and State of Domicile: _____ SSN: _____

Attach in triplicate the legal description of real estate or other property to be released.

iNET

Send to: Florida Department of Revenue, 5050 W. Tennessee St., Tallahassee, FL 32399-0155

Value of the property to be released:	$
Value of remaining real property in Florida if release is issued:	$
Value of all other property having tax situs in Florida:	$
Total gross value of decedent's estate:	$
Estimated taxable estate for federal estate tax purposes:	$

    I, the undersigned, by making this request do hereby personally guarantee to furnish the Department of Revenue of the State of Florida a copy of the Federal Estate Tax Return (Form 706) if it is required under the Federal Revenue Acts, as and when it is filed with the Internal Revenue Service in the above estate, if it has not already been done. I further guarantee to furnish copies of all documents issued by the Internal Revenue Service, and the several states or territories of the United States, in connection with the above estate, as may be required by the State of Florida to determine the amount of estate tax due, if any. I further guarantee the payment of any tax that might hereafter be found due to the State of Florida for estate tax from the above estate.

    I understand that the State of Florida might require the posting of a deposit to be applied against any tax that might be found due the State of Florida prior to the issuance of the above requested release. I am willing to post such deposit as may reasonably be required. I further understand that if the tax as finally determined is less than the deposit posted, a refund of the excess will be made.

I, _____ , hereby acknowledge under oath that I have read the foregoing instrument and to the best of my knowledge and belief, the statements therein contained are true and correctly disclose all of the requested information.

_____   _____
Signature of Applicant/Printed Name   Applicant's Mailing Address

    _____

_____
Relationship to Estate, i.e., Executor, Administrator, Surviving Spouse, etc.

State of: _____ County of: _____

Sworn to (or affirmed) and subscribed before me this _____ day of _____ , _____
                                               Day   Month   Year

_____
Signature of Notary

Personally Known _____
or Produced Identification _____
Type of Identification Produced _____   _____
                                                               Print, Type or Stamp Name of Notary Public

INDEX

SPHINX® PUBLISHING'S NATIONAL TITLES

Valid in All 50 States

LEGAL SURVIVAL IN BUSINESS

How to Form a Delaware Corporation from Any State	$24.95
How to Form a Limited Liability Company	$22.95
How to Form a Nevada Corporation from Any State	$24.95
How to Form a Nonprofit Corporation	$24.95
How to Form Your Own Corporation (3E)	$24.95
How to Form Your Own Partnership	$22.95
How to Register Your Own Copyright (3E)	$21.95
How to Register Your Own Trademark (3E)	$21.95
Most Valuable Business Legal Forms You'll Ever Need (2E)	$19.95
Most Valuable Corporate Forms You'll Ever Need (2E)	$24.95

LEGAL SURVIVAL IN COURT

Debtors' Rights (3E)	$14.95
Grandparents' Rights (3E)	$24.95
Help Your Lawyer Win Your Case (2E)	$14.95
Jurors' Rights (2E)	$12.95
Legal Research Made Easy (2E)	$16.95
Winning Your Personal Injury Claim (2E)	$24.95

LEGAL SURVIVAL IN REAL ESTATE

How to Buy a Condominium or Townhome	$19.95
How to Negotiate Real Estate Contracts (3E)	$18.95
How to Negotiate Real Estate Leases (3E)	$18.95

LEGAL SURVIVAL IN PERSONAL AFFAIRS

Como Hacer su Propio Testamento	$16.95
Guia de Inmigracion a Estados Unidos (2E)	$24.95
Como Solicitar su Propio Divorcio	$24.95
How to File Your Own Bankruptcy (4E)	$21.95
How to File Your Own Divorce (4E)	$24.95
How to Make Your Own Will (2E)	$16.95
How to Write Your Own Living Will (2E)	$16.95
How to Write Your Own Premarital Agreement (2E)	$21.95
How to Win Your Unemployment Compensation Claim	$21.95
Living Trusts and Simple Ways to Avoid Probate (2E)	$22.95
Most Valuable Personal Legal Forms You'll Ever Need	$24.95
Neighbor v. Neighbor (2E)	$16.95
The Nanny and Domestic Help Legal Kit	$22.95
The Power of Attorney Handbook (3E)	$19.95
Repair Your Own Credit and Deal with Debt	$18.95
Social Security Benefits Handbook (2E)	$16.95
Unmarried Parents' Rights	$19.95
U.S.A. Immigration Guide (3E)	$19.95
Your Right to Child Custody, Visitation and Support	$22.95

Legal Survival Guides are directly available from Sourcebooks, Inc., or from your local bookstores.
Prices are subject to change without notice.

For credit card orders call 1–800–432–7444, write P.O. Box 4410, Naperville, IL 60567-4410
or fax 630-961-2168

SPHINX® PUBLISHING ORDER FORM

BILL TO:		SHIP TO:		
Phone #	**Terms**	**F.O.B.** Chicago, IL	**Ship Date**	

Charge my: ☐ VISA   ☐ MasterCard   ☐ American Express

☐ **Money Order or Personal Check**

Credit Card Number

Expiration Date

Qty	ISBN	Title	Retail	Ext.
		SPHINX PUBLISHING NATIONAL TITLES		
_____	1-57248-148-X	Como Hacer su Propio Testamento	$16.95	_____
_____	1-57248-147-1	Como Solicitar su Propio Divorcio	$24.95	_____
_____	1-57071-342-1	Debtors' Rights (3E)	$14.95	_____
_____	1-57248-139-0	Grandparents' Rights (3E)	$24.95	_____
_____	1-57248-087-4	Guia de Inmigracion a Estados Unidos (2E)	$24.95	_____
_____	1-57248-103-X	Help Your Lawyer Win Your Case (2E)	$14.95	_____
_____	1-57071-164-X	How to Buy a Condominium or Townhome	$19.95	_____
_____	1-57071-223-9	How to File Your Own Bankruptcy (4E)	$21.95	_____
_____	1-57248-132-3	How to File Your Own Divorce (4E)	$24.95	_____
_____	1-57248-100-5	How to Form a DE Corporation from Any State	$24.95	_____
_____	1-57248-083-1	How to Form a Limited Liability Company	$22.95	_____
_____	1-57248-101-3	How to Form a NV Corporation from Any State	$24.95	_____
_____	1-57248-099-8	How to Form a Nonprofit Corporation	$24.95	_____
_____	1-57248-133-1	How to Form Your Own Corporation (3E)	$24.95	_____
_____	1-57071-343-X	How to Form Your Own Partnership	$22.95	_____
_____	1-57248-119-6	How to Make Your Own Will (2E)	$16.95	_____
_____	1-57071-331-6	How to Negotiate Real Estate Contracts (3E)	$18.95	_____
_____	1-57071-332-4	How to Negotiate Real Estate Leases (3E)	$18.95	_____
_____	1-57248-124-2	How to Register Your Own Copyright (3E)	$21.95	_____
_____	1-57248-104-8	How to Register Your Own Trademark (3E)	$21.95	_____
_____	1-57071-349-9	How to Win Your Unemployment Compensation Claim	$21.95	_____
_____	1-57248-118-8	How to Write Your Own Living Will (2E)	$16.95	_____
_____	1-57071-344-8	How to Write Your Own Premarital Agreement (2E)	$21.95	_____
_____	1-57071-333-2	Jurors' Rights (2E)	$12.95	_____
_____	1-57071-400-2	Legal Research Made Easy (2E)	$16.95	_____
_____	1-57071-336-7	Living Trusts and Simple Ways to Avoid Probate (2E)	$22.95	_____
_____	1-57071-345-6	Most Valuable Bus. Legal Forms You'll Ever Need (2E)	$19.95	_____
_____	1-57071-346-4	Most Valuable Corporate Forms You'll Ever Need (2E)	$24.95	_____
_____	1-57248-130-7	Most Valuable Personal Legal Forms You'll Ever Need	$24.95	_____
_____	1-57248-098-X	The Nanny and Domestic Help Legal Kit	$22.95	_____
_____	1-57248-089-0	Neighbor v. Neighbor (2E)	$16.95	_____
_____	1-57071-348-0	The Power of Attorney Handbook (3E)	$19.95	_____
_____	1-57248-149-8	Repair Your Own Credit and Deal with Debt	$18.95	_____
_____	1-57071-337-5	Social Security Benefits Handbook (2E)	$16.95	_____
_____	1-57071-399-5	Unmarried Parents' Rights	$19.95	_____
_____	1-57071-354-5	U.S.A. Immigration Guide (3E)	$19.95	_____
_____	1-57248-138-2	Winning Your Personal Injury Claim (2E)	$24.95	_____
_____	1-57248-097-1	Your Right to Child Custody, Visitation and Support	$22.95	_____
		CALIFORNIA TITLES		
_____	1-57248-150-1	CA Power of Attorney Handbook (2E)	$18.95	_____
_____	1-57248-151-X	How to File for Divorce in CA (3E)	$26.95	_____
_____	1-57071-356-1	How to Make a CA Will	$16.95	_____
_____	1-57248-145-5	How to Probate and Settle an Estate in California	$26.95	_____
_____	1-57248-146-3	How to Start a Business in CA	$18.95	_____
_____	1-57071-358-8	How to Win in Small Claims Court in CA	$16.95	_____
_____	1-57071-359-6	Landlords' Rights and Duties in CA	$21.95	_____
		FLORIDA TITLES		
_____	1-57071-363-4	Florida Power of Attorney Handbook (2E)	$16.95	_____
_____	1-57248-093-9	How to File for Divorce in FL (6E)	$24.95	_____
_____	1-57071-380-4	How to Form a Corporation in FL (4E)	$24.95	_____
_____	1-57248-086-6	How to Form a Limited Liability Co. in FL	$22.95	_____
_____	1-57071-401-0	How to Form a Partnership in FL	$22.95	_____
_____	1-57248-113-7	How to Make a FL Will (6E)	$16.95	_____

Form Continued on Following Page   **SUBTOTAL**

To order, call Sourcebooks at 1-800-432-7444 or FAX (630) 961-2168 (Bookstores, libraries, wholesalers—please call for discount)

Prices are subject to change without notice.

SPHINX® PUBLISHING ORDER FORM

Qty	ISBN	Title	Retail	Ext.
_____	1-57248-088-2	How to Modify Your FL Divorce Judgment (4E)	$24.95	_____
_____	1-57248-081-5	How to Start a Business in FL (5E)	$16.95	_____
_____	1-57071-362-6	How to Win in Small Claims Court in FL (6E)	$16.95	_____
_____	1-57248-123-4	Landlords' Rights and Duties in FL (8E)	$21.95	_____

GEORGIA TITLES

Qty	ISBN	Title	Retail	Ext.
_____	1-57248-137-4	How to File for Divorce in GA (4E)	$21.95	_____
_____	1-57248-075-0	How to Make a GA Will (3E)	$16.95	_____
_____	1-57248-140-4	How to Start a Business in Georgia (2E)	$16.95	_____

ILLINOIS TITLES

Qty	ISBN	Title	Retail	Ext.
_____	1-57071-405-3	How to File for Divorce in IL (2E)	$21.95	_____
_____	1-57071-415-0	How to Make an IL Will (2E)	$16.95	_____
_____	1-57071-416-9	How to Start a Business in IL (2E)	$18.95	_____
_____	1-57248-078-5	Landlords' Rights & Duties in IL	$21.95	_____

MASSACHUSETTS TITLES

Qty	ISBN	Title	Retail	Ext.
_____	1-57248-128-5	How to File for Divorce in MA (3E)	$24.95	_____
_____	1-57248-115-3	How to Form a Corporation in MA	$24.95	_____
_____	1-57248-108-0	How to Make a MA Will (2E)	$16.95	_____
_____	1-57248-106-4	How to Start a Business in MA (2E)	$18.95	_____
_____	1-57248-107-2	Landlords' Rights and Duties in MA (2E)	$21.95	_____

MICHIGAN TITLES

Qty	ISBN	Title	Retail	Ext.
_____	1-57071-409-6	How to File for Divorce in MI (2E)	$21.95	_____
_____	1-57248-077-7	How to Make a MI Will (2E)	$16.95	_____
_____	1-57071-407-X	How to Start a Business in MI (2E)	$16.95	_____

MINNESOTA TITLES

Qty	ISBN	Title	Retail	Ext.
_____	1-57248-142-0	How to File for Divorce in MN	$21.95	_____

NEW YORK TITLES

Qty	ISBN	Title	Retail	Ext.
_____	1-57248-141-2	How to File for Divorce in NY (2E)	$26.95	_____
_____	1-57248-105-6	How to Form a Corporation in NY	$24.95	_____
_____	1-57248-095-5	How to Make a NY Will (2E)	$16.95	_____
_____	1-57071-185-2	How to Start a Business in NY	$18.95	_____
_____	1-57071-187-9	How to Win in Small Claims Court in NY	$16.95	_____

Qty	ISBN	Title	Retail	Ext.
_____	1-57071-186-0	Landlords' Rights and Duties in NY	$21.95	_____
_____	1-57071-188-7	New York Power of Attorney Handbook	$19.95	_____
_____	1-57248-122-6	Tenants' Rights in NY	$21..95	_____

NORTH CAROLINA TITLES

Qty	ISBN	Title	Retail	Ext.
_____	1-57071-326-X	How to File for Divorce in NC (2E)	$22.95	_____
_____	1-57248-129-3	How to Make a NC Will (3E)	$16.95	_____
_____	1-57248-096-3	How to Start a Business in NC (2E)	$16.95	_____
_____	1-57248-091-2	Landlords' Rights & Duties in NC	$21.95	_____

OHIO TITLES

Qty	ISBN	Title	Retail	Ext.
_____	1-57248-102-1	How to File for Divorce in OH	$24.95	_____

PENNSYLVANIA TITLES

Qty	ISBN	Title	Retail	Ext.
_____	1-57248-127-7	How to File for Divorce in PA (2E)	$24.95	_____
_____	1-57248-094-7	How to Make a PA Will (2E)	$16.95	_____
_____	1-57248-112-9	How to Start a Business in PA (2E)	$18.95	_____
_____	1-57071-179-8	Landlords' Rights and Duties in PA	$19.95	_____

TEXAS TITLES

Qty	ISBN	Title	Retail	Ext.
_____	1-57071-330-8	How to File for Divorce in TX (2E)	$21.95	_____
_____	1-57248-114-5	How to Form a Corporation in TX (2E)	$24.95	_____
_____	1-57071-417-7	How to Make a TX Will (2E)	$16.95	_____
_____	1-57071-418-5	How to Probate an Estate in TX (2E)	$22.95	_____
_____	1-57071-365-0	How to Start a Business in TX (2E)	$18.95	_____
_____	1-57248-111-0	How to Win in Small Claims Court in TX (2E)	$16.95	_____
_____	1-57248-110-2	Landlords' Rights and Duties in TX (2E)	$21.95	_____

SUBTOTAL THIS PAGE _____

SUBTOTAL PREVIOUS PAGE _____

Shipping — $5.00 for 1st book, $1.00 each additional _____

Illinois residents add 6.75% sales tax _____

Connecticut residents add 6.00% sales tax _____

TOTAL _____

To order, call Sourcebooks at 1-800-432-7444 or FAX (630) 961-2168 (Bookstores, libraries, wholesalers—please call for discount)
Prices are subject to change without notice.